MODERN EVENTING
WITH
PHILLIP DUTTON

**The Complete Resource—
Training, Conditioning, and Competing
in All Three Phases**

Phillip Dutton

with Amber Heintzberger

Foreword by Wayne Roycroft • Introduction by Boyd Martin

Trafalgar Square
North Pomfret, Vermont

First published in 2013 by
Trafalgar Square Books
North Pomfret, Vermont 05053

Printed in China

Copyright © 2013 Phillip Dutton

All rights reserved. No part of this book may be reproduced, by any means, without written permission of the publisher, except by a reviewer quoting brief excerpts for a review in a magazine, newspaper, or website.

Disclaimer of Liability
The authors and publisher shall have neither liability nor responsibility to any person or entity with respect to any loss or damage caused or alleged to be caused directly or indirectly by the information contained in this book. While the book is as accurate as the authors can make it, there may be errors, omissions, and inaccuracies.

Trafalgar Square Books encourages the use of approved safety helmets in all equestrian sports and activities.

Library of Congress Cataloging-in-Publication Data

Dutton, Phillip, 1963-
  Modern eventing with Phillip Dutton : the complete resource—training, conditioning, and competing in all three phases / Phillip Dutton with Amber Heintzberger.
     pages cm
  Includes index.
    ISBN 978-1-57076-489-9 (hardback)
  1. Eventing (Horsemanship)--Handbooks, manuals, etc. I. Heintzberger, Amber. II. Title.
  SF295.7.D88 2013
  798.2'42--dc23
                       2012049868

All photographs by Amber Heintzberger except 4.1 D by Hannah Bennett
    and 3.2 A–C courtesy of RZ Dutton Saddles
Book design and diagrams by Lauryl Eddlemon
Cover design by RM Didier
Typefaces: Poppl-Pontifex, Myriad

10 9 8 7 6 5 4 3 2 1

Dedication

*I dedicate this book to my parents,
Peter and Mary Dutton. I was fortunate to grow up
with their love and support, which gave me the strength
and confidence to leave our farm in the Outback of
Australia to pursue my sport and my passion.*

Contents

Foreword *by Wayne Roycroft*   v
Introduction *by Boyd Martin*   vii
Preface   ix
Eventing Past and Present   xi

Part I: Introduction to Modern Eventing   1

1 The Successful Event Rider   3
   Setting Goals and Planning Ahead   4
   A Team Effort   5

2 Selecting Your Event Horse   13
   Planning Ahead   13
   Trying the Horse Out   19

3 Tack and Equipment for the Horse   35
   Tack   35
   Equipment   48

4 Apparel and Equipment for the Rider   55
   Apparel   55
   Equipment   63

5 Horse and Rider Fitness   68
   Horse Fitness   68
   Rider Fitness   75

Part II: Schooling and Training   81

6 Basic Dressage: Teaching Your Horse Correctly   83
   The Correct Horse   83

7 Riding Cross-Country: No Jumping   111
   Getting Out of the Arena   112

8 Introducing Cross-Country Jumping   123

9 Show Jumping Training   149
   Problems You May Encounter   164

Part III: Competing   167

10 Mental Preparation for Rider and Horse   169

11 Warming Up and Riding Your Dressage Test   177
   Warming Up   177
   Riding the Test   185

12 Walking the Cross-Country Course   191
   Developing a Plan   191

13 Warming Up and Riding Cross-Country **203**
Warming Up 203
Riding the Course 211

14 Walking and Riding the Show Jumping Course **221**
Walking the Course 221
Warming Up 225
Riding Your Show Jumping Round 230

Part IV: Care and Maintenance 233

15 Grooming **235**
Maintenance 236
Competition Grooming 246
At the Competition 254

16 Commonsense Nutrition **259**

17 Hoof Care and Shoeing **271**

18 Horse Health and Veterinary Care **283**
The Ideal Role of the Veterinarian 284
Common Problems 287
Care of the Horse During a Competition 304

Glossary of Eventing Terms 309

Quick Reference: Scoring Cross-Country and Show Jumping 314

Event Packing List 315

Jumping Exercises 316

My Horse Hall of Fame 320

Acknowledgments 326

Index 328

Foreword

by Wayne Roycroft

It is a great pleasure to write a foreword for Phillip's book, *Modern Eventing*. I first met Phillip some 25 years ago when he came to a clinic in Sydney, Australia. He was already an accomplished horseman, coming from an Outback farming community. I was impressed by the quiet, confident way that he rode and managed his horses.

Some time after this Phillip moved to the United States, and his success there has been truly inspiring. We joined forces at major events in Europe while I was Coach of the Australian Eventing Team, and we formed a great coach/pupil relationship, as well as being good friends.

One of my fondest memories was riding and galloping horses with Phillip, leading into the Atlanta Games, on the beautiful hills overlooking his and Evie's property at True Prospect Farm in Pennsylvania. The Australian team won the gold medal and Phillip's team spirit, help, and advice, as well as his performance on his great horse True Blue Girdwood, was instrumental in the team winning by an extraordinary 60 points.

Phillip came back to Australia some months before the Sydney Olympic Games with his two horses, Show of Heart and House Doctor. He stayed at my property at Mt. White and we had the best time, training and just working out how to get the best out of the horses. As always, we worked well together, and I continued to be impressed by Phillip's knowledge and skill.

This was followed by his selection to the Australian Team and a wonderful performance to win team gold on his very young horse, House Doctor.

This book reflects on a truly amazing horseman, coach, husband, father, and most of all, to me, a great friend.

Wayne Roycroft
Australian Olympic Medalist and Team Coach

Introduction

by Boyd Martin

For those of you who don't already know, Phillip Dutton was born and raised in a small, country town called Nyngan in Australia. There are no coaches or riding instructors within two hours' drive from there, there are simply people called "horsemen." Phillip's early training and understanding in the art of horses was not your typical, structured, riding-school education, but about working with horses to do what you needed to do. He has learned the hard way that you cannot tell the horse what to do, but must make him *want* to do what you ask of him.

In 2006 I was privileged and honored to meet Phillip while I prepared my horse Ying Yang Yo for the Rolex Kentucky Three-Day Event. After watching Ying Yang jump a few fences, he knew what type of horse he was, the exercises that would improve him, and he knew how hard he could test and challenge the rider. I was blown away every day by the number of exercises he had up his sleeve to teach and train all types of horses to become successful eventers. He was so brilliant in the way he did this and I knew that I had to change my career path and take the opportunity to learn more from this great horseman if I was to become all I had dreamed I could be.

I quickly abandoned my native Australia and became a working pupil/assistant trainer for Phillip for the next three years. The thousands of hours I was lucky enough to spend observing him and his horses was life-changing. You could never put a price on it. While he is a man of few words, he speaks a thousand words through "feel" to every horse he sits on. On a day-to-day basis Phillip is dealing with horses of every level—from three-year-olds getting broken in and four-year-olds starting their first event, right up to preparing horses for the Olympic Games.

The first ten years of my career in Australia I spent trying to get myself onto an Australian team, with no success. Either my horses did not perform well at the correct event, or they were unsound at the most critical moment. Within two years of studying with Phillip I tasted my first team experience, riding Neville Bardos at the 2010 World Equestrian Games in Lexington, Kentucky. Two years later I experienced my first Olympics with Otis Barbotiere riding for the United States (along with Phillip) in London. Without question both team representations were thanks to the guidance of Phillip every step of the way, and not only did he train me to be selected for the US Team, I was riding with him as a teammate in both instances.

The most extraordinary thing about Phillip is that he could take you on a course walk or on a training session and tell you precisely how your horse would react. This is the brilliance of Phillip and his decades of experience with every type of horse put on the planet. Now that I'm off on my own, running my own business, I often get cornered by a challenge with a particular horse. I stop and ask myself, "What would Phillip do?"

For a very quiet and humble person, Phillip Dutton has had an enormous impact on producing the best event riders in America, without question. If you look at the top 50 riders in this country at any point in the last ten years, the majority of them have been influenced by the greatest trainer this country has ever seen. No one has matched in American history the number of advanced horses produced by Phillip and no one has come close to his record of USEA Rider of the Year twelve times.

In 2011 whilst renting the upper barn at Phillip's training facility in Pennsylvania the unthinkable happened when an electrical fire completely destroyed the barn. As much media hype and recognition as I received for pulling my horse Neville out of the burning barn, at the end of the night, the true unsung hero was Phillip Dutton. He arrived at the fire and went in on his own to search for horses. He was solely responsible for retrieving Caitlin Silliman's mare Catch A Star from the barn, guiding her down the blazing aisle to safety. Catch A Star had third-degree burns over 70 percent of her skin, which shows the immense danger Phillip put himself in to retrieve this magnificent mare. If that wasn't enough, once again unprompted, he chased me into the barn and allowed me an extra set of hands to retrieve Neville from the inferno. As always he showed unselfishness helping get Neville out of the barn, never thinking twice about the danger he put himself in.

The riders on the 2012 Olympic Games shortlist were all sent to a training camp in England. Most of us were "first-timers" who had never experienced the pressure and intensity of being placed in this unusual situation. After the team was announced, the feelings in the camp ranged from deep depression and hostility to joy. It was Phillip who privately took aside the riders whose dreams had been shattered, and gave them the guidance they needed to go on and train.

He also played a huge role for his teammates, giving us direction over the weeks leading up to the Games. Everyone turned to Phillip for his thoughts and suggestions. At the Games he was almost like a primary grade school teacher, making sure everything was as perfect as it could be for the rest of us. He was more than a teammate, he was the leader, the coach, and a guide. When my horse Otis Barbotiere failed the final horse inspection, it was Phil who came over and gave me the first hug. A champion coach is not only there when things are going great, but he is there when it all falls apart.

If you watch a Rolex, or a Burghley, or an Olympics on television, you will notice top US riders entering into the start box with a nervous look on their face. The majority of times you will also notice Phillip in the background, standing close by, giving comforting advice in those final moments before the rider sets out on course. He does not do this for money, or to be seen in public, or because he has nothing else to do; he does this because a great trainer leaves nothing to chance; a great trainer knows that the thousands of hours of practice comes down to this moment, and he is there.

Boyd Martin
Member of the US Eventing Team at the 2010 World Equestrian Games in Lexington, Kentucky, and the 2012 Olympic Games in London, England

Preface

The sport of eventing has grown so much in recent times that there is a place within it for virtually any rider and horse. We have competitions from the very low introductory level right up to the highest level–the CCI Four-Star. The number of horse-and-rider combinations competing in events each weekend throughout the United States and the rest of the world is impressive.

Although not all horses and riders can or want to compete at the highest level, the horse and rider at every level should have a good, clear understanding of the basics of riding, training, and competing. I will try to explain my methods in this book and share a lot of my experiences, as well.

The first phase of an eventing competition is the dressage, and in most cases this is the area where we spend the most time training. For those of you who have followed the sport's progression, you will know that the required movements have gotten more difficult and the standard has risen sharply. If you win the dressage and you jump faultlessly you can't be beaten!

Traditionally, event horses have moved up the levels when their cross-country and show jumping skills were up to standard but not necessarily their dressage education. That has changed a lot; now if you want to be competitive

Team Australia accepting Gold Medals at the 1996 Olympic Games in Atlanta. From left to right: Andrew Hoy, Wendy Schaeffer, me, and Gillian Rolton.

at any level, improving your dressage training before you move up is a must.

The effect of improved dressage at all levels has changed what we look for in a potential horse as well. A "soft," loose-moving, quiet horse requires much less training to achieve good dressage scores and therefore is more desirable.

Cross-country courses have evolved as well; increased efforts to improve the safety of horse and rider on course has demanded this evolution, and the attention of course designers to safety has truly decreased the chances of a serious accident occurring. Courses are challenging while technologies such as frangible pins and collapsible jumps are now being used to make them safer.

Over time cross-country courses have become more technical so that you see a lot more combinations and narrow jumps where riders must hold their line. In an effort to make the cross-country phase still have an effect on the outcome of the competition, designers have had to come up with jumps that "slow" riders down to negotiate them. From this idea, narrow jumps and apexes have been used more and more. It is then a balance for the designer to get the flow of the course right so that it still has enough forward-riding jumps to keep both horse and rider confident.

At the Four-Star Level, the courses are now shorter in length. Therefore the endurance aspect of the cross-country phase in some ways plays less of a part than it used to. However, a designer can still have the maximum number of jumping efforts, as long as the course is over 11 minutes long. Therefore, with shorter courses and the same number of jumps, it is harder to complete the course within the allowed time; the horse winds up doing more sprinting, which requires more "wind" fitness.

It used to be a traditional mindset as an eventer that you finished your cross-country course at all costs. I am sure this came from eventing's military and fox hunting background. There was a notable case at the Rome Olympics in 1960 where the great Australian rider Bill Roycroft fell and then remounted, completed the cross-country and then show jumped the next day with a broken collarbone to help the Australian team win a gold medal. Even in my day, my teammate on the Australian team at the Atlanta Olympics, Gillian Rolton, slipped on a turn and fell between jumps early on the course, remounted then had a spectacular fall at the water jump where she broke her collarbone, remounted again, and finished the course.

As brave and gritty as these performances were, there are so many cases where this kind of action has not been fair to the horse and in some cases, not fair to the rider. Currently the rules state that if you have one fall you are eliminated. The general thought now is, or should be, that there is always another day! The rider should understand that more training for your horse is necessary and retiring before more damage is done is a much better course of action than pushing your and your horse's limits.

The show jumping is the last phase of an event and often the one where the competition is won or lost. The horse and rider must really understand the difference needed in the horse's approach to the jumps compared to the cross-country. Show jumping courses generally include related, or measured, distances so that horses need to be adjustable and riders need a good understanding of what is being asked from the course.

Our goal as event riders is to excel at all three phases. This requires a lot of training and knowledge, but successfully completing an event at any level can be a very rewarding challenge. I hope to help give you the tools to meet these challenges and have fun in the process!

Phillip Dutton

*Twelve-Time USEA Leading Rider
of the Year and Five-Time Olympian
2009 Developing Rider Coach of the Year*

Eventing Past and Present

The Three-Day Event was first introduced at the Olympic Games in Stockholm, Sweden, in 1912, based on the training and testing of military chargers. Spread over three consecutive days, it was a complete test for the army horse. As of the Paris Olympics in 1924, eventing was open to civilians; women were not allowed to participate until 1964. But now, as in all equestrian sports, men and women compete on equal terms.

Up until very recently, the format of the Three-Day Event included a dressage test on the first day. An endurance test followed on the second day in what is now known as the "classic" or "long format, which included a short roads and tracks (Phase A); followed immediately by a steeplechase (Phase B); then by a long roads and tracks (Phase C). A compulsory halt (10 minutes) was instituted after Phase C for a veterinary examination, after which the competitor began Phase D, the cross-country. The third and final day was the show jumping phase.

Today, however, the second phase has been changed (in nearly all events) to a "short" format whereby Phases A to C (roads and tracks and steeplechase) have been eliminated and replaced by the cross-country course alone—Phase D.

LEVELS

The United States Equestrian Federation (USEF) and the United States Eventing Association (USEA) recognize three types of eventing competition: Tests (Individual or Combined); Horse Trials; and Three-Day Events. Run under USEF rules, there are six levels of eventing in the United States:

1 Beginner Novice Level is designed to introduce green horses and riders to Horse Trials, combining dressage, cross-country, and beginner jumping tests.

2 Novice Level is a continuing introduction to Horse Trials. It is designed for competitors and horses with some experience at lower levels or for experienced riders and horses new to the sport.

3 Training Level is an elementary examination of competitors and horses with some experience and training.

4 Preliminary ("Prelim") Level is a moderate examination of competitors and horses in a regular training program preparing for One-Star Events.

5 Intermediate Level is an examination of increasing technical difficulty that prepares competitors and horses for Two-Star Events.

6 Advanced Level is the highest national level of Horse Trials, of a difficulty designed to prepare competitors and horses for either Three- or Four-Star Events.

International events are run under the rules of the Fédération Equestre Internationale (FEI). The international levels of eventing are the Concours International Combiné (CIC) and the Concours Complet Internationale (CCI). The CIC events occur at One-, Two- and Three-Star Levels, while the CCI events range from

United States Equestrian Federation (USEF) Regulations

HORSE TRIALS

1 The Horse Trials comprises three distinct tests, usually taking place on one or two days, during which a competitor rides the same horse throughout, namely:
- Dressage
- Cross-country
- Show jumping
- The dressage test must be first. The cross-country and jumping tests may follow in either order.

2 Relative influence of the tests: In principle, the cross-country test should be the most influential of the three tests of a Horse Trials. The dressage test, while less influential than the cross-country test, should be slightly more influential than the jumping test.

3 Levels: The following levels of competition may be offered at a Horse Trials:
- Beginner Novice
- Novice
- Training
- Preliminary
- Intermediate
- Advanced

THREE-DAY EVENT

1 The Three-Day Event comprises three distinct tests, taking place on separate days, during which a competitor rides the same horse throughout, namely:
- A dressage test spread over one or more consecutive days, depending on the number of competitors, directly followed on the next day by a cross-country test (see below).
- A cross-country jumping test. Sometimes this test comprises four Phases as described in the long format on p. xiii: Phases A and C (roads and tracks); Phase B (steeplechase); Phase D (cross-country obstacles).

One to Four Stars (Championship). One-, Two- and Three-Star CIC competitions are roughly comparable to Preliminary, Intermediate, and Advanced Levels of American national competition; and to the Novice, Intermediate and Advanced Levels of British national competition (see sidebar).

The traditional difference between the CCI and the CIC was that the four phases of cross-country (A, B, C, and D) were held in a CCI competition, while CIC competition only ran the D, or cross-country phase. With the advent of the new "short" format (no roads and tracks or steeplechase), the FEI agreed to increase the distance and difficulty of the CCI cross-country courses to make them harder than those run in CIC competitions. Thus, CIC competitions have fewer obstacles on a shorter course.

Today, all championships held under the auspices of the FEI are held in the short format, although in the United States, at the One-Star Level, the "long" format continues to be used to test the proper development and training of the event horse. For educational purposes,

---

- A show jumping test.

2 Categories indicate the extent of foreign participation in a Three-Day Event. The four categories of Three-Day Events are:

- National Three-Day Event (CCN)
- International Three-Day Event (CIC) and (CCI)
- Official International Three-Day Event (CCIO)
- International Championship Three-Day Event (CH)

3 Levels of Three-Day Events are indicated by stars. The five levels of Three-Day Events are:

- Training Three-Day Event: An educational introduction to the Three-Day Event at the Training Level. It's sometimes referred to as a "Half-Star."
- One-Star (*): An introduction to the Three-Day Event for competitors and horses.
- Two-Star (**): For competitors with some experience in Three-Day Events on horses just beginning International competition.
- Three-Star (***): For competitors and horses with some International experience.
- Four-Star (****): For experienced and successful combinations of International competitors and horses.

All Three-Day Events in the United States will be denoted by their category and their level, for example, a CCN** is a National Three-Day Event at the Two-Star Level. Events limited to Seniors are indicated by the letters noted above, for example: a CCN***. Events limited to Young Riders are indicated by the addition of the letter "Y," for example: CCN-Y**. Events limited to Juniors are indicated by the addition of the letter "J," for example: CCN-J*.

(Continued on p. xvi.)

long-format events at the lower levels have also become popular, although at the time of writing, they are fairly uncommon.

Thanks to the new "shorter" format cross-country phase, upper-level horses can return to competition more quickly so horses tend to compete nearly year-round. Many professionals, including myself, spend the summer in one location and the winter in a warmer climate. (Ocala, Florida, and Aiken, South Carolina, are two popular winter destinations with numerous Horse Trials and Three-Day Events within a short drive.)

USEF Regulations continued

LEVELS OF NATIONAL HORSE TRIALS AND THREE-DAY EVENTS

"QR" means Qualifying Result

"NQR" means National Qualifying Result

"IQR" means International Qualifying Result

1 Beginner Novice (B): Open to competitors of any age, on horses four years of age and older.

2 Novice (N): Open to competitors of any age, on horses four years of age or older.

3 Training (T): Open to competitors of any age, on horses four years of age or older.

4 Preliminary (P): Open to competitors from the beginning of the calendar year of their fourteenth birthday, on horses five years of age or older. The competitor must have obtained an NQR at four Horse Trials at the Training Level or higher.

5 Training Three-Day Event: Open to competitors of any age, on horses four years of age or older. Both the competitor and the horse must have obtained NQRs at four Horse Trials at the Training Level or higher, one of which must be attained as a combination. A competitor established at the Preliminary Level may compete on a horse that has obtained two NQRs at Training Level or higher.

6 Preliminary Three-Day Event: Open to competitors beginning the calendar year of their fourteenth birthday, on horses five years of age or older. Both the competitor and the horse, though not necessarily as a combination, must have obtained an NQR at four Horse Trials at the Preliminary Level or higher.

7 Intermediate (I): Open to competitors from the beginning of the calendar year of their sixteenth birthday, on horses six years of age or older. Both the competitor and the horse, though not necessarily as a combination, must have obtained an NQR at three Horse Trials at the Preliminary Level or higher, plus an additional NQR with no more than 20 jumping penalties at obstacles on the cross-country test.

8 Advanced (A): Open to competitors from the beginning of the calendar year of their eighteenth birthday, on horses six years of age or older. Both the competitor and the horse, though not necessarily as a combination, must have obtained an NQR at

SAFETY

Eventing is not without risk. Rules protecting the rider include a requirement to wear a safety vest (body protector) during cross-country, as well as an ASTM/SEI or ISO approved equestrian helmet equipped with a safety harness, which must be fastened while on the horse, although riders over 18 on horses seven years and older may wear a top hat in the dressage phase. Many riders also choose to wear an inflatable safety vest over the regular body protector on cross-country.

In an increased effort to improve safety three Horse Trials at the Intermediate Level or higher, plus an additional NQR with no more than 20 jumping penalties at obstacles on the cross-country test.

LEVELS OF INTERNATIONAL HORSE TRIALS AND THREE-DAY EVENTS

In all instances, at least one of the QRs must have been obtained in the current or preceding calendar year. All competitors and horses must meet the minimum requirements published by the Fédération Equestre International (FEI).

1 CIC* (Competition International Combined): Both the competitor and the horse, though not necessarily as a combination, must have achieved three NQRs at either National Preliminary Horse Trials (CNC*) or National One-Star Three-Day Events (CCN*).

2 CCI* (Competition Complete International): Both the competitor and the horse, though not necessarily as a combination, must have achieved four NQRs at any combination of CNC*, CCN*, and CIC*.

3 CIC**: Horse and rider, though not necessarily as a combination, must have achieved two IQRs at a CNC** or higher.

4 CCI**: Having met the minimum requirements of the FEI, the horse and rider, though not necessarily as a combination, must have achieved three IQRs at a CNC** or higher.

5 CIC***: Having met the minimum requirements of the FEI, the horse and rider, though not necessarily as a combination, must have achieved two IQRs at a CNC*** or higher.

6 CCI***: The horse and rider must meet the minimum requirements of the FEI.

7 CCI****: The horse and rider must meet the minimum requirements of the FEI.

COMBINED TESTS

Combined Tests consist of two distinct tests during which a competitor rides the same horse throughout. The tests may include two of the following—dressage, cross-country, jumping; or may include one discipline (such as cross-country) repeated twice under different conditions. Combined Tests will be conducted under guidelines published by the USEA.

on cross-country by preventing rotational falls (falls in which a horse somersaults), some fences are now being constructed with frangible pins, which support regular timber and break under a certain amount of pressure. There are also "breakable" logs that collapse when a horse falls on them.

SCORING

Dressage is scored with penalty points, and the goal is the lowest score possible. Time and jumping penalties are added to this score from cross-country and show jumping, and the horse and rider with the lowest score at the end of the event is the winner. See the Appendix for a quick reference list of scoring (p. 314).

RULES

The rules for eventing are constantly under revision. In the United States the current rulebook for eventing is available online at the USEA and USEF websites: www.useventing.com and www.usef.org. In other countries, check with the national governing body and for FEI events visit www.fei.org.

GLOSSARY

See page 309 in the Appendix for an extensive glossary of eventing terms.

PART 1

Introduction to MODERN EVENTING

1.1 Connaught and I after winning the 2008 Rolex Kentucky Three-Day Event.

CHAPTER 1

The Successful Event Rider

Success in eventing can be defined in different ways for different people. A child on her first pony will be happy to complete her first Beginner Novice, and while a professional rider's idea of success may be representing her country and winning prizes at the Four-Star Level, an adult amateur who has a fulltime job or is raising a family may be thrilled to complete a Training Level Horse Trials with no cross-country jumping penalties. Whether you ride as a hobby or as a career, the experience should be enjoyable and you should mark your success to your own individual standards (fig. 1.1).

THE LEARNING PROCESS

The purpose of eventing is to test the horse and rider in three very different phases: *dressage, cross-country* and *show jumping*. For anyone at any level to be successful they need to embrace each phase of the sport. All three phases are equally important and you have to put in the time to train for each of them if you want to have a chance at competitive success.

- You should honestly evaluate yourself and your horse and decide how to most wisely invest your time and money as you strive to improve. For example, if you are very good at dressage but nervous about cross-country, you need to find time in the saddle to become confident in that phase. If you're weak in dressage or show jumping, find a way to catch up so you are comparatively strong in both these phases. It's advantageous to compete in individual dressage or jumper shows to spend more time in the ring and give you and your horse more "mileage" in these areas.

- Mainly because of the trust and faith that needs to be developed between horse and rider, it is just not feasible to buy a "made" horse to get into eventing (see chapter 2, "Selecting Your Event Horse"). Cross-country riding takes understanding and experience from the rider, who needs to give confidence to the horse. A more experienced horse is generally helpful to the rider, especially someone just starting out, but he does not guarantee instant success.

- There is a lot of practice required to be a safe and successful cross-country rider. This means a commitment to riding on a regular basis. If you want to ride at the highest level, it means riding many hours a day, seven days a week, until it becomes second nature. For somebody that is going to be more part-time it is still necessary to commit to improving your riding coordination and skills on a regular basis in order to be safe in the saddle.

- There also needs to be the desire to conquer each eventing level before moving up to the next one. There is no point in moving up if you do not feel solidly prepared for all three phases at the level you are currently competing. All the successful riders are aware of this and work hard to have a solid base before moving on up.

- Each young horse also has to start at the beginning and learn all the steps. Even when he's winning the dressage phase and is brave going cross-country, there's no point moving him up if he has three rails down in the show jumping every time out. It's a slow process to develop and train a green horse—the same as an inexperienced rider. When starting a young horse, even Olympic riders have to go back to the basics and build that foundation for the horse's development.

SETTING GOALS AND PLANNING AHEAD

Things don't always go as planned, so a successful event rider must also be able to adapt. There are many obstacles that you will come against and you can't let them upset you and get you down; instead embrace the challenges and look ahead. A positive attitude is so important in our sport. There are many variables and things that can and do happen, and being able to keep your eye on the big picture and enjoy the sport and your horse is essential.

Event riders need to be good long- and short-range planners. Having a training plan on a week-to-week and year-to-year basis can help

The Successful Event Rider

you set and achieve realistic goals. Improving your dressage training is a week-to-week goal, while achieving a certain competitive level by the end of the year would be a long-term goal. Having this mentality will keep you and your horse improving on a steady basis.

Keep in mind, though, that you might have to change or abbreviate your long-term goals as things go along. And, it's the same with your riding on a week-to-week basis: You need to have a realistic approach for what you feel you can work on that week and be flexible in your training plan.

The sport is such that you have to really enjoy the process of getting there because it takes a long time to gain success. Eventing is not like some other riding sports, say hunter/jumpers or dressage, where you go into the ring several times in a day, if you wish, with the chance to win lots of ribbons. It's a more gradual process with long-term satisfaction rather than instant gratification.

The people I see who are successful at all levels usually have a good sense of humor and are able to both accept the lows and not get too caught up in the highs—that is, they don't think they're invincible once they start winning because they know every week is going to be different in what they can achieve. Accepting this with a good attitude can make a big difference in how much you enjoy the sport—and the experiences you have along the way.

1.2 The happiness and well-being of the horse should be every rider's first priority. Head Girl Emma Ford, pictured here at Millbrook Horse Trials, taking excellent care of all my horses.

A TEAM EFFORT

Put Your Horse First

The most important member of your team is, of course, your horse (fig. 1.2). Always have the horse's best interest in mind: You can have ambitious goals but you must take into account what is best for your particular horse. Only enter an event that you and your horse are prepared for, not just because you want to go

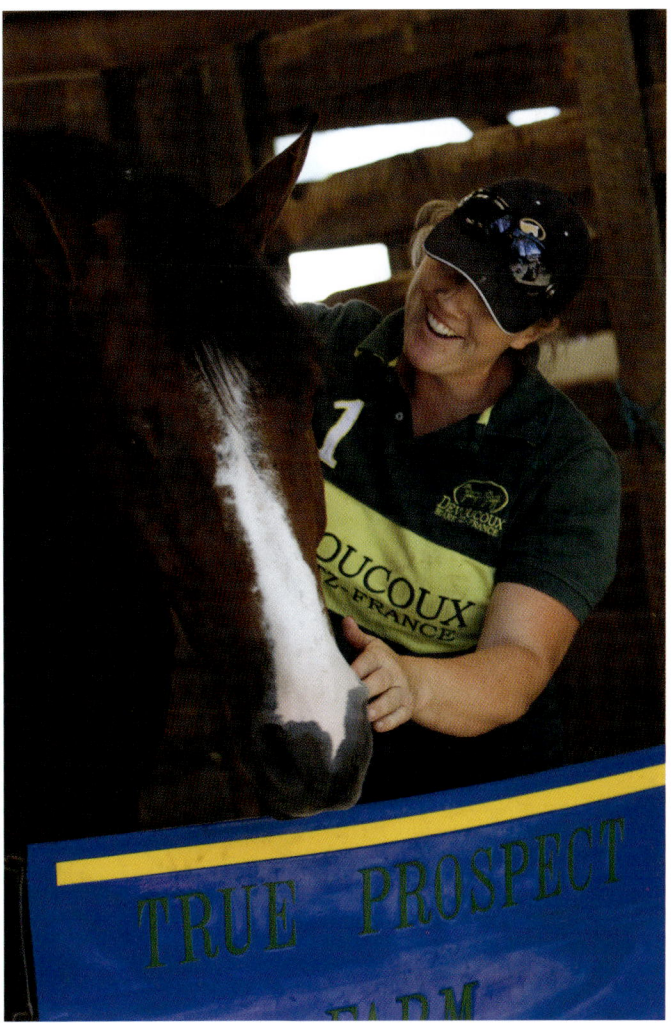

MODERN EVENTING WITH PHILLIP DUTTON 5

1.3 Acknowledging your supporters is key to success. Here are some of mine, with me. From left: Olivia Dutton, Evie Dutton, and Annie Jones.

there. And always be prepared to forego a competition when things aren't going right; then head home and train more for another day.

General Support

To be a successful event rider, you have to recognize that you can't go it alone, at any level. Assistance can be something as simple as a friend or family member helping you drive to the event, or holding a horse while you walk the course. Other people can help you afford to participate by owning a horse for you to ride, or sponsoring you financially. You will also need a coach or trainer, a veterinarian and farrier who understand the sport, and a groom or "helpers" when you compete, especially when you have more than one horse in a competition (fig. 1.3).

It is important to surround yourself with people you get along with and who create a team atmosphere. You, in turn, need an attitude that makes people want to help and support you.

Financial Aid

- If you are a young rider and your parents or other relatives and friends are supporting you, think of this as your first chance to "ride

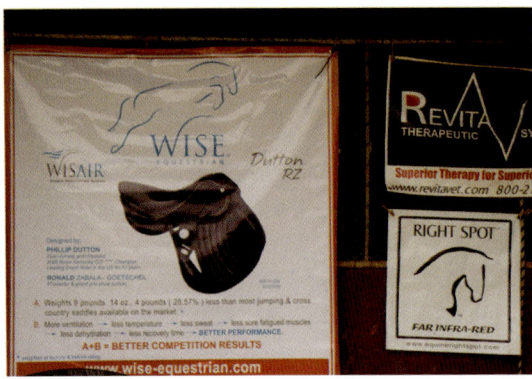

1.4 A & B Hanging banners on your competition stabling is one way to promote sponsors (A). Boyd Martin and his 2012 Olympic mount Otis Barbotiere, showing off their sponsored gear and looking confident at the 2011 Jersey Fresh Three-Day Event (B).

The Successful Event Rider 1

1.5 Assistant rider Ryan Wood, a successful Four-Star event rider from Australia, is listening carefully to my advice.

for an owner." This will prepare you for riding for somebody else in the future when the opportunity presents itself.

- Take time to think about what the owner of the horse wants from the sport and why he (or she) is involved rather than just asking for help on your terms. The same applies to asking a company to sponsor you: What will you be able to give back in return for the company's support (figs. 1.4 A & B)?

- When you are riding for a horse owner you may have to find ways to make it enticing, fun and rewarding. I have found that everybody I ride for has different goals. Some people like the big events like Rolex Kentucky, the World Championships or the Olympic Games and really enjoy being part of a huge sporting spectacle; others who are breeders like to see their progeny brought on, produced well and then sold. Still other people simply want to help the rider: While they are not so interested in the individual horse, they get

MODERN EVENTING WITH PHILLIP DUTTON 7

satisfaction from seeing the rider fulfilling her passion and dreams.

- The first step when somebody is interested in supporting you is to work out what you need to do to satisfy his or her goals and wishes. Communication is often the key, keeping the horse owner or your sponsor updated during good and bad times. Some of the hardest phone calls I've had to make are when I feel I have not lived up to an owner's expectations, or to tell him his horse has been injured. Nevertheless, it is important to be upfront and share information when all is going well … and when it isn't.

Accepting Instruction: Coach or Trainer

Enlisting the help of a coach or someone experienced in the sport is a good way to help you set and meet realistic goals (fig. 1.5). I think that the successful event rider has to have a desire and a mindset to accept instruction without taking constructive criticism negatively.

That said, you have to be strong and independent enough so you can ride without an instructor watching all the time, "holding your hand," and doing everything for you. Eventing is a sport where you are out there on your own, especially on the cross-country phase. Your instructor can help you gain skills and improve your riding but you have to develop your mind and confidence so that when you're on course you can do it on your own.

In training sessions with your instructor it is very important to be able to be like a

1.6 A & B Here, I'm coaching Boyd Martin on Ying Yang Yo at the 2011 Fair Hill International. Even Boyd, an Olympian who has won at the Four-Star Level, needs "eyes on the ground" (A). US Eventing Team Member Becky Holder on Can't Fire Me is getting some coaching from me in the warm-up arena at the 2011 Fair Hill International (B).

"sponge" for knowledge and instruction, taking in as much as you can.

Everybody needs a set of "eyes on the ground." It doesn't matter what level you ride or how experienced you are, there is always room for improvement and having a good relationship with a knowledgeable coach whom you trust is essential (figs. 1.6 A & B).

I don't see a great advantage in changing coaches on a regular basis or getting information from too many people. There is not just one way to coach a horse or rider, but I think that you can become confused if you hear too many different ways to go about it. Having said that, there is a time when you reach a certain stage that you may need to move on to a different coach who will help take you to the next level.

No matter how good your coach is, he or she cannot help you if you are not willing to put yourself out there and learn. There is an art to being a good student and to listening and accepting criticism without taking it personally. In most cases, when coaches are shown your commitment and loyalty, they will go beyond the standard help they usually give in return for being paid. If you want to really succeed, you need to make your coach feel truly a part of your riding career.

Veterinarian

Your relationship with your horse's veterinarian is equally important as your relationship with your supporters and coach. There will be times when you really rely on your vet, and the higher up the levels you go, the more integral this partnership becomes. I find that for the best results my vet needs to get to know my horses well, understanding what is normal for each particular individual.

If you can demonstrate your passion and commitment to your horse, a lot of times you will get much more from your veterinarian than just a commercial interest. Depending on your goals for your horse and your vet's background, try to educate your vet about the sport. For instance, it is very important for your vet to know the rules about the use of various drugs and medications in competition.

There is much more veterinary information in chapter 18, "Horse Health and Veterinary Care" where I introduce my vet, Kevin

TIPS: Choosing a Coach

- The United States Eventing Association (USEA) Instructor Certification Program provides a list of coaches who are guaranteed to have some education on everything from teaching to safety.
- Find someone who is going to suit your personality and style.
- Depending on the level you are riding, you don't necessarily need to have an advanced coach.
- Getting the foundation right is the first step, so someone who will coach you in the basics, as well as help you get ready for competitions, will help you to build a base of knowledge that will stay with you for life.
- Everybody coaches differently; some people can be quite aggressive, intense, and talk a lot while others tend to be quiet and don't say as much. There is no right—or wrong—way to coach, it's what gets the best out of you and teaches you the most.

1.7 Head Girl Emma Ford holding William Penn.

Keane, DVM, who has taken care of my horses for years. He offers you a great deal of medical advice and shares some experiences about his work with event horses.

Farrier

Event riders rely heavily on their farriers (see chapter 17, "Hoof Care and Shoeing"). Without your horse's feet you don't have much, and getting a good rapport going with your farrier is crucial. Educate yourself well about your horse's feet so that you can, if needed, express any thoughts on improving them to your farrier, taking into account that he will have more knowledge than you do about feet and shoeing.

However, as a rider there are often things you can share: for example, tell him if your horse is forging (when the horse's back feet clip the front shoes during motion); if the farrier is unfamiliar with the sport, explain the need for stud holes in the shoes; and talk about the different conditions you may be faced with in the next shoeing cycle.

In consultation with your vet, your farrier can also work on adjusting the horse's shoeing in different ways to improve his comfort level: pads to protect the sole; bar shoes to prevent bruising of the heels; and glue-on shoes that don't need nails are all examples. You need your farrier to help your horse perform his best and stay sound.

Groom or Helper

It is nearly essential, especially when traveling to events, to have someone along to help. If you only have one horse you could possibly get by on your own (see chapter 15, "Grooming"), but when you have to walk the course and your horse has to stand on the trailer, having someone with you makes it easier—and safer.

More urgently, if you happen to have a mishap at the event you will really definitely need help. It is ideal when your helpers (or helper) are competent with horses, able to tack up, and understand the horse's well-being. It is also practical for them to be able to drive the truck and trailer should you be unable to do it yourself.

The further up the eventing levels you go and the more horses you ride, the more necessary it becomes to employ a professional groom (fig.1.7). Again, you need to forge a good relationship so your helper or groom does everything she can to enable you to have a successful and well-organized competition. Many riders can be irritable when under pressure, but it is important to try not to take your anxiety out on the people around you. It will be hard to encourage them to come back and help you again if they do not have a good experience (fig. 1.8).

On this note of trying to be friendly and nice to people, it is essential to recognize event organizers, warm-up arena stewards, and everybody else who is helping with the event. These people are usually volunteers, and it is common sense that being courteous and expressing your thanks is appropriate. It may also help you get a special favor sometime when your entry arrives late, or you need to ask for a different time to ride.

1.8 Here, I'm with one of my number-one supporters, Olivia, at Fair Hill 2011.

1.9 There is nothing like the exhilaration of crossing the finish line after a successful ride. Jes Hargrave congratulates friend Fiona Allen after a successful Preliminary cross-country run at The Fork in North Carolina.

CHAPTER 2

Selecting Your Event Horse

Before you can begin to compete in eventing you need to find a suitable partner. You can spend a small fortune on high-end tack and equipment and riding lessons with all the top trainers but without a suitable horse you are at a serious disadvantage. This does not mean that you need to spend a lot of money on a horse that has competed to the upper levels or even one with the potential to do so: When you are just starting out, a reasonably priced horse—one with experience at the lower levels—may be just right for you.

When you are looking, there are literally hundreds of factors to take into account. There is never the perfect horse for any rider: one horse may have had the right training but has an old injury that is of concern; another, with a lot of potential, is greener than you want. Ultimately, you have to prioritize what you can live with and what you cannot.

PLANNING AHEAD

Buying a horse is very exciting, but, in reality, it is also quite daunting. You put a great deal of time, money and energy into your horse's training, maintenance and competing so you want to be as certain as you can be that you find the right horse. Start with this check list to help define your search:

- Care and well-being: Will you keep the horse at home or board him? If the latter, what are the stables like? Turnout? Who will be in charge of overseeing his care?

- Facilities: Where will you ride and train? If you live in a cold or wet climate will you have access to an indoor arena? Is there good footing for dressage training and are there schooling jumps for stadium and cross-country?

- Your schedule: Are you working, in school, or raising a family? Realistically, how much time will you have to spend with your horse? Will you have enough time for a high maintenance horse that needs lots of work every day or should you look for a horse that can run around a Novice course now and then with minimal time spent on training and fitness work?

- Finances: Do you have the money for a fancy, well-trained horse or will you need to get an older one with good training but also lots of miles? Do you want a young horse that still needs a lot of work?

- Transportation: Do you have a truck and trailer or other means for traveling to

2.1 A truck and trailer are just two of the things you will probably need before you bring home a horse.

competitions? Can you borrow one from a friend or hire a horse transporter (2.1)?

- Breeding: Traditionally Thoroughbreds excelled in eventing because of their athleticism and endurance, but Warmbloods have become popular for their way of moving, which tends to score better in the dressage phase. Crosses between Warmbloods and Thoroughbreds are also popular. Fancy European Warmblood pedigrees come at a cost, however, so before you head out shopping, consider your realistic budget. For the junior or adult amateur competing at the lower levels, a grade or cross-bred horse may be more suitable and more fun to ride.

- What preferences do you have? Consider basics like color, breed, mare or gelding, and whether you can tolerate any vices or bad habits, such as cribbing or teeth-grinding.

- What do you know about training, fitness work, and the general care and welfare of your horse?

- Do you have, or know of, a coach or trainer who will give you lessons and oversee your work, riding and education?

The more organized and prepared you are before you start the search, the better you'll be able to make an educated decision. Think through all of these areas so that you are comfortable with the parameters of the type of horse you are looking for and how things will work once you own the horse.

Below are four common scenarios:

1 Inexperienced Rider

You are a rider new to eventing, or you have decided that you would like to go up the levels. It would be beneficial to find an experienced horse on which to learn. The first priority in your search is his temperament: He should be compatible to your personality and not get upset when you make a mistake. It's a great advantage when you can arrange to take the horse on a short trial.

Dressage: A nervous or aggressive horse is unsuitable, as is one not forward enough, that is, won't respond immediately to your leg. You should aim for a horse that is educated in dressage but not one with huge, expressive movement. This can make it harder for the novice rider to sit correctly in the saddle, especially at sitting trot. He should move through the test efficiently and give the inexperienced rider a feel for how a correct horse should go.

Cross-Country: You do not want a horse that will get too strong. You do want an honest, forward-thinking horse that is not going to get offended if you make the occasional mistake on course, for example, pulling on his mouth in the air, or coming to a jump without the perfect striding or line. The right kind of horse here knows his job and works out how to get to the other side of the jump. The horse that lacks some speed would not be a concern to me—you want an agile, well-educated cross-country horse.

Show Jumping: Again you want an, educated, relaxed horse. He should be quite adjustable in the show jumping, have had really good training, and be able to canter a course quietly and obediently.

History: A lot of the horse's suitability can be determined in your trial period. The horse's record should also play a big part here. Often, the horse will be coming down a level or more from where he has been competing. Pay attention to the consistency of his dressage scores; also his cross-country jumping and show-jumping penalties. Every horse can have a rail or two down, but I would be dubious about him if he's had three or more rails down consistently.

Compatibility: I would also take into account your strengths and weaknesses as a rider. If your strongest phase is dressage, you should put more emphasis on the horse's ability in the jumping phases, and vice versa.

Vetting: Most horses that have done a lot in the sport are not going to vet 100 percent clean. If the horse is moving back down a level to compete with you, it is usually easier on his body, so you need to make it clear to your vet what your goals are in this respect. In a lot of cases, older experienced horses' soundness can be managed easily as long as you know what you're dealing with.

2 Green Prospect

The first thing I would look at is the movement of the horse and his potential to jump. In simple terms you want a really athletic, naturally balanced horse. Some horses from the track (known as off-the-track Thoroughbreds, or OTTBs), because of their galloping training, have tight muscles and tension. There is a bit of an art in horse selection to look into the future and see whether this type of horse can be developed. You need to feel potential for greatness as well as room for improvement.

I try to analyze how the horse learns. With a green prospect, you're dealing with a horse with absolutely no experience or training in eventing, so I like a horse that quickly picks up what I'm asking him to do and improves during the trial period. This gives me confidence that over a year or two the horse will improve even more and excel at his job.

Dressage: In addition to you riding the horse, in general, the horse's regular rider needs to ride him too so you can see him go and picture whether you can imagine him developing into a good-moving prospect. As I watch the horse walk, trot, canter, and jump a few small fences with his regular rider, I am looking for the following:

- How quiet and sensible is he?
- Does he want to buck, spook, and play up?
- Is he prepared to walk, trot, and canter forward, or does it look like the rider has to push him all the time?
- What is his movement like?

Jumping: It is more difficult to tell how a green horse will jump, but if the horse has balanced gaits and the right education, I believe you can usually count on the horse developing into an acceptable jumper if his conformation allows. For a horse like this I put a lot of emphasis on his conformation (see p. 20); you still have years of educating the horse ahead and it will be harder for him when he is not naturally built for it.

Temperament: This is a little harder to determine in young horses since they all change a little once they get into the day-to-day training grind. When the horse is from the track, remember a lot of race trainers encourage the horses to be wound up and tight; I would stay away from the extremely nervous ones because in most cases they are hard to settle. I've had quite a few OTTBs that were nervous and difficult at the beginning, but over time, mellowed out. It's not easy, though, especially for the first six months of competing.

Compatibility: It is important to understand that a really green rider and really green horse are not a good combination. A less experienced rider should have a horse that is fun, one she can learn with. If you're not confident and don't know how to train a green horse, you should look for an experienced horse. There are some exceptions, for instance, when you have a good trainer to guide you through the entire process.

Vetting: Soundness is very important so your vetting will play a big role in your decision. Again, you will not be able to educate the horse if he cannot stand up to day-to-day training.

3 Potential Upper-Level Horse

A horse with potential for the upper levels is probably already competing in Novice through Intermediate Level. The first thing I look for is whether he has the scope and potential to go on to becoming a Four-Star horse.

Dressage: Check his natural movement, ability to lengthen his stride, and the ease with which he can do the movements. It is nice to have an overstep in the walk, natural suspension in the trot and a naturally airy, balanced canter. Some horses that are naturally gifted can perform without a great deal of effort.

The flying changes are important at the Four-Star Level and some horses find them easier than others.

Jumping: At the upper levels the horse needs to be able to jump a bigger fence, at least 4 feet high with a wide spread; it must not be a big struggle for him. When I'm trying out a Novice horse I wouldn't jump him that big, but I would set the jump up a couple of levels from what he is doing to test his potential to jump a big fence.

Cross-Country: The gallop becomes more important at the upper levels and you have to estimate the horse's ability to be able to gallop consistently at 570 meters per minute and to have the endurance to go for 11 to 12 minutes. Certainly if the horse is a Thoroughbred, you will have a lot of confidence in his endurance but with a Warmblood you have to take into account the way he gallops: he should cover the ground well, not go "up and down" with his leg movement, which makes him slower, less efficient, and also wastes energy. The depth of his chest will give you an indication of his heart and lung capacity. The ability to gallop is a hard one to confidently predict: The speed of the horse is important, but efficiency of the gallop probably takes higher priority.

Temperament: By this stage the horse should have a good attitude to work and not be nervous and tight when training; he should be honest and brave cross-country and not back off when he sees a big fence.

History: I would also take into account the horse's record, but if he fits the other criteria I would not pass him over because he's had some trouble in competition. Who has been riding him? When it's been a good rider you respect, you should take his record into account, but if he's been ridden by a less experienced rider then chances are you can probably improve him when you take over the training.

Vetting: This is important. You want to know he has still got a good future ahead of him. It takes a lot of training and galloping to get fit for the upper levels, so you and your vet should come to an agreement about what you can deal with—or not. If the horse has some degeneration in the joints he can often be managed successfully, however any soft-tissue injury will require close to a year off should it become a problem. When he has good tendons and suspensory ligaments, you have an advantage.

4 Upper-Level Horse

When trying a horse that is already competing at the upper levels, I would first check his record. Generally an upper-level horse has had a good rider, so look at his results and honestly evaluate your own strengths and weaknesses. If he has had rather too high dressage scores but you're a good rider on the flat, he might be something you're willing to take a chance on, particularly if he has a good record over fences. The same is true when he's had some difficulty on cross-country: If you're a very confident rider, you might feel comfortable about improving his performance. I'd be careful about taking on a horse that doesn't have a good show-jumping record though, because from my experience this is the hardest area to improve at these levels.

I would evaluate the horse's education: You would expect all upper-level horses to be well educated, but in some cases the horse is lacking a lot of the basics. You may find a really good horse this way, but you will need the time to go back a level and retrain him. A few horses that I've had in the past—Hannigan, Simply Red, and Connaught—did not have good cross-country records before I got them. When I tried out each one of them it was apparent to me that the correct education was not there, but there was an enormous amount of potential. I took a gamble that this would shine through once I had reeducated them and they all became phenomenal event horses.

Jumping: Take into account the horse's scope. How easy is it for him to gallop and jump the upper-level fences? The horse that naturally has jump and movement will find the Four-Star Level easier than a horse that has to work much harder at it.

Temperament: This is key. You want to feel you get along with the horse and can work with him on a day-to-day basis.

Vetting: Most of these horses are not going to vet cleanly. Looking over the record, when the horse has had quite a lot of withdrawals from events or hasn't completed FEI competitions, you are seeing "red flags" warning you about the future of his soundness. I'm not too concerned how a horse looks on X-rays because he has already shown, through his record, whether he stands up to the job at the upper levels. You and your vet should discuss how to best manage the horse's soundness.

TRYING THE HORSE OUT

When I look at a new horse, I have a specific routine:

1 I have a checklist of questions to ask the seller—usually on the phone before I go to see the horse.

2 I assess the horse from the ground looking at his conformation while he stands square without any tack or a rider, and also being trotted out on a firm surface.

3 I evaluate the horse's character, disposition and individual personality qualities like willingness and boldness.

4 I assess the horse's action and watch him being ridden on the flat and over fences.

5 I try out the horse myself on the flat and over fences.

6 When I am interested in buying the horse, I have my veterinarian perform a thorough pre-purchase examination.

1 Checklist

Here is a checklist of things to ask about the horse. To avoid wasting time you can do this over the phone before you go to see him.

- His age.

- His experience: When he has experience he should have an official competition record that you can look up through the USEA.

- If he is a Thoroughbred, did he race? If he stood up to racing, it is a good sign because he can probably also withstand the demands of eventing.

- Has he been able to consistently compete at his current level?

- Does he have any prior injuries? Old tendon and suspensory injuries need to have healed well and the horse should be back in full work to show that this old injury isn't going to be a problem in the future. When a horse that has done little work has problems, these will only be exacerbated by the stress of training.

- Any stable vices like kicking or cribbing?
- The horse's general turnout and feeding routine.
- How many days of the week does he usually get ridden?
- Why is he for sale?

2 First Impression

The first time you see your prospective horse, he may be groomed to the nines or standing in a muddy paddock. Try to look beyond the superficial details but don't ignore your first impression. Most people like an attractive horse with a balanced, athletic body type and a pretty face.

Look for an arching neck, a sloping shoulder, and a back that is on the shorter, stronger side rather than long and weaker. The horse should have an overall athletic appearance with plenty of room in his chest for his heart and lungs, and should not have overly bulky musculature. His hindquarters should be strong and somewhat sloping for strength and jumping ability.

Riders are not all aiming for the Olympics or the Rolex Kentucky Four-Star, but everyone needs a horse with the talent or scope to carry out their own specific goals. Being proud of your horse and wanting to be around him is also important. When I go to try a horse and I like the way he looks, I hope that the trial goes well and that I will like the feel I get from riding that horse.

That said the way the horse goes for you and his ability to work and learn is by far the most important thing to consider. Try not to overlook the horse's shortcomings just because you fall in love with a pretty face.

3 Assess the Horse's Conformation from the Ground

With the horse standing still, evaluate his conformation. I like to look at the horse standing square without any tack. This gives me a complete first impression, including his conformation, soundness and the way he carries himself naturally.

And later I like to watch him trotted in hand on a firm surface (see p. 23).

Soundness

At the top of my list, I stress soundness. The definition for "sound" varies depending on what you are aiming to do with your horse. Most horses are up to the physical demands of competing at Novice and Training Level, with proper management. As you move up the levels and the jumps become higher, the speeds get faster and the courses longer, and the horse must have the conformation and foundation to bear the increased demands placed on him.

General Impression

I usually find it is more important how the horse's conformation affects his movement than how he looks when he's standing; however, it can be a useful guide as well as a time-saver if you rule a horse not suitable from your initial impression. Do not feel pressured to ride a horse that you are not really interested in after assessing him from the ground; it is better to move on and spend your time and energy finding a horse that does suit your needs.

A horse that is built slightly uphill, or with his head and withers slightly above his hind end, generally makes a better eventer. Instead of the rider having to gather the horse up and balance him, the well conformed horse will naturally carry himself. When the horse has a nice uphill build, analyze the rest of him. (Review the excellent book on this subject, *Sport Horse Conformation: Evaluating Athletic Potential in Dressage, Jumping, and Event Prospects* by veterinarian Christian Schacht.)

Feet

The horse's feet are important: They are the foundation on which the rest of the horse is built (see chapter 17, "Hoof Care and Shoeing").

- The horse with really small feet is not ideal: When they are bigger, there is more surface area to support his load.

- You want to make sure that the horse's feet are fairly similar in shape.

- Beware of flat feet, hooves with thin walls, or contracted heels. These types of feet will need extra care and really good management, which can lead to extra expense and worry, not to mention training time lost if he is unsound.

- I also suspect unevenly sized feet. Some horses are born this way, some with what is termed a club foot, which is generally smaller and more upright than a normal foot. I have found that the smaller foot tends to deteriorate more quickly and suffer more pain from training. A smaller foot can also atrophy as a result of his using it less. When the horse has pain on that side he will not put his full weight on that foot and over time it will shrink. You can never categorically say this will happen; when you're looking at an experienced horse that is sound and with good X-rays, his different-sized feet aren't causing him a problem so I wouldn't be as concerned.

Legs

A horse with turned-in or turned-out legs will sustain a lot more stress in his daily use than a horse with correct or straight legs. Over time this can play a part in causing inflammation, resulting in deteriorating soundness. A lot of horses have an action called "winging": While the legs are in the air, the lower half of the leg will be pushed or swing out before it comes back to the ground—noticeable when the horse is trotting or cantering toward you. Generally, I find these horses not as clever, especially at jumping, which can be attributed to this labored action.

That said, remember that each individual compensates in different ways, and a horse with less than ideal conformation may perform better and be sounder than expected. If you find a horse that you like and his leg conformation is not ideal you should have him thoroughly evaluated by a veterinarian.

Neck and Shoulders

You want the horse to be supple enough here to either reach down and stretch, or when needed, be more elevated and collected in his work.

- A neck with good muscling on the top is preferred.

- When the neck has heavy muscling underneath this generally means it will be harder to get him to stretch, release and soften.

- A horse with a neck that is a bit swan-shaped is usually more difficult to train. This neck is quite long: Under tack the horse tends to be upright at the base of the neck, then at the fourth vertebrae from the poll, goes to "round." This is not desirable because this type tends to want to go behind the vertical.

Back and Hindquarters

Considering that the neck connects to the back, the way the horse uses his neck will directly affect the way he uses his back.

- You want the back to swing up and down as he moves. The back should be shaped to allow for this, not sunken down so much that it won't swing up, and not too straight or inverted ("roach-backed") so that it won't swing down.

- The hindquarters need to be strong and powerful, not "falling away" or weak.

- Being too powerful compared to the rest of the body is not ideal either; when the horse is more powerful behind and the front end can't keep up, the horse will tend to be more downhill and harder to ride.

4 Evaluating the Horse's Personality

Temperament

The horse with a good temperament and attitude toward learning is going to be quicker, easier and more enjoyable to teach. I nearly always pick a less talented horse with a good temperament over a talented but nervous horse, or one with a difficult attitude. Riding your horse each day should be rewarding and fun. My advice is to leave the difficult, temperamental horses to the professionals.

Willingness

The horse should come out of the barn eager to please his rider and willing to work. If he is "nappy" and tries to head back to the barn before you make it to the arena, you are wasting your energy just getting him out of the door. Even at the lower levels the horse should be willing to do his work and to attempt new challenges. Some spookiness or freshness is okay but continued bad behavior means there will be a lot more required on your part, and it can indicate the horse does not have a great attitude toward working.

My belief—or motto—when trying out a horse is that you can never change him, you can only improve him. Chances are—much like a fiancé—a prospective horse will continue to do the things that make you happy, as well as those that annoy you to no end, even after you "marry" him (bring him home). Don't assume you will be able to fix all his flaws once he's yours!

Boldness

Boldness and bravery are important in an event horse, especially out on cross-country; however, you don't want what I call "nervous" bold, or a horse that just runs at the fences. Look for one that goes forward to the jump in a sensible way and enjoys jumping. Try to jump a jump that is a little different, such as a Liverpool or a jump with filler, or even take a different angle to a jump. I would like the horse to jump confidently and leave the ground committed to clearing it, even if he is a little green and unsure of himself.

Self-Preservation

It is important to me that the horse is careful and possesses self-preservation. If the horse does knock down a pole, I want to see him react at the next jump by snapping his knees up higher, and getting extra clearance rather than being lazy and hitting the pole again.

Remember that out on cross-country, while you want the horse to be brave and bold, you also want him to be clever and not just rush around the course. He should pay attention to the jumps, reacting appropriately to the question at hand and to your aids as you guide him around.

5 Assess the Horse's Action

As I mentioned before, the horse's standing conformation assessment is a guide. The important part is how the horse carries himself when he is moving.

Athletic Ability

- Watching the horse trot in hand, I try to get an impression of how he moves and more importantly, an overall impression of the horses' soundness. This is not the pre-vetting of the horse. It just gives you confidence the horse is fine to ride and not suffering from any obvious soundness problem. It also gives you the chance to see the horse walk and trot without a rider.

- The canter is probably the most important gait because it takes the most time and effort to improve. I look for a horse that naturally canters easily in a nice, uphill balance. Horses with a good canter are often the horses that are good jumpers. If the horse struggles to keep an even canter, riding to a jump will be that much harder.

- It is interesting that in the racing world, most horses are bought and sold at a very young age before they can show if they have any speed. A lot is based on the conformation of the horse and a big emphasis is put on the horse's walk. Most people believe in a correlation between a big overstep in the walk and having a fast gallop.

I like to watch the horse being ridden by his usual rider—first on the flat and then over jumps. From this I am able to get an idea of how he goes and his potential. It is normal to ask this demo rider to show you what the horse is capable of. I wouldn't rule out a horse if he can't perform certain movements, but it gives you an idea of the horse's level of training.

A lot of what you can find out will depend on his level of experience. If you are a novice rider bring your trainer and have him or her sit on the horse before you ride, to help assess whether the horse is appropriate for you.

Watching the Horse Being Ridden

On the Flat

As I watch his rider put the horse through his paces on the flat, I look for a supple, loose-moving horse. I like to see a regular rhythm in his trot and he should keep this rhythm when leg-yielding or changing direction. A horse whose rhythm changes frequently is not going to score as well in dressage as a steady horse. I also look for the potential for an "uphill" canter (see p. 23). A horse that naturally canters on his forehand will be much harder to collect. This will negatively affect his performance in all phases of an event.

Here is the first chance to look at the horse's education. By watching the horse being ridden, usually by his regular rider, I can start to form an opinion on the suitability of the horse for what I am looking for. Generally, the rider will show what the horse is educated to do. So for an OTTB or a green horse prospect, this will be walk, trot, and canter in each direction and on each lead—on a soft contact. Obviously, the more experienced the horse, the more that can be shown. Try to pay close attention to the horse's attitude to the work: Is he slow to go on the bit? Is he nervous, tight, stiff, or aggressive at the beginning? Is he willing to work? Pinning ears and swishing the tail can be signs of an unhappy horse. How established is the horse's education?

Over Fences

When jumping an inexperienced horse, I look for a natural instinct to jump cleanly and carefully while going forward to the fence and a horse that is attentive and clever with his legs.

You can keep the jumps small: A simple cross-rail or vertical will do. You want to assess his potential, not back him off by testing beyond his ability and confidence level (fig. 2.2).

In evaluating what the horse is like to ride to the jump I assess the following:

- How educated is he to the jumping?

- Does he rush on the approach?

- What kind of shape does he make with his body when he jumps?

- What does he do with his front and back legs?

- What is he like on the landing side?

There is no need to have the horse jumped excessively by his rider. It is more a time to get an idea of the way the horse approaches, executes, and travels away from the jump. It also helps form an opinion on the way the horse has been trained and ridden. With the green horse, you are looking for a forward-thinking horse that is respectful of the jumps. On the approach, whether in trot or canter, it is ideal when the horse's rhythm doesn't change drastically, that is, not speeding up or backing off too much.

The jump is important, and watching from the ground is probably the best way to evaluate this. Straightness is imperative. A horse that

2.2 Watch the horse's current rider school him before you get on for a ride.

drifts left or right is not ideal. Generally, the drift will take away from the horse's jump and he won't go as high. Drifting is also difficult on course, especially on cross-country, where it is important to hold your line.

Ideally, you want the horse's front legs to come up so his knees are in front of him, both legs coming up together, knees even and the horse rounding in the air, using his back to execute the jump, and pulling his hind legs up high enough to clear the fence as he goes through the air. I like the horse to be able to land on either lead. The horse that wants to land on the same lead all the time will need more training than a horse that is balanced and adjustable.

However, although the way he uses his front legs is important, it is not a deal breaker. There have been many great event horses that haven't folded their front legs tightly. The Foreman is a classic example. Most photos of him jumping show his legs only partly folded. However, he always got them out of the way and left the ground confidently.

It is also better when the horse rounds or bascules over the jump. When he does this he is using his back while jumping. A basculed jump will have the horse's withers up over the jump, his neck reaching forward and round. As the horse's back legs leave the ground, his rump and back legs go high up over the jump. A horse that jumps flat and or quickly in the air is generally not as good in the show jumping. Also, he would not be that desirable on the cross-county. The back legs of the horse should be able to stretch out behind him in the air. A horse that doesn't do this will struggle.

Overall, the horse should take his time with the jump but still have a forward instinct. A horse that hesitates at the jumps and then goes really high, isn't going forward enough and more than likely will struggle, especially where there are related, striding jumps, because he isn't covering the ground while jumping.

The other extreme is a horse that rushes at the jump. This is probably the hardest type to ride. The tendency here is to hold on to try to stop the horse from getting too aggressive at the jump—so the ride to the jump becomes backward. You end up pulling back on the reins on the approach.

6 Trying the Horse Out Yourself

On the Flat

After watching the horse being ridden, the next step is for you to try the horse. If, after watching the horse go, you really feel he's not for you, don't feel obligated to ride him. It is perfectly okay to say so and not waste everyone's time and energy.

I want to see if we have a good connection and "chemistry." I try to ride him the way I would want to train him if I owned him. If the horse is green I try to get an idea of the quality of his gaits and how he will be to get "round" in his frame. I look for his potential for improvement and pay attention to his temperament and attitude toward working.

On all horses, whether they are green or well educated, it is a good idea to take some time in the walk to get a feel for the horse. Gradually, put your leg on and evaluate the horse's reaction and also slowly take a feel of the horse's mouth. Is it sensitive? Or, a little heavy? With the more educated horse, I would push him forward then ask him to accept the contact and go on the bit.

If he is a green horse with no training your main priority is to get the horse moving straight and forward and gradually accepting the contact. With the green horse, you don't necessarily have to get him on the bit, but you want to get an idea of whether or not you will be able to improve his education in the future.

I walk, trot, and canter each direction, getting a feel for the horse's balance, his ease of staying in the gait, and his suppleness, looseness in his movement, acceptance in the connection when changing directions, and quality of his transitions.

You can also get an idea of the horse's temperament. Is he a sensitive horse that you have to sit on quietly or is he a bit "cold," needing to be pushed along?

Once you have an overall impression you can then work on specific exercises depending on the education of the horse. How well does the *green horse* understand picking up each lead? Does he get wound up if you lengthen the trot or canter? How balanced is he on a 15-meter trot and canter circle? Will he accept your lower leg and accept a simple leg yield? How is his mouth? A very tight mouth makes it hard to take any contact, a heavy or numb mouth makes for a slow-reacting horse.

With a *more educated horse*, you can test the horse's education: leg-yielding; shoulder-in; half-pass; lengthening and collecting; 10-meter circles; counter-canter; lengthening and shortening the canter; and flying changes.

How comfortable is he to sit to? What you ask of the horse should be related to the horse's education and, obviously, your own knowledge and education.

Having someone teach you through the trial can be helpful; try to be fair to the horse. Don't ask him to do movements that he has not yet learned. The main idea of this ride is to try to estimate how you would be able to get along with him and his potential on the flat.

Jumping

Once you have had a good evaluation on the flat, I shorten my stirrups and move on to jumping.

With the *green horse*, you will be trying to estimate the horse's potential to jump and how he might develop if you were going to train him over time. The green horse should give you a confident feeling and about his potential for the future. Test to see if he has enough ability to go to the level that you are aspiring to ride.

With the *more experienced horse* you are able to test more and see how he reacts to you as a rider. From watching the other rider on him, you should already have an idea of the kind of ride you need: either aggressive and forward for the "colder" horse or more sensitive and quiet for the "hotter" kind.

It is important to try the horse with different kinds of "tests" as well. This isn't going to be possible on a very green horse that has limited jumping experience. First, you want to get a good feel for the rhythm of the horse and how he jumps. It is good to then mix up the canter approach to evaluate how he will react,

Personal Stories

Let me tell you about a couple of my own personal experiences trying out horses who went on to become successful Four-Star competitors.

The Foreman

The Foreman was a four-year-old Thoroughbred who had just finished racing when Bruce Fenwick brought him to my farm for me to try, along with three or four other horses. I remember "Chip" having a very regular, "floating" trot, which I liked. He spent time in the air with his legs and had natural suspension. His canter was uphill even though his standing conformation was a bit downhill, and when I rode him he had a great feel. He was a bit nervous being in a new environment, but relaxed in the walk, which I liked. In those days, I didn't put as much emphasis on the nervousness, so this didn't worry me too much.

The Foreman showed me from the very first jump that he would rather go very high over the jump rather than hit it. He was pretty brave considering he had just started jumping. Because he jumped so high, he did land a bit unbalanced, but not too bad. His front knees did not come up in front of him over the jump, but because his instinct was to go so high, I didn't rule him out. That style of jumping is still with him today.

Connaught

I flew to Atlanta to try Connaught, the horse I rode to win the 2008 Rolex Kentucky CCI**** and at the Beijing Olympic Games, at his previous owners', Jim and Julie Richards, farm. Julie had ridden him to the Three-Star Level, so I went through all the movements that are required at that level. He had flamboyant movement but was very green and unbalanced. I got the feeling that the potential was there but would take some time to get established. I remember that he had quite small steps in the walk and one flying change was pretty bad; those shortcomings have stuck with him his whole career!

Connaught was just amazing to jump and gave me an unbelievable feeling. I don't think it would have mattered how he went for me on the flat after I jumped him! I started with a small vertical and then another a bit bigger. I then jumped a sloping Oxer until it got to be about 4 feet, which is about how high he would have to jump if I bought him. I mixed up the approach to the oxer, jumping out of a galloping approach, short canter, and an angle. I got the feeling that with every jump he cared about how he jumped and did what he could to get his legs out of the way. His knees were up in front and tight and he kicked up his back hind legs. After I jumped him, I gave him a sprint on the flat for about a quarter of a mile. Although he isn't a Thoroughbred, I felt he had enough gallop for the Four-Star Level.

From all my experience trying horses and then watching them progress, I don't think you ever really *change* them, but what you can do is *improve* them. The Foreman's jumping technique improved but will never be classic. Connaught's walk did improve but it is never his best gait. This theory applies to other areas as well. If a horse bolts when you are trying him, chances are that might get better but won't completely disappear. If the horse grinds his teeth when you try him, I bet he will still grind his teeth five years down the road. I like to picture the horse in two to three years and how I think he will progress. I take all the information into consideration as I come to my decision.

but always being fair and always with enough power in the approach.

Test the horse's rideability when approaching the jumps on a short canter stride, and also on a forward canter or gallop approach. Also, try a not-straight approach to the jump but on a slight angle (this should only be done if you have the riding skills to do so). After the forward or gallop ride, I then canter to a jump on a short canter stride and evaluate how the horse deals with the change of ride. Does he pull after the forward ride? Does his jump change and get flatter? When he is ridden in a shorter stride does he keep his confidence?

It is hard to give advice on how high and wide to jump. Certainly you shouldn't overface yourself or the horse. It doesn't hurt to ask the owner (or representative) if she is okay with the height you are jumping. Similarly to when you are watching the horse being ridden, it is important to evaluate straightness when he is jumping, and how he approaches, jumps, and departs from the fence.

You also need to evaluate the horse's self-carriage between the jumps. You don't want the horse to be too heavy or race on. Lastly, does he make you feel comfortable and confident?

Cross-Country

If he has passed this part of the test, then it is ideal to try some cross-country jumps. Obviously, this isn't always possible in some venues. Arguably, the most important part of our sport is the cross-country, so finding a way to try the horse on a course is advisable. Transporting the horse to a cross-country venue on another day is an option. If that is not possible, where it's appropriate, make a corner jump in the arena, jump a Liverpool, a jump with filler underneath, or put someone's coat on the ground underneath a jump.

All of these things will give you more knowledge as to how the horse will react to different settings and jumps. It is also important to gallop the horse in an open field when you can. The last thing you want is to get the horse home to find out his gallop is too strong for you. Ideally, this can be done when trying the horse out on cross-country. Take the horse to the speed he will be competing at and then bring him back again.

When trying him cross-country you need to start off getting a feel for how the horse goes over some forward-riding cross-country jumps. After this it is important to find out how he reacts to various jumps such as water, ditches, narrow fences, angles, banks, and more. Keep to a level at which you and the horse are confident. With the very green horse, you need to keep this very simple. Introduce him to walking in the water and trotting over logs.

Again, evaluate the horse's attitude and reactions. Does he "think" *forward?* Is he still controllable and adjustable? Do you get a confident feel? How does he react if you don't ride him perfectly or lose your balance?

From experience, I would advise you to then go home to think about your experience and watch the video replay before making your decision.

2.3 A–C Have your veterinarian thoroughly examine any horse that you are considering for purchase. Here Dr. Kevin Keane performs flexion tests on a sale prospect at True Prospect Farm as helpers look on and assess the horse's soundness.

7 The Pre-Purchase Exam

If you decide that this could be the horse for you, it is worth the money to have a thorough pre-purchase exam performed by your own veterinarian or a local vet that you trust and can openly communicate with. The horse's regular veterinarian can also be a good source of information.

When you are planning to compete at the lower levels, the horse may get by with some minor soundness issues if you follow a careful maintenance program of fitness and veterinary care. For the FEI levels, however, you will need a truly sound and fit horse, and your veterinarian will be your best guide as you find a suitable partner.

The higher the level the horse will be competing, the more particular the vetting should be. You should tell your vet the level that you want to ride when you do the pre-purchase exam so he can evaluate the horse objectively (2.3 A–C).

Most horses can continue to perform with mild arthritic changes. If there are changes, I would rather both sides of the horse are similar, that is, if the horse has some arthritis in his hock, I'd prefer it in both hocks rather than just on one side. Supplements such as Nutramax Cosequin® can help, and in some instances it may be necessary to give your horse joint injections so that he stays comfortable.

Advice from a Veterinarian

My longtime veterinarian Dr. Kevin Keane (see p. 283 for a more about him) has traveled extensively with the US and Australian equestrian teams. His practice is unique in that it treats both sport horses and racehorses. He is also an upper-level eventing competitor and has competed to the CCI** Level with his horse Fernhill Flutter. Kevin says:

"Acquiring an event horse frequently begins with an evaluation by your veterinarian to determine if that horse is the right model for you as far as health and soundness. The vet's role is to assess the animal; there is probably no horse that is perfect, so we basically try to determine the risks that the exam discloses and put them together in a synopsis to discuss with the trainer/rider/potential owner to determine if they want to go forward with the sale.

"Horses come from a lot of different backgrounds: unraced Thoroughbreds, horses with a previous career like show jumpers—it is not uncommon in eventing to have OTTBs and sport horses from other disciplines that were considered more suitable for eventing. Some people also pick out a nice young prospect that is unexposed to any discipline and develop the horse on their own. While the young prospect is not likely to have many problems, a horse with a previous career may have some old injuries that need to be assessed.

"You want to have a baseline image of the horse's overall health and soundness, especially for an upper-level horse. An evaluation includes a physical and a soundness exam in which we take X-rays to look for abnormalities that could influence the horse's soundness in the future. In former times it was not common, but these days it is becoming more usual to ultrasound the horse to determine if there have been injuries to soft tissue that is otherwise hard to detect. This is uncommon with young horses because most abnormalities can be detected with a good palpation.

"The veterinarian's role is to basically help guide you through your acquisition, but not to make the decision for you. I think the most successful system is to have your coach with you *and* a vet that has some level of experience with event horses and is familiar with the discipline. That is very important. There are textbooks now (for example, *Diagnosis and Management of Lameness in the Horse* by Michael W. Ross and Sue J. Dyson) that specifically deal with unsoundness in horses for the discipline

Taking a Horse on Trial

It is hard to evaluate a horse's potential in a day. When you go to try a horse, you are there to get a feel of how you would progress with him. If you have the option of taking the horse home on trial, say for a week or two, it is a great opportunity and a much surer way of picking the right horse, no question (fig. 2.4). You will then be able to see how he behaves in a new environment and have more time to get to know him and make up your mind whether he is your ideal partner. A trial is a big advantage, but I would not consider taking a horse on trial unless you are nearly certain that you want to buy him.

A lot of owners understandably are not that keen on letting a horse go on trial, because they're not sure that the care of the horse will be up to standard. Give the owner confidence by insuring the horse and write up an agreement that spells out in detail that you take on the risk.

Another option is to try the horse at another place. This helps you to see the horse's personality and how he reacts at a show ground, public jumping facility, or some other venue where you can meet the owner and ride the horse.

Usually, when you try the horse for the first time, he is ridden in front of you before you get on. This is as it should be, but if you go back a second time to try him out, request that you can sit on him first, because when you take him home you will not have someone else ride him before you get on.

2.4 Lee Lee Jones and Olivia Dutton out for a ride. Suitable horses come in all shapes and sizes.

that the horse is performing in. For example, event horses tend to have specific injuries that are more prevalent in their sport and the vet should be familiar with these. There are many things to consider when purchasing a horse for eventing and your team will help guide you through the decision-making process."

The Off-the-Track Thoroughbred (OTTB)

Kevin also says, "The OTTB is very commonly seen in eventing. Depending on the level you want to compete, there are many abnormalities that—once healed well—the horse can probably live with. For example, a horse that had a bowed tendon at age three that was rehabilitated and put back in work at age six, may have healed well. Many horses with tendon injuries go on to compete again, so this may not be a reason to overlook an otherwise promising horse. Because racing tests the horse's soundness so well at an early age, an injury as a racehorse may not necessarily preclude an OTTB's usefulness as an event horse; there can be many variations here, and it is best left up to the veterinarian to decide whether a horse is suitable for your intended purpose."

3.1 The tack room at True Prospect Farm on a busy work day.

CHAPTER 3

Tack and Equipment for the Horse

TACK

As a sport that involves three separate phases, eventing requires a great deal of equipment for both horse and rider (fig. 3.1). Riders just starting out may be tempted to purchase less expensive equipment, but if you plan to stay in it for the long haul, it is a good idea to buy the best quality you can afford.

Used tack shops can be an excellent source of inexpensive but high quality equipment; just make sure to check for damage or wear and have a good saddler make any necessary repairs to keep things in safe working condition. You also may be able to borrow nice show tack for your first event so that you can decide if competing is for you before you make a big investment.

Saddles

The most essential pieces of tack are a saddle and bridle. In an ideal world you would have three saddles, one for each phase of competition, but when you are starting off at the lower levels this is not imperative. There are numerous different designs and types of saddles on the

market. Generally, the most important thing, after making sure the saddle fits the horse, is that you the rider are comfortable in whichever saddle(s) you choose.

Just recently I have come up with a line of saddles, the Dutton RZ, that are lightweight and incorporate ease of fitting to different types of horses, as well as a ventilation system that helps to keep the horse's back cool. I'm really pleased with how these are working on my horses (figs.3.2 A–C).

All Purpose

While an all-purpose saddle may not be as ideal as one made for a specific purpose, it can be used for both show jumping and cross-country. Popular with pleasure riders, these are an acceptable and more economical alternative to having separate saddles. It usually has a forward flap to allow for jumping, and short

3.2 A The dressage saddle has longer flaps and a deep seat, which allow the rider to sit up tall with a long leg, as is appropriate for dressage riding. In addition to the patented WisAir™ airflow system, the Dutton RZ saddles feature a standard exchangeable gullet system so the width of the saddle can be adjusted to fit different horses' backs.

3.2 B A cross-country saddle—the Dutton RZ. The forward flaps help the rider maintain a correct galloping and jumping position cross-country, and the extra ventilation, unique to this saddle, helps prevent the horse from overheating as he exerts himself.

3.2 C The Dutton RZ show jumping saddle, which I designed in cooperation with eventer Ronald Zabala-Goetschel's Wise Equestrian brand. These saddles are lightweight and have a patented WisAir ventilation system to keep the horse's back cool during performance.

billets for use with a long girth. When you are just starting out it is a good option to help you financially "ease" into the sport.

Dressage

A dressage saddle has a deeper seat and a longer flap than a jumping saddle (see fig. 3.2 A). This helps you sit down comfortably into the saddle at sitting trot and feel at one with your horse. Everyone's shape and size is different and there are numerous saddles on the market. Take the time to get the right fit not only for you but for your horse. To a degree, a saddle can be customized to you and your horse, and I feel the extra expense is worthwhile. Padding can also help the fit to the horse, although keep in mind that the more padding you put between you and the horse takes away from that feel of being "one" with him.

If you are not sure about the length of time you are going to have the horse that you are currently riding, your saddle can be adjusted to your next horse as well. In a situation like mine, where I ride lots of horses, I have a couple of different fitting saddles: one that fits narrow-bodied Thoroughbred-type horses and another that fits broader ones. The same saddle will go on the same type of horse all the time, with minor adjustments made with padding.

Cross-Country

On cross-country weight is important, especially at the higher levels, because a heavy saddle fatigues the horse more quickly. There are saddles on the market specifically designed for cross-country riding and I feel they make it safer and easier to ride (see fig. 3.2 B). The seat is longer so when riding a drop fence or in the situation where you get a little bit left behind, you are still kept nicely in the saddle. The flap where the rider's lower leg sits is also designed for riding with a shorter stirrup, as you do on cross-country. Bear in mind, these cross-country saddles with the longer seat tend to keep your position back in the saddle more than you'd like at slower speeds so they are not ideal for show jumping.

Show Jumping

For show jumping, the saddle has a more forward fit with a flatter seat that allows you to come back into the saddle and also the freedom to go with the horse as he jumps (see fig. 3.2 C). I would look at the shape of how the saddle holds your lower leg. You want to get one where your lower leg comfortably stays on the horse and doesn't slide back.

The fit to the horse is again important but not quite as crucial as in the dressage phase, so padding can be used to make up for a saddle that is not quite custom-fitted to your horse.

Saddle Pads

The saddle pad is designed to provide a protective, cushioning barrier between the horse and saddle. You want something that protects against shock and abrasion without adding too much bulk and without creating unnecessary heat buildup, which can create problems for the horse's skin and prevent proper cooling as the horse works, especially in hot weather.

Saddle pads come in all different styles and materials. Sheepskin pads have been the norm for many years; these days, memory foam and synthetic pads have also become popular and are very good at preventing soreness and impact on the horse's back.

- In dressage, it's nice to have something smart looking that creates an attractive overall picture and does not take away from the natural beauty of the horse.

- On cross-country, go a little more practical: A saddle pad should be lightweight. There is no benefit to having a big square or rectangular saddle pad that covers more of the horse than needs to be covered, which creates extra heat and weight. A pad shaped around the saddle is appropriate.

- In show jumping too, excess padding that can flap around is not ideal so something more shaped to your saddle is better.

The fit of the saddle and saddle pad is not to be taken lightly: the horse's performance can be severely affected by a sore or tender back, and this can be hard to diagnose since many horses do not react to back palpation because they are just tight and stiff there anyway.

Keeping saddle pads washed and clean so they are not abrasive to the horse's back is important, as dirty patches can cause painful pressure points on the horse's back.

In some cases, you need extra padding under the saddle but, to me, this should be a short-term solution only; for the long-term you should get your saddle correctly fitted to your horse. As mentioned, if you have one saddle but ride several horses with different types of withers, saddle pads can help create a more customized fit. When you place the saddle on the horse's back you should be able to fit at least three fingers between the pommel and the withers: If the saddle sits too low, you can raise it with a pad.

Non-slip pads are cheap and a good buffer, and help to hold the saddle in place. This is the first thing I would try—before adding a breastplate—to keep a saddle from slipping.

Girths

- A lot of dressage saddles nowadays have long billets, which are used with a short girth (fig.

3.3 A short dressage girth with long billets keeps the buckles out from underneath from the rider's leg.

3.3). These allow your leg to be closer to the horse without interference from the girth's buckles, since they will rest below where your leg is in contact with the saddle. They are a great idea and are just as effective at holding the saddle in place as a long girth. Short billets are also on some jumping saddles, and I think this is a great addition.

- Traditional, longer girths also come in elastic-sided models: Even when the girth is tight, should the horse need to make a big effort over a jump, the elastic allows for extra movement. Be sure not to overdo the tightness, however—you want it secure but don't crank it up so the elastic is stretched to the maximum.

Most girths are made from leather but there are some soft, lighter synthetic girths available. Certainly for training they are practical because they are easier to clean. Some girths are contoured to fit the horse's shape and, in some cases, this can be useful in preventing rubbing and pinching of the sensitive skin behind the horse's elbows.

Rubbing and chafing occurs for various reasons. As a first measure of prevention, be sure your leather girth is clean and flexible. A simple sheepskin cover that slides over the girth can be useful in preventing chafing and can be taken off and washed when needed. String girths are also used for horses more subject to being chafed: They are often used in racing and for younger horses.

Stud Guard

Girths also come with an attachment called a "stud guard": When they jump, some horses mark themselves underneath their chests with their front feet. This affects the way they jump because they worry about hurting themselves. You can use a stud guard for show jumping and cross-country, and, for some horses, it is an important addition. Connaught, for instance, used to hit himself frequently, and I found a stud guard an important addition. It's lightweight and only a small piece of extra tack to put on, but it is not something you need to use unless your horse has this problem.

Overgirth

An overgirth is sometimes appropriate for extra safety in case a billet breaks on cross-country. The first line of defense, however, is to regularly maintain your saddle and make sure the billets are in good shape. This is money well spent. I've had stirrup leathers and breastplates and attachments break on cross-country, but fortunately not in a major competition, touch wood!

Breastplate

The purpose of a breastplate is to keep the saddle from slipping back too far without restricting the horse's shoulder and movement. It is not usually appropriate in the dressage phase because the place the saddle moves to comfortably on the horse is where the rider should be sitting anyway—in most cases.

Your position should be forward over the horse's withers for jumping, and you do not want the saddle to slip back because it is harder to stay with the horse: When he takes off, you'll be sitting too far back and then get catapulted forward. So, in some cases it's a good idea to find a breastplate that keeps the saddle in place while you gallop and jump.

However, there is no point in using an accessory unless it works. There are a lot of breastplates on the market, but I don't feel that many of them work all that well. Also, riders don't always use them to their full advantage. They feel that if it's there, it's good enough.

The breastplate should fit tightly enough to stop the saddle slipping back (see fig. 3.5). I like one with elastic at the junctions that stretches to allow the horse to use his shoulders (see fig. 3.6). Some of the new breastplates not only attach near the saddle but at the girth. This provides more security while still allowing the horse to use his shoulders.

Bridles

Most of the time you'll be using a normal snaffle bridle (fig. 3.4). There are many different styles on the market, and you can find something that flatters your horse's head. A big heavy horse will look better in a heavy bridle with broader straps while a Thoroughbred or other finely built horse looks better with a lighter version.

The main concern with the bridle is the fit. Make sure that the head piece that goes over the horse's ears is big enough and that the cheek pieces are long enough so the bit hangs in the mouth comfortably. There are a variety of nosebands on the market, which can be purchased with the bridle or separately, depending on your horse's needs (see p. 41). It is popular, but by no means necessary, to have some sort of decoration on the browband, such as brass clinchers or fancy stitching.

Reins

Reins vary greatly: The most important thing is to find reins in a width that fit your hands comfortably. Too wide and they may feel like too much of a handful; too narrow, they will cut into your hands.

Reins are different lengths, too. Some horses have a short neck—or shorten their neck a lot, especially for jumping—and it's not a good idea to have a lot of extra rein length hanging down because you or your horse could get a foot caught in it.

There are different styles of reins. Some have a rubber grip, which is quite helpful for jumping, especially in wet or muddy conditions, or even hot conditions when the horse gets sweaty (see fig. 3.6). Plain leather reins look nice for dressage, and there are some leather reins that are lined with rubber on the inside for a sleeker look. One thing rubber tends to do on a day to day basis is rub the horse's neck and take the hair off, which is unsightly, so you may want to have another type of rein to swap out.

For cross-country you can tie a knot at the buckle in the middle of your reins for extra security, since it is possible for the buckle to come undone, leaving you with two separate, flapping reins. Be sure to secure the keeper, too; having reins with a longer "tongue" to go through the buckle can also help prevent this issue.

Note: A double bridle that has both a snaffle bit and a curb bit with separate reins for each

Tack and Equipment for the Horse 3

3.4 For most horses, a simple snaffle bridle is preferable.

can be used for dressage at the higher levels. It can also be used on cross-country, although this is not something to try just for the heck of it. It could be used under expert supervision and on the advice of an instructor who thinks it would be advantageous to your horse.

Nosebands

The noseband is an important part of the bridle. In some horses changing the noseband can really affect contact and the way the horse goes, particularly in the two jumping phases. If you are having an issue with your horse getting too strong, the first line of defense is to try a few different nosebands and work on the fit to make sure it's effective before you go to a stronger bit.

Some of the better-made nosebands have

3.5 A flash noseband with a loose ring snaffle bit, a leather hunting-style breastplate, and rubber reins.

3.6 A figure-eight noseband with a "Wonder" Bit, rubber reins, and elasticized breastplate. The horse is also wearing an ear net to keep flies away.

padding and are quite comfortable for the horse. A tight noseband will restrict how much he can cross his jaw and be strong, but it's not ideal to go out on course with his mouth closed really tightly. This is uncomfortable for him and can create resistance.

A few common types of nosebands:

- A *flash noseband* has a drop attachment on the regular cavesson that fits below the bit to keep the mouth closed (fig. 3.5).

- The *figure-eight* works well for a lot of horses because it puts pressure higher up on the horse's face and keeps his mouth closed with a softer effect (fig. 3.6).

- A regular *drop noseband* can be helpful on the flat to help keep the horse's mouth closed. It fits lower on the face, which is more comfortable for some horses.

- A noseband that I have some experience with has a *flat metal plate* on either side of the horse's mouth. For horses that tend to cross their jaw and get strong while galloping, this helps to give the rider a little extra control.

Hackamore

The hackamore, or bitless bridle, is popular in show jumping (figs. 3.7 A & B). The control of the horse comes from pressure on the poll

Tack and Equipment for the Horse 3

3.7 A & B A hackamore: I find that a hackamore can work well on a horse that resists in show jumping by encouraging him to jump in a freer style than when wearing a bit. Turning and control are not as effective as with a bit, and I would definitely not recommend using a hackamore on the cross-country course, for safety reasons (A). The metal links in the noseband of this type of hackamore apply extra pressure to the front of the horse's face, which gives the rider more control (B).

and the front of the horse's nose. Hackamores can work well on a horse that resists in the show jumping phase by encouraging him to jump in a freer style than when wearing a bit.

Turning and control with a hackamore is a lot less effective than with a bit, so this is definitely one you want to practice with at home to make sure that you can ride safely with it. I would definitely *not* recommend using a hackamore on the

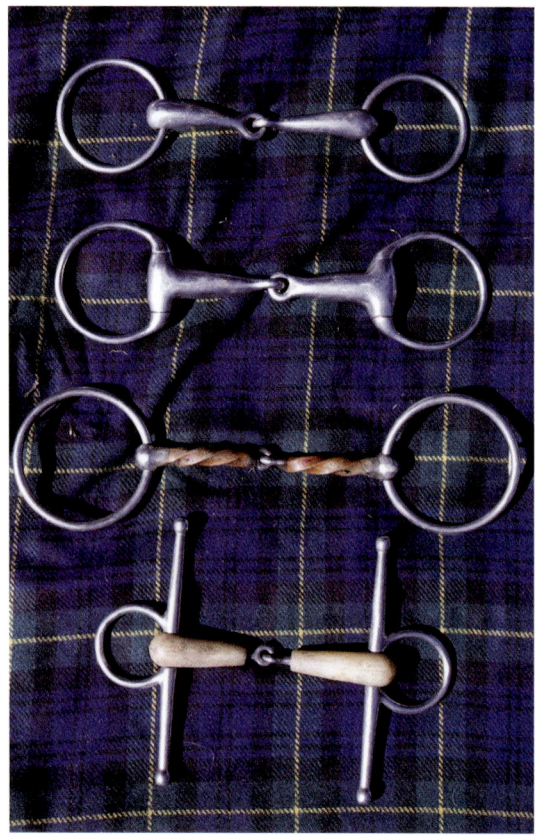

3.8 A few of my favorite bits are (top to bottom) a loose ring snaffle; eggbutt snaffle; slow twist copper mouth loose ring snaffle; and full cheek "Happy Mouth" snaffle.

cross-country course because it would be a risk to both horse and rider. When the horse starts galloping fast you need the security of a bit in his mouth.

Bits

In general, the goal is to ride all three phases of an event in a soft snaffle bit (fig. 3.8). Before you use a stronger bit you need to understand why you are doing it. Ideally, you should educate your horse so that you don't need a stronger bit. I've had several horses, including Nova Top, True Blue Girdwood, The Foreman, and Truluck, go in a snaffle at the upper levels.

If your horse becomes unsafe in a snaffle when you are riding at speed, you should use a different bit for training. A stronger bit can also help to rebalance a strong horse in preparation for the jump.

My horses Connaught and House Doctor both didn't really get strong in the gallop but needed help getting prepared for the jump. As they become more trained, balanced, and experienced I was able to use "less" bit than I had earlier in their training. Early on, House Doctor had various bits because I found that after some time in one bit he would not be as responsive; I used a three-ring Pessoa bit most commonly with him. Connaught used an Attached Wonder Bit: I actually had one made for him that was just a little stronger than the one you can buy off the shelf.

Because of my horses' needs, these are the bits I have used throughout my career, but there are many different ones on the market.

Bits for Dressage

There are restrictions on the bit you can use for dressage, and I would encourage people to stick to a normal snaffle or an abbreviation of a normal snaffle.

- Types of snaffle bit include a variety of *loose ring, eggbutt* (see fig. 3.8) and *dee ring* bits. You want a snaffle that your horse will not resist: A loose ring with a medium-width mouthpiece will encourage the horse to take the bit forward while still staying soft and submissive, so it's a good bit to start. A horse with a small mouth will not be comfortable in a big, heavy bit–be sure to choose accordingly.

- A double bridle, which consists of a curb bit and a small snaffle (or "bradoon"), can be used at Intermediate Level and up. The point of a double bridle is to enhance collection, not to hold a stronger horse or to give you more stopping power. As mentioned, its use is best reserved for an experienced, knowledgeable rider with an independent seat and quiet hands.

Dr. Bristol and French Link Bits

These types have an extra link in the mouthpiece that is sometimes good for horses a little dull in their mouth. They fit comfortably in the horse's mouth and the extra link allows you to move the bit a little, which lets your horse go in a somewhat softer way. I wouldn't use one of these on a horse whose mouth structure is very light; I'd use it on a horse that's a bit heavier. With a lighter horse the bit would likely have too much effect and cause him to travel behind the vertical, with his nose tucked in toward his chest.

Leverage Bits

Some bits, such as the Baucher, provide leverage and encourage the horse to be more responsive to the rider. "Leverage" refers to the pounds of pressure transmitted through the horse's bit per pounds of pressure from the rider's hands through the reins. Some horses are more sensitive than others to this pressure, so proceed gently when testing a leverage bit on your horse.

Bits for Jumping

There are many different types of bits one might choose for jumping. Again, it is ideal to keep your horse in a lighter, snaffle type of bit, if you can. Remember that during the approach to the jump, the more you take back, the more you are taking away from the horse's power. However, in a lot of cases, having a different kind of bit will actually help the horse's performance, especially in competition, since it is a waste of energy when the horse is constantly fighting and pulling against you.

It is best if you can train the horse in lessons or at home in a mild snaffle bit and save the stronger bit for competitions. A lot of times when you use a stronger bit for training, after a while, you just have to keep going to an even stronger bit because the horse's reaction becomes dull. Also, the bigger, stronger bit very often isn't as helpful in your daily training as it is on the "big day," when your horse is excited by the atmosphere and the opportunity to gallop and jump cross-country, and when you need a little extra stopping power.

Stronger Bit Options

When choosing a stronger bit, the first thing you have to recognize is why your horse needs more bit. Also, take into consideration what sort of action each bit has and what you really need for your horse.

3.9 A full-cheek gag snaffle.

3.10 "Wonder" Bit and FLAIR™ Nasal Strip, which aids the horse's breathing during intense exercise.

The Gag

A *gag* is a very common snaffle bit: It has a pulley action so that as you use the reins the bit is lifted in the mouth and helps elevate the horse up in front of you (fig. 3.9). This is perfect for the horse that wants to carry himself low and drag you along in the approach to the jumps. The gag can be quite an aggressive bit: the idea behind it is so you use *less* hand, not more strength.

The *cherry roller gag* is the ultimate bit for a very strong, pulling horse. The bit has smooth rollers on the mouthpiece so the horse finds it nearly impossible to "lock on" and take a grip onto this bit. It has the same action as a regular gag snaffle.

The gag can be ridden with two reins, as can the *pelham* (see p. 47), the idea being that when the horse is going well you can use just the rein attached to the snaffle and when you need more strength you can use the other rein attached to the curb bit. Practically speaking, it is difficult to hold two reins and a whip and maintain your galloping position. I have done this, but it is not suitable for all riders. If you want to you need to think about finding thin reins that you can fit in your hands and still grip with, since many cross-country reins are fairly wide to begin with.

Three-Ring Bit

A *three-ring* bit is a good, safe bit to use. You have the option of putting the reins on different settings, depending on how strong the horse is on the day. The lower the ring you attach the rein to, the more leverage you have to bring the horse up in front and slow the horse down. The downside, I feel, is in the steering: Because of the longer shank where the rein attaches, there's a slower reaction when you turn your horse. But if your horse is sensitive about turning, this is a softer alternative to the gag snaffle.

Wonder Bit

A "*Wonder*" Bit, where the bridle and rein attachment are both fixed to the bit, has an action of elevating the bit in the horse's mouth as you use the rein, as well as applying pressure to the poll (fig. 3.10). This bit is not as strong as a gag, and I think horses tend to go well in it and are not as resistant as they are with a gag. Horses may submit and come back better than with a gag thanks to the softer action. They also tend to have a better turning action due to the way the bit is shaped on the side of the horse's face.

Pelham and Kimberwicke

A *pelham*, which applies leverage to the poll when the shanks are pulled back as well as pressure under the chin with the curb chain, is another option. The chain can be adjusted to give the bit more influence. These are not as popular as they used to be, when they came more from the hunt field. I don't like the fact that the pressure is on the horse's mouth virtually all the time, especially when the chain is tight. Some horses really go well in it while others, at the end of the course after some time galloping, may not be as respectful of the bit as you would like.

The *Kimberwicke* has a similar action to the pelham, but the reins are attached to holes in the rings of the bit. The Kimberwicke also uses a curb chain.

Both the pelham and the Kimberwicke can also be used with an *equalizer*–or *converter*–a leather strap that buckles to the bit, which you can attach the rein to then use just one rein. It's not perfect but as the horse gets stronger you still have more control than with just a snaffle.

All the bits I've just discussed for jumping can be used for both the cross-country and show jumping phases. In the show jumping, it is important for the horse to jump in a nice shape; when he's resistant or worried about his bit, chances are he'll jump with his head up and back hollow and not pay attention to where his legs are. So, it's important to find a bit that fits well, keeps the horse responsive to your aids and careful about jumping, while still giving you the extra control you need.

On cross-country, the emphasis is on controlling the horse's speed and making sure the horse respects the bit throughout the whole course, not just at the beginning. While schooling at home it's hard to determine how your horse will react to a bit when competing on cross-country. Not only are training sessions usually at a slower speed, but the horse behaves differently at home, so there can be some trial and error figuring out which cross-country bit is most suitable to your horse at competitions.

EQUIPMENT

Horse Boots

The main reason we use boots on the horse is to protect his legs. You can protect the horse from hitting himself, such as when a back hoof catches a front leg or he brushes or interferes when traveling across the ground, and from trauma, such as hitting a jump or running into something when he spooks. Properly fitted boots can prevent a potentially serious injury, especially in the jumping phases. Their downside is that if they are not fitted correctly they can slip down, come off, or restrict the horse in some way, and when they are too tight they can put pressure on the tendons. In some cases, they can cause rubbing and chafing, especially if

3.11 Dressage boots protect the horse's legs in the warm-up area. Note: They are not allowed in the dressage test.

dirt or sand gets underneath them, which can be quite painful for the horse the next day.

Dressage Boots

While horse boots are not allowed in the actual dressage phase, it's not a bad idea to have them on for the dressage warm-up (fig. 3.11). Boots help prevent injury if the horse stumbles and hits a nerve, which can make him sore enough you can't continue to ride. Again, for preventing injury, boots are a good idea while schooling dressage at home.

Exercise Bandages/Polo Wraps

Elastic exercise bandages or fleece polo wraps also can help prevent injury but since it is imperative they are applied correctly, you should get some training in how to put them on (fig. 3.12). The downside is that when they come undone they can unravel, and if you don't realize it in time, the horse can spook, or they can get tangled around a leg. Bandages provide more of a custom fit and move quite well with the horse as compared to a fixed boot. When put on correctly, they are an excellent form of protection, especially for dressage schooling (see sidebar, p. 49). They are a little bit more time-consuming to use and are not suitable for use in wet weather or when the horse has to travel through water or water jumps. They also require constant laundering to keep them free of dirt and debris.

Cross-Country Boots

(*Note:* See p. 204 in "Warming Up and Riding Cross-Country" for photos.)

Cross-country poses the most risk to the

horse's legs as you are galloping over varied terrain and jumping fixed obstacles. The boot needs to be strong enough to protect the front of the horse's front legs from knocking a jump, and the back of the front legs from the toe of the hind foot, which can injure a tendon. Generally the tendons of the hind legs are out of harm's way.

You want a boot that will hold as little heat as possible: When one gets hot enough you can break it–even steel can be bent or broken when heat is applied–so it makes sense that horses are at a higher risk of injury when their legs get hot. Current studies show that heat in the tendons is a major factor in injury. Finding a boot made of a lightweight material that will give protection without heating the leg is important. You also want a material that does not absorb and hold water because the extra weight may cause the horse to alter his gait and be more likely to injure himself.

Show Jumping Boots

For show jumping, the main protection you are looking for is for the tendons and inner aspect of the front legs. An open-front boot has straps that come around the front and hold the boot in place, leaving the front of the leg exposed (fig. 3.13). This means that while the tendons are protected, the horse can still feel the rail with the front of his leg when he makes a jumping error, which should encourage him to pick up his legs and clear the jumps the next time. Fetlock boots protect the ankles on the hind legs from brushing while leaving the fronts of the legs exposed so that again, if the horse hits a rail he feels it.

3.12 A polo wrap correctly applied.

Bandaging

To apply an exercise bandage or polo wrap, start midway down the leg on the inner aspect. Place the end of the bandage in the groove between tendon and cannon bone, and maintain an even tension as you wrap it around the front of the leg then toward the back, using your free hand to smooth the bandage as you go. You must be certain that the tension remains the same and there are no wrinkles because they can damage a horse's tendons. Ideally, the end of the bandage should be near the top of the leg with the Velcro fasteners pointing toward the rear of the horse.

3.13 Open-front jumping boots protect the tendons at the back of the leg while allowing the horse to notice when he hits a rail with the front of his legs. Feeling this encourages him to pick up his feet higher, thus leaving the rail up next time.

Bell Boots

Usually used on the front legs, *bell boots* go around the pastern of the horse and cover down to ground level, mainly protecting the coronary band and bulbs of the horse's heel. These are great for a horse that tends to overreach with the back legs and clip the front; they can also help prevent pulling off front shoes and minimize injury from the back legs coming through and clipping the front feet and legs. Because of the padding around the coronary band these are not ideal, in my opinion, for training at home because they do minimize the feeling when the horse hits a jump rail.

It's important to fit these well: They can't be too tight, or they will cause chafing. They should be able to move around, with maybe a finger's gap around the pastern, but not so loose that they can come off.

Accessories

Running Martingale

A *running martingale* is particularly helpful for a horse with a high natural head carriage, and for a rider who is not as steady in her hands and is going to inadvertently pull on the horse at the wrong time. It will keep your hands action similar all the time. It helps with high head carriage in that when you use your hand it encourages the horse to stay in a shape and not hollow out as much. I often use one. It needs to be fitted properly and you must use rein stoppers so the rings don't get caught on the buckles of the reins (see fig. 3.6).

The running martingale should be fitted so that when the horse is cantering or galloping normally his movement is not restricted, but short enough so it has an effect when his head comes up too high. To fit the martingale when the horse is standing normally, the rings should reach his throatlatch when the straps of the martingale are stretched out to their full length.

There is also a running martingale attachment for the breastplate, useful because it's one less piece of tack. However, there is a problem getting the straps long enough, especially for taller horses.

Standing Martingale

A *standing martingale*, which has a strap that attaches to the back of the noseband to help hold the horse's head down, is not allowed in eventing. I often use one in training, however, especially with a horse that violently tosses his head.

Chambon

A *chambon* consists of a strap that attaches at the bottom of the girth or surcingle, runs forward between the forelegs, and forks. These two straps now continue to a ring on either side of the bridle or halter, at the base of the crownpiece. Running through those rings, the straps follow the cheek pieces to the bit. They may attach to the bit or pass through the bit rings and attach to themselves below the horse's neck.

It works for a horse with a naturally high head carriage because the pressure is on the top of the poll instead of the bit. This is good for teaching the horse that when you push with your leg he should reach down for the bit. It's mainly used for longeing, flatwork, and galloping fitness, and it's nice not to have to deal with extra reins.

Draw Reins

Useful in training (but illegal in competition), when in the wrong hands, *draw reins* are no good at all. When used in the right way they can help encourage the horse to stay "round." As long as you have the horse going forward, they tend to be accepted, and they create less fight and disturbance when encouraging the horse to be submissive to the hand.

Draw reins are a training aid that should

Longeing

Longeing can be useful in certain circumstances. I haven't relied on it that much in my career but I think for some horses it's particularly helpful, such as a horse that is naturally a bit fresh and frisky when you first get on, or for settling the horse in at competitions. It can be a way of letting the horse's energy and excitement wear down a little without having to ride the horse for a long time to wear him down.

I don't see much benefit to longeing your horse without side reins. With side reins, the horse longes on the bit, then when you get on to ride he is already accustomed to accepting the bit and going forward. Without side reins he can trot around with his head in the air, not necessarily using the correct muscles as he works.

Side reins can attach to a saddle or to a longeing surcingle. They are quite easy to attach and come in elastic-sided and adjustable lengths. Some of them have a rubber "donut" that allows a little extra give. Side reins don't need to be so short that they restrict the horse, but make sure there is enough contact to encourage the horse to go on the bit.

When longeing your horse it is important to try to get him to be obedient and not just race around. There is a knack to longeing and having the whip behind the horse so he has the feeling of staying in front of the "leg" and going forward. If you are not familiar with the technique you should have a professional show you how to longe correctly.

Longeing isn't the easiest on the horse's soundness since it means working on a circle for an extended period of time, so be sure to find good footing and at least a partially enclosed area to help maintain control of the horse. Also, be sure to take safety for yourself and others into account, especially when you are longeing at show grounds where lots of people are riding.

not be overused. The horse ridden in draw reins all the time gets a bit "set" in his neck and is not encouraged to reach and stretch into the bit, so I do not use them regularly when training since this is not a correct way of going.

The time it can be appropriate to use draw reins is once the horse is going forward quite well. Their use is not a good idea for the horse that is just broken in since he has not yet established an understanding of going forward. A nervous racehorse just off the track might be an appropriate candidate because draw reins give a bit of security about having contact, and help teach the horse to go on the bit in an easier way than the rider struggling with his mouth.

Once the horse understands the concept of yielding to the hand, take the draw reins off. You might use the draw reins on Monday and Tuesday and ride the rest of the week without, or start your ride with them on and once the horse is soft and submissive, remove them to finish the work.

Another situation where draw reins can be useful is in fitness work where you don't want

TIPS: Looking after Tack and Equipment

By Emma Ford, Former Head Girl at True Prospect Farm

General Tips

- Tack is cleaned on a daily basis: I tend to wipe it with a damp cloth, then use whatever conditioner I have on hand.
- I remove bits from bridles every day to be washed in plain water.
- Bridles should be taken completely apart at least once a week to ensure that the leather remains clean and supple, especially at the stress points (such as where the bit rings apply pressure).
- Phillip has a preference for rubber reins. I wipe these over with a damp sponge on a daily basis, and at least once a week, use a scrub brush (a nail brush works well) and liquid dish soap on the rubber to remove grime. Be sure to check for wear and either repair or replace the reins when the rubber starts to fall apart. Any competent saddler should be able to restore the rubber, as long as the leather is still in good condition.
- For really dirty tack I dilute ammonia with water (about 2 fluid ounces ammonia to a quart or so of water) to help lift grease off the tack. You just wipe it over the tack with a sponge or a damp towel before you soap the leather. I use this every other day for heavily used tack. Obviously bits are not to be washed in this solution!
- There are many products available for conditioning the leather. For a homemade version that is suitable for daily use you can take a bar of glycerin soap and add a cup of water and a cup of milk, melt it all in the microwave and let it set before use.
- For show tack at the end of the season I take all the leather products apart and use a water-repellent tack cleaner called Ko-cho-line Leather Dressing®. Using latex gloves I rub this into the leather, wrap individual bridle pieces in newspaper to keep away mildew, then store them in an airtight container. When they are brought out at the

to use a stronger bit but find it difficult to rate and balance the horse in a normal snaffle. You can use the draw reins for both trotting and galloping; just remember that while they are an aid for training, they should not replace basic correct training and riding.

Conclusion

There is a great deal of equipment on the market, and it can be tempting to buy more than you need or to try new gadgets when you see them hanging on the wall at the tack shop. However, it is generally best to keep things as simple as possible and get the best quality equipment that you can afford. If you want to try something new, it can be advantageous to borrow it from a friend or your trainer first and give it a try, but always focus on your horse's correct basic training before you start throwing gadgets at a problem.

---

beginning of the next season, the tack will be mold- and mildew-free and supple.

- I do have my two favorite products for metal polishing: Cape Cod® metal wipes and Simichrome. For the most part, I only use this on bit rings and the brass on show halters. I try very hard not to have a lot of brass buckles and decorations, like clincher browbands, to have to keep clean!

Rules for Wear and Repair
- Check stitching and repair.
- When leather is cracked, replace it.
- Check buckles and rein hooks regularly.
- Replace elastic that has stretched.
- Replace stretched stirrup leathers.
- Get rid of a saddle with a broken tree. Do *not* use it.
- Look for signs of wear on the bit: Rough edges can cut the horse's mouth, and when a bit gets worn out, the metal can actually break.

Horse Boots
We have a variety of horse boots. Some I can scrub in a bucket, some go in the washing machine, and

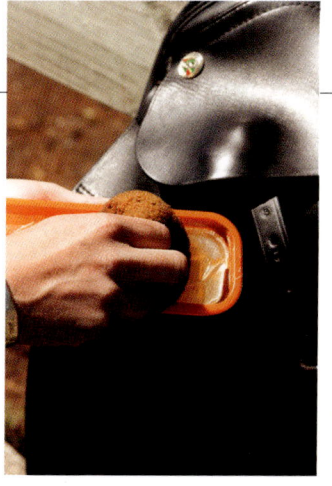 

3.14 A & B Regular cleaning keeps tack safe and looking its best (A). Emma cleaning bridles at an event (B).

others have complicated parts that you have to remove before cleaning. Follow the manufacturer's instructions. I try very hard when washing them in the machine not to put them in with anything fuzzy like polo wraps so that the Velcro maintains its grip.

Saddle Pads
We use Ecogold™ Pads, which are made of a synthetic material and have to be air-dried. To keep them white I add a product like OxiClean® or use whitening toothpaste on areas that get stained—for example, by the girth's buckles—before washing.

CHAPTER 4

Apparel and Equipment for the Rider

APPAREL

Fashion trends come and go, but basic riding apparel is classic in style. If you buy good quality clothing and accessories you can expect to use your purchases for a long time. Before you head to the tack shop and start buying, assess your needs at home.

Though riding equipment is available at various price points, keep in mind that if you are in it for the long haul it usually pays to buy the best quality you can afford because "quality" lasts longer, performs better, and in some cases, is safer than cheaper options. That doesn't mean that you have to start out with top-of-the-line equipment from head to toe: You may be able to purchase used equipment to save a few dollars. If you are unsure about the quality, safety, or fit of any equipment or apparel, seek the opinion of a professional or an experienced friend (figs. 4.1 A–F).

Headgear

Helmet

It has been a big change for me wearing a helmet every day. Growing up in the heat of Australia we wore an Akubra hat every day, but it has

4.1 A–C Appropriate dress for the higher levels. Young Man and I are correctly turned out for upper-level dressage at Jersey Fresh. I am wearing a shadbelly coat with canary vest points, a top hat (note that helmets are now widely accepted as part of FEI dressage apparel), white gloves, white breeches, and well-polished, tall, black dress boots with spurs (A).

US Eventing Team member Karen O'Connor on Mandiba is impeccably turned out for the cross-country phase at the 2010 Alltech World Equestrian Games (B).

Appropriately attired for upper-level show jumping at Fair Hill, I am wearing my approved helmet with harness and chinstrap fastened, red ("pink") Eventing Team riding coat, dark gloves, white breeches, and tall black field boots, which have laces at the front of the ankle, and spurs. While I am wearing a white necktie, a stock tie or choker with stock pin is also appropriate for both men and women. I am carrying a short jumping crop. Note that I still need to put on the required medical armband (C).

Apparel and Equipment for the Rider 4

4.1 D–F Appropriate dress for the lower levels: Natalie Wales of Virginia riding See Spot Run is correctly attired for the dressage phase at the lower levels. She is wearing a navy short dressage coat with four buttons, buff breeches, and tall black field boots. Her dark gloves will not attract attention if her hands are unsteady, and she carries an appropriate dressage whip. Her approved hunt cap has a securely fitted and fastened safety harness and chin strap (D).

Jennie Brannigan and Cambalda are ready for Preliminary cross-country at the 2010 Millbrook Horse Trials. Jennie's dress is appropriate for any level of competition. Her white and navy clothing are tasteful and coordinated, and although it is not required, she is wearing an air vest over her mandatory body protector for extra safety. On her head is an approved helmet with harness and chinstrap fastened, and she has her (required) armband containing medical information (E).

Holly Payne riding Madeline at the Millbrook Horse Trials in 2008. Her attire is correct for any level of show jumping. Note: while Holly is wearing a stock tie in this photo, a ratcatcher-style shirt with a choker is also acceptable (F).

been brought home to me how important it is to wear protective headgear.

One of the most important considerations in riding apparel is the helmet. Aside from purchasing something that makes a pretty picture, keep in mind that the helmet is a vital piece of safety equipment, protecting you against injury and even death. Helmets come in different shapes, sizes, and colors. There are specific helmets designed for show jumping, dressage, and cross-country, but their safety rating is the same; the reasons for using one rather than another in any given phase are more cosmetic than technical.

It is always preferable to buy a new helmet; even if a secondhand one looks okay, it may have sustained an impact and not offer sufficient protection. The USEA has a rule that any helmet has to be approved to the ASTM/SEI Standard for use in any phase of eventing competition (though at the time of publication a top hat can be worn for dressage in FEI recognized competitions). Whether you are planning to compete at recognized events or not, it's a good idea to use that as your base standard.

Fitting of your helmet is important as well: Certainly getting help from someone at a store to find your correct size is a good idea, and sizes will vary from brand to brand. A good rule of thumb is that the helmet should grip the skin on your forehead so that it stays in place when you move your head around, without being too tight or uncomfortable for you to wear. The helmet should not be so loose that it slips down and impairs your vision or it could easily come off in a fall.

The chin-strap attachment is important and also varies from brand to brand. Remember: You are often wearing your gloves or holding the reins and trying to attach and detach your chin strap, so it's important to take into account what is best going to suit you and be easy for you to operate. Remember to always wear your helmet with the chin strap fastened while mounted.

Helmets should always be replaced immediately if they suffer a severe impact such as from a fall or being dropped onto a hard surface; even if no damage is visible, any severe impact can result in diminished protective properties. Also keep in mind that in addition to evolving technology and standards, the protection offered by any riding hat diminishes over time as the material deteriorates, so you should routinely replace your helmet every five years or so, even when there are no visible signs of damage.

Helmets

Important Points to Consider

- When trying on any riding hat, it is important that it fits comfortably and securely. Any helmet has to be approved to the ASTM/SEI Standard.
- Check the fit and adjust if necessary each time you wear the helmet.
- Adjust harness chin strap first, then back strap.
- If the hat sustains a severe impact—even dropping onto a hard surface—it should be thrown away and a new one purchased. (Remember, your head is priceless!)

Top Hat

When you compete at the FEI levels you can wear a top hat in the dressage phase. Remember, more riders every day are opting to wear a helmet in the dressage, even at these levels, though some riders still prefer the traditional appearance of a top hat. A helmet is not only more protective but a more economical option since a quality top hat ranges from around $150 to more than $500.

If you decide to wear a top hat make sure that the fit is comfortable and height of the hat flattering to you. If it is at all loose, secure it firmly with hair pins so it does not fly off in the middle of your test—especially on a windy day.

BODYWEAR

Body Protector

This is another piece of mandatory equipment for the cross-country phase at USEA-recognized events, and I would suggest that any time you are cross-country schooling you wear one also. Again, they come in lots of different styles and brands. Your body protector should be a comfortable fit so that you can ride and

4.2 A & B Canadian Eventing Team member Jessica Phoenix on Exponential splashes through The Head of the Lake Water Complex at the 2010 World Equestrian Games. The rip cord for her air safety vest is clearly visible above the pommel of her saddle. While horse and rider landed with a big splash, the air vest did not deploy since Jessica stayed in the tack (A).

Kyle Carter riding Madison Park, also for Canada, heads for the finish line. Kyle's red air vest fits snugly over his regular body protector, which is just visible at the shoulders. The rip cord can be seen just behind his right hand, and stopwatch (B).

function easily, as well as give you some protection if you fall.

The fit of a safety vest is crucial for optimum protection: the back section should come down and protect, but not quite cover, the end of your tailbone. This part is important because when you are sitting in the saddle you don't want the back of the body protector coming into contact with the cantle and pushing the vest upward, which is uncomfortable and unwieldy.

Air Safety Vest

At the moment inflatable air vests are not compulsory equipment, but they do offer extra protection in a fall. I don't see any disadvantage in wearing these and for the cross-country phase I recommend them (figs. 4.2 A & B).

An air vest can be used *in addition to* a body protector, *not* instead of one. It uses a CO_2 cartridge to inflate the vest, which happens when a ripcord that is attached to the saddle pulls free from the vest (in a fall).

There are various brands on the market at different price points. An air vest is available for adults and children, and fitting one is quite simple: It needs to be snug around your body leaving some allowance for inflation. Wearing one does take some getting used to: When you dismount, be sure to disconnect the cord first, otherwise the vest inflates when you least expect it! The cartridge that comes with it is for a one-time use only so mistakes like this can get expensive. That said, you should pack a couple of spare cartridges in your tack trunk.

Clothing

Breeches

Worn with tall boots, breeches come in a variety of styles, colors, and materials designed for schooling and show. Personal preference is key in finding breeches you like: They come in tight or looser fits with different cuts for different body types. The color should be white or light for dressage and show jumping, while a darker color can be worn for cross-country. Breeches are available with a knee patch or a full seat made of a "grippy" synthetic material or leather. A leather full seat is comfortable and provides extra grip in the saddle, though is admittedly more expensive and the breeches can be harder to launder and maintain.

Children can wear cuffed jodhpurs with short jodhpur boots and garter straps (see "Boots" on p. 63).

Shirt

Typically a white short- or long-sleeved "ratcatcher" shirt is worn underneath a hunt coat. This also comes in a variety of fabrics now, including high-performance moisture-wicking materials to keep you cool in hot weather. Your shirt should be tailored to fit without a lot of excess material but have enough room in the shoulders so you can comfortably follow the horse's motion.

When coats are "excused" (due to hot weather) you must wear a white or light-colored, short- or long-sleeved shirt with a collar, such as a ratcatcher shirt or a polo shirt. Do not wear a choker or stock tie when not wearing a coat.

Stock Tie or Tie

Stock ties come in the traditional style that have to be tied and secured with a pin, which takes some learning, or in a pre-tied version that can be fastened on with Velcro. A jacket and tie—or stock tie—can be worn in both the dressage and show jumping phases.

Coat or Jacket

For dressage and show jumping, a jacket or hunt coat is required at USEA-recognized events. These can range in color from charcoal gray to navy or black. The fit of the riding jacket is important: A well-fitting coat can enhance your overall look in the saddle, while a baggy coat looks sloppy, and one that is too tight, straining at the buttons, is unflattering. If your coat does not fit well you should have it tailored, or get a new one.

At Preliminary Level and above Horse Trials, and at the FEI levels, you can wear a Shadbelly riding coat with tails in either black or navy blue (black is traditional for men while blue is traditional for women, but both sexes can wear either color) over a ratcatcher shirt with a stock tie and a vest (most commonly seen in canary yellow). The outfit is accompanied by a top hat or helmet.

Cross-Country Attire

For cross-country it is important to wear something that is going to feel comfortable underneath your body protector and air safety vest (optional, see p. 60) and cross-country number or pinny. I find technical fabrics made for bike racing and other athletic endeavors ideal.

Though it may be tempting to overdress in cold weather it is not a good idea because once you warm up, you can easily overheat. I prefer to put a coat on while I'm warming up and then remove the coat in the warm-up area before I go out on course. If it is raining then a light, waterproof athletic raincoat is ideal as the top layer.

While dress for dressage and show jumping tends to be more traditional and conservative, you can choose your own style and color for cross-country. Have a little fun and let your personal style show with dark or brightly colored breeches, a shirt in the color of your choosing, and perhaps a coordinating helmet cover and gloves.

Gloves

I think gloves are very important because once the horse's neck starts to sweat and the reins get slippery, it makes steering harder if you can't hold on to the reins. There are lots of good gloves for working through this. My preference is for SSG riding gloves and I tend to use a different pair for each phase.

For *dressage,* there is an element of how you look, so I usually wear white gloves. Tight-fitting gloves provide the best function and look neat.

For *cross-country*, the glove is going to come under more pressure because of the speed and effort that can go into steering and turning. You'll be going through water jumps and sometimes mud, so I generally go with a tougher, stronger glove that is still thin enough to provide feel and function. There are gloves available that are very thin but have extra gripping material where you need it so you have the

4.3 A–E There are many types of spurs, suitable to different types of horses. A spur with a longer shank that allows the rider to use the spur without moving the leg excessively during dressage should only be used by riders with excellent control of the lower leg (A). I often use roller ball spurs in dressage (B). A short Prince of Wales spur is a good general-use spur (C). The Prince of Wales spur can come with a rounded tip, and decorative detail on the side (D), or with a rounded disc to increase the horse's response to the leg aid (E).

feel of a lighter glove with the performance of a stronger glove. Inexpensive knit gloves with rubber material on the palms are also adequate.

In the *show jumping* I feel either type of glove can be used, depending on your preference. There are so many gloves and materials and brands and everybody's hands are a little different, so trial and error is the best way to find what works for you.

Boots

Tall boots, although somewhat uncomfortable to walk in, are very comfortable to ride in and will enhance your feel and grip on the horse. Getting the right fit is essential: There is a break-in phase for a new pair of boots, so don't be discouraged if they hurt for the first ride or two. When they are broken in they will mold to your feet and legs and be more comfortable. I find the ones with a zipper at the back much more practical than the older style of boot where you have to get the boot on and off without being able to open the shaft that goes over the calf.

Boots can be an expensive investment and one pair is sufficient for all three phases. If you want to specialize and buy boots for each phase, generally a dressage boot is made of stiffer, more rigid leather in the leg while the jumping boot has softer, more flexible leather so you can ride with shorter stirrups. I find that the spur rest on the back of the boot is helpful in keeping your spur in place.

For children who are still growing, a short jodhpur boot is more appropriate. These should be worn with jodhpur pants and garter straps, which fit just below the knee to keep the pants from riding up or twisting.

For schooling, paddock boots and half chaps are fine and will keep your tall boots from wearing out as quickly, but do school in your tall boots from time to time because there is a different feel in the way the leather grips the saddle.

EQUIPMENT

Spurs

There are many types available to suit all horses (figs. 4.3 A–E).

Spurs are useful for refining and reinforcing the leg aids. The length of spur allowed is $1\frac{3}{8}$ inches. It must be made of smooth metal and not capable of wounding a horse. The shank must point downward and rowels, if used in dressage, must be smooth and free-rotating. *Swan-neck* and *shank-less* spurs are allowed, as are *roller-ball* spurs (plastic or metal). Spurs are mandatory at the Intermediate and Advanced Levels.

The more involved you get with the sport, you will find that different spurs have varying effects on your horse. A *Prince of Wales* is a good all-purpose spur. Roller-ball spurs are helpful if used in the right way to keep the horse in front of your leg. Sometimes having a more effective spur rather than a rounded, dull spur is better because you don't have to use your leg as much, as opposed to kicking all the time with a dull spur; however, it must be taken into consideration whether you are educated with the leg and have the control to use the spur only when you want to.

The rider's experience and leg control, and

Dressed for Success: The Jog Outfit

If you compete at a Three-Day Event you will need a couple of nice outfits for the veterinary inspection, also commonly known as "the jog" or "the trot-up" (fig. 4.4). While you won't be sent home for wearing jeans and a T-shirt, out of respect for the ground jury it is common practice to dress nicely or in matching outfits or uniforms in the case of a team competition. With spectators attending the jog, many competitions even offer a special award for the "best turned out" horse and rider. With long-format events taking place at the lower levels these days, even Beginner Novice riders may experience the jog.

It is important to wear something comfortable enough to jog in, which will not distract you or the ground jury from the main focus: your horse. Men are safe wearing khaki pants and a sport coat, adding a touch of style with an accessory like a hat or cowboy boots. Women can be a little more daring with skirts or dresses and fancy shoes, but a flapping mini skirt or tottering heels is unprofessional and distracting. Keep your style classic and simple for the best results, especially when it comes to footwear. Unless you are really comfortable jogging along next to a thousand pounds of horseflesh while wearing 3-inch heels, opt for something a little more practical.

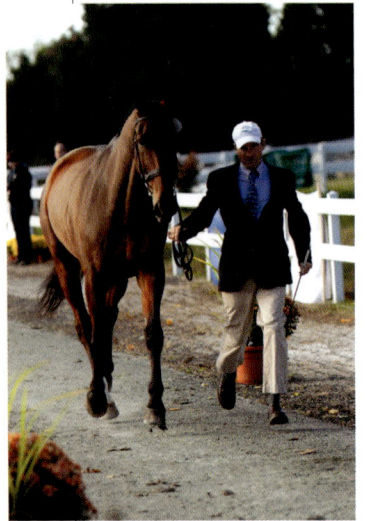

4.4 Clean, conservative clothing is always appropriate for the veterinary inspection at a three-day event. Women can be a bit more daring (though not distracting) in dress.

Fashion Dos and Don'ts

DO

- Wear pants that fit well. It may be worth hiring a tailor to get the right length and cut.
- Coordinate your outfit to complement your horse. This is your chance to highlight your assets—take advantage of the opportunity.
- Polish your shoes. You polish your riding boots, you polish your horse's hooves, so take the time to polish your "jog" shoes, as well. Whether they are old paddock boots or Italian dress shoes, make sure they are clean and shiny.
- Wear something that you like that flatters your body type. Fashion trends come and go, but nothing compares to feeling your best in whatever clothes you wear. If you like to take fashion risks, feel free to express yourself within reason, but if your style is more conservative, that's fine too.

DON'T

- Wear clogs. Sprawling head over heels as you twist an ankle in these barn favorites will not earn favor with the ground jury.
- Wear a skirt shorter than knee length. It should be of a heavy enough fabric that it does not flap around.
- Wear a big floppy hat without securing it to your head.
- Dress as if you are going out clubbing or to a dance party.
- Wear anything with stains on it. Yes, it's hard to stay clean when you are working with horses. Wear something over your nice clothes to keep them clean while you are getting ready, or have someone help you with your horse.

the horse's personality and reaction to the different types are all important when choosing which spur to use. Generally, I use the rollerball spurs in dressage where you don't want to be asking from your leg all the time but need a reaction when you give an aid. In show jumping, I generally use a more rounded, "quieter" spur so the horse's reaction is more relaxed. On cross-country, I also use a small spur, but not quite as rounded on the end.

Whip

Dressage Whip

A dressage whip is now legal at USEA competitions, though not in championship divisions—or at FEI competitions. (A whip is allowed in the warm-up at all of these.) It does have to be less than 47.2 inches, including the lash.

A dressage whip can be helpful in encouraging a lazy horse forward rather than kicking all the time to make him go, which makes him dull to your leg. With some horses, the whip creates tension, so choose whether to carry one in dressage based on your horse's personality.

Jumping Whip

Because stopping or hesitating can be dangerous when galloping and jumping at speed, it is important to always carry a whip on cross-country. If your horse gets worried about the whip the answer is to get him used to it, not to avoid carrying one. You can try a smaller whip to begin with, but in any case, I feel the whip is a necessity on cross-country.

When choosing a jumping whip, consider the grip and your ability to hold it. I'm not a big fan of tiny whips because I don't feel they can be effective. I'd rather have a whip the horse respects and understands and then not have to use it very often. The USEF rules (EV 114.3) state that any jumping whip must not exceed 30 inches in length or be weighted at the end. "Jockey" whips can be customized in length, stiffness, and color, so they are a great resource.

Dropping a whip on the course will leave you badly equipped should you encounter a refusal or hesitation so I have a rubber band on the handle of mine, which I attach around my middle finger. This means that if I lose my grip, I am not going to lose my whip. You can also a hair band or anything similar; some people like to put a rubber martingale stop over the handle to keep the whip from slipping out of their hand.

The same whip that you carry on cross-country can be used in the show jumping phase.

CHAPTER 5

Horse and Rider Fitness

Eventing is by definition an endurance sport, and fitness for both yourself and your horse is an important area to focus on as you train and prepare for competition. Considering the time, energy, and finances involved, it is not fair to you or your horse to show up at a competition and not be in good enough shape to compete and do so easily, without causing undue stress and exhaustion. Your horse must also be fit enough to easily handle the demands placed on him without unnecessarily risking injury. Fitness is not attainable overnight: It takes time, planning, and hard work.

HORSE FITNESS

There are many variables that go into getting your horse fit, most notably what he has done prior to starting a fitness program.

- The ex-racehorse comes with a really good, solid base of fitness, therefore horses that have raced or have been in race training are much quicker (easier) to get fit, especially for lower-level eventing.

- Any general riding can improve the horse's fitness, but while a horse that has been training and/or competing in show jumping or dressage, for example, will be fit for that discipline, he may need more endurance training before tackling a cross-country course.

- The horse that has just been broken in or hasn't been in a serious work program will take much more time and work to get fit enough to compete.

Because cross-country is the most physically demanding phase of an event it is easy to get stuck focusing on cross-country fitness. But the point is to prepare the horse's whole body so that he can do the entire event easily and not put stress on his tendons, ligaments, and joints, as well as his musculature and respiratory system. By preparing the horse with a slow, gradual fitness program, his mind and body will become accustomed to the work required and grow stronger with time.

During any activity a horse is more prone to injury when he is fatigued. A horse that is starting to get really tired on course will not be as clever and careful in his gallop stride or when he is jumping. Once his muscles tire and get weak they don't support the various parts of the body efficiently, putting more strain on soft tissue. When the horse is really fit and strong he is much more likely to stand up to the demands of training and competition.

Wind (respiratory) fitness really comes into play over longer courses like the CCI events. Most Horse Trials, even at the Advanced Level, take about six minutes—a CIC is a little bit longer—so the wind fitness is not as essential as over the longer courses where the horse needs extra endurance.

At the other end of the spectrum I see no point in having your horse overly fit for what you want to achieve. An over-fit horse is often harder to handle and more difficult to ride because he is often more exuberant: He'll need to be ridden a lot more to be quiet and sensible, especially to get him relaxed and rideable for the dressage. Added to this, in my opinion, it is a waste of your horse's legs to make him endure more conditioning work than is needed.

You have to find a balance between preparing the horse for the physical demands of the level you are competing in while not wearing your horse out doing more miles than he needs to reach optimum fitness.

The Plan

The following is a basic fitness plan that can be adapted depending on your horse's fitness base when you start. You have to work on two main areas with your horse: first, strength and conditioning, or aerobic training, and later faster, anaerobic work (see sidebar, p. 69).

- Aerobic training is slow work that can be done in walk, trot, or canter. The idea behind this work is to slowly but surely put a good base of muscle on your horse and prepare his overall body as you strengthen the important soft-tissue areas, including tendons and ligaments.

- Anaerobic work is done at a faster pace so the heart rate is elevated to increase the horse's lung and wind capacity and fitness.

Lower Levels

At the lower levels of eventing—I would say Training Level and below—there is not really much stress on the horse's lungs or wind because the speed required in the cross-country for these levels never gets the heart rate to a point where the aerobic phase of training is necessary. So for the lower levels, things are a little easier: You can focus your horse's training program on getting him strong enough to handle regular work.

Preliminary and Above

For Preliminary Level and above Horse Trials and Three-Day Events, I make sure my horses are prepared with both long, slow work and

---

Aerobic vs. Anaerobic Exercise

Strictly speaking, the terms "aerobic" and "anaerobic" refer to the presence and absence of oxygen, respectively. During exercise with adequate fuel and oxygen (*aerobic*), muscle cells can contract repeatedly without fatigue. During non-oxygen (*anaerobic*) conditions, in higher intensity exercise such as sprinting, muscle cells must rely on other reactions that do not require oxygen to fuel muscle contraction.

Initially during increased exertion, muscle glycogen is broken down to produce glucose, which undergoes glycolysis, producing pyruvate, which then reacts with oxygen (Krebs cycle) to produce carbon dioxide and water and releases energy. When there is a shortage of oxygen (anaerobic exercise or short bursts of speed) carbohydrate is consumed more rapidly because the pyruvate ferments into lactate. If the intensity of the exercise exceeds the rate with which the cardiovascular system can supply muscles with oxygen, it results in buildup of lactate and quickly makes it difficult or impossible to continue the exercise. Over time, short amounts of anaerobic exercise can be beneficial in building strength (see below).

The two types of exercise differ by the duration and intensity of muscular contractions involved, as well as by how energy is generated within the muscle.

Among the recognized benefits of doing regular *aerobic* exercise are:

- Strengthening the muscles involved in respiration.
- Strengthening and enlarging the heart muscle, to improve its pumping efficiency and reduce the resting heart rate.
- Strengthening muscles throughout the body.
- Improving circulation efficiency and reducing blood pressure.
- Increasing the total number of red blood cells in the body, facilitating transport of oxygen.

Among the recognized benefits of regular anaerobic exercise are:

- Increased power.
- Increased muscle mass.
- Improved bone density.
- Strengthening joints.

some fast work. If you are training for a Three-Day Event, the cross-country course is much longer than a regular Horse Trial so endurance is very important. I suggest that you have a proper, mapped-out fitness program tailored to your specific goals and individual horse, especially before tackling the One-Star Level and above.

This means starting with a conditioning/legging-up/slow-work phase and then adding a regulated, fast-work phase where I gallop my horse every five days. Competing in a Horse Trials leading up to a Three-Day Event can be used as one of these gallop days.

Legging Up

Competing at any level, your horse needs a base of fitness. If your horse has been turned out to pasture or has been out of work and you are starting his fitness program from scratch, I think it is important to start with about five to seven days of just walking. This means relaxed walking under tack for about 45 minutes at a time, just to get his body and muscles toned and used to carrying your weight in the saddle.

Note: If your horse is coming back from an injury, you need to follow your veterinarian's recommendation how to bring him back.

I know lots of people who ride seven days a week and feel it's good for their horse. I usually work on a six-day week so the horse gets one day of rest. This is not compulsory and I'm not sure the horse needs it, but with everyone's busy lifestyle, it is good to plan for a day away from the barn, and I think sometimes it's good to let the horse have a rest day. That said, some horses' behavior is not as good after a day off: When your horse is fresh or hard to handle,

5.1 Trotting builds fitness gradually. Ryan Wood is trotting a young horse called Davinci on the gallops (a strip of prepared footing) at True Prospect Farm in Pennsylvania.

just take him for a relaxing walk instead of giving him a complete rest.

Once I have completed the first week of walking I start on a trotting or jogging phase of the program (fig. 5.1). When the horse is comfortable with 20 minutes of trotting I cut back how many days I trot and will add some flatwork. This means that his schedule will look something like this:

Week One
  45 minutes of walking each day.

Week Two
  30 minute walk followed by 15 minutes of trotting each day.

Week Three
  30 minute walk and a 20 minute trot each day.

Week Four
  Sunday: Rest.
  Monday: 15 minute walk, 20 minute jog, and light flatwork (having the horse on the bit, mostly rising trot, some canter work, mostly on a circle with some changes of direction and some transitions).
  Tuesday: 30 minute walk and flatwork.
  Wednesday: 15 minute walk, 20 minute jog, and flatwork.
  Thursday: Same as Tuesday.
  Friday: 30 minute walk and flatwork.
  Saturday: 20 minute jog and flatwork.
  Sunday: Rest.

Training Level and Below
Keep the same daily program but add jumping.

Week Five
  Monday: Same as previous week.
  Tuesday: 15 minute walk, some flatwork, and an introduction to jumping, including poles on the ground, cross-rails (see p. 149 "Show Jumping Training" for ideas). Remember, this is still a simple introduction to get the horse physically ready to jump, not a full training session over fences.
  Wednesday: 15 minute walk, 20 minute jog, and flatwork.
  Thursday: 30 minute walk and flatwork.
  Friday: Flatwork and light jumping again.
  Saturday: 15 minute walk, 20 minute jog, and flatwork.

Week Six through Week Eight
  Keep your program similar to above. Then your horse will be ready for cross-country schooling in preparation for your first event.

Preliminary Level and CIC*/CCI*
For Preliminary Level, I get to the same stage as above and then on Tuesday and Saturday add some long, slow cantering: about 400 meters per minute (mpm), or show-jumping speed. The first week I go one mile at 450 mpm (see p. 74 for advice on how to gauge your speed). I start with 15 minutes of walking, some flatwork to warm up, and then the canter.

Week Six
   Canter 2 miles (all at once) on Tuesday and again on Saturday.

Week Seven
   Canter 3 miles on Tuesday and again on Saturday.

Once the horse is up to cantering 3 miles, he should be sufficiently conditioned to compete in a Preliminary Level Horse Trial.

Intermediate Level and CCI**
(Continuing on from the "Preliminary Level and CIC*/CCI* plan.)

Week Eight Onward
   Monday: Jog for 30 minutes and do flatwork.
   Tuesday: Flatwork and light jumping, then build up to five, one-mile slow canters. (Preliminary Level horses got up to doing 3-mile canters, so just keep building up gradually.)
   Wednesday: 30-minute walk plus flatwork.
   Thursday: 20-minute jog plus flatwork.
   Friday: Flatwork and jumping.
   Saturday: Flatwork and slow canters, over time building up to 5 miles at a stretch.

Once the horse has established that level of fitness, maintain the program for two weeks. At this point the long, slow work is complete and you can start on the fast work (see sidebar).

5.2. Cantering, especially on hills, prepares your horse for faster work. Assistant rider Jennie Brannigan canters Dreamboat up a hill at True Prospect Farm.

Wind and Respiratory Fitness

Fast Work

At the end of this program your horse will have muscle and body condition. To do a CCI* and above, you will need to add some wind or anaerobic conditioning to the program. To achieve this I don't do more of the long, slow cantering at this stage; instead, every five days I substitute what we call a "fast work" to increase the horse's wind capacity. Before competing in a CCI*, the horse will need approximately six of these "fast works." If you meanwhile compete in a Horse Trials it can be a substitute for one of the fast works.

These fast works should consist of one mile at 550 mpm. If you have a good hill to canter up this will vary (see p. 74), but it is a good rule of thumb (fig. 5.2).

- Start with walking and 15 minutes of flatwork as well as a warm-up canter before you go faster.
- Try to do the last gallop about five days before cross-country day at your event.

Week with "Fast Work"

Monday: 30 minutes trot and flatwork.

Tuesday: Flatwork and jumping.

Wednesday: Walk 30 minutes and flatwork.

Thursday: Flatwork and jumping.

Friday: Gallop day: Warm up with trotting or flatwork and cantering. Then do one mile at 600 mpm, which is equivalent to 20 seconds every, 200 meters. I do this every five days. A horse preparing for an Intermediate Horse Trials or a CIC event (One, Two and Three-Star CIC competitions are roughly comparable to Preliminary, Intermediate, and Advanced Levels of American national competition, respectively) needs to do just one or two of these before he is ready; a horse going to a CCI** needs to do about seven or eight of these "fast works" before the event—remember, a Horse Trials would count as one fast work.

Advanced Level Horse Trials, CCI *** and CCI****

At this level I add slow cantering three times a week.

Monday: 35-minute trot plus flatwork.

Tuesday: Flatwork and build up to five, 1-mile, slow canters.

Wednesday: 30-minute walk and flatwork.

Thursday: Flatwork and slow canters.

Friday: Flatwork and jumping.

Saturday: Flatwork and slow canters.

Fitness required is the same for a CCI*** as it is for a CCI**, and likewise Advanced Level Horse Trials fitness is the same as for Intermediate Level Horse Trials. To get to the CCI*** level, the horse needs to do nine or ten "fast works" (18 seconds every 200 meters, or 690 meters per minute). And, finally, to a CCI**** the horse needs 11 "fast works" in order to be prepared for the event.

Footing

Joint and Tendon Fitness

One of the most important things to consider when doing all of this work is the footing. Whether you are trotting or cantering, or most certainly before you ask him to do any fast work (anaerobic), your horse's fitness conditioning needs to take place on an even, "forgiving" surface. Hard ground is tough on the joints, and deep ground puts more stress on the horse's soft tissue. An uneven surface can also cause lameness should the horse take a bad step.

For trotting and slow cantering, when you haven't got good surfaces outside (or there is bad weather) you can actually do this work in an all-weather arena (a dressage or jumping arena with sand or other suitable footing). The downside: It requires making more turns than when working out in the open—turning that can put stress on the horse's body. It also gets monotonous going around and around an arena—for both horse and rider.

For the long, slow cantering during the winter months we do our fitness in our indoor arena: Because of the constant turning I give the horses a break for about 30 seconds in between each mile, and make sure I change direction on a regular basis so the horse is conditioned evenly on both sides of his body.

To do fast work you unquestionably need a really good surface outside; fast work can't be done in an arena because it needs to be measured out over a distance, whether this means heading to a racetrack or a good, grassy field. I would not expect a horse to do fast work unless you have access to a suitable space with good footing.

Time and Distance

Knowing the distance that you are working your horse can help you learn how to judge your pace as well as create a more accurate conditioning program. You can measure distance with a meter wheel and place markers such as buckets, traffic cones (or anything that will be easily visible while you are riding) every 200 meters to get the timing right (see "Riding for Time," p. 196).

Muscle Fitness

Riding Hills
Riding hills is an ideal addition to any conditioning program: The horse has to work harder, pushing with his hindquarters and developing new musculature. I think going down a hill, especially a steep one, can be hard on the horse's soundness, though a little downhill work is good for him to learn to balance and develop coordination. I would encourage you to walk downhill and trot uphill. Try to estimate how much time is spent at the walk and add that to your time actually trotting.

For anaerobic work, I prefer to use a hill if possible because you can go slower and still get the horse's heart rate up; however, each incline will be different so it's hard to generalize. As you get to know your hill you can measure it and figure out a plan that is equivalent to doing a mile at 690 mpm. This might mean going up the hill twice at 500 mpm, for example.

More on Fast Work
Review the sidebar on p. 72 where I discussed fast work (anaerobic) and its contribution to wind and conditioning.

For slow canter work (aerobic), I usually ride in a two-point seat position, which is comfortable for the horse and good fitness work for the rider since it develops your leg strength and position. You can shorten the stirrups to jumping length for the slow canters and faster work, which makes your leg muscles work a little harder.

It is important to gradually build up to the fast work, and to include a walking, cooling-down period after any conditioning work. Let the horse walk afterward for a good 10 minutes to let his muscles loosen and relax as he cools down.

It is also important after the stressful fast works to really cool down your horse's legs and try to keep inflammation out of the joints and soft tissue. Icing the legs is recommended; applying some kind of poultice on the legs that evening, under stable wraps, will also help to reduce inflammation and soreness (see chapter 15, "Grooming"). Check your horse's legs the next morning for heat and inflammation and ice or cold hose again, if necessary.

RIDER FITNESS

The Importance of Rider Fitness

Rider fitness is just as important as the horse's fitness. Riding is quite unique in that riding itself is the best conditioner for your sport. However, when you only have one horse to ride and you are not in the saddle all day, there are many alternative forms of fitness training that will benefit your strength as a rider.

Every person and every body type is going to require an individualized approach to fitness training. While you may not develop the physique of a marathon runner, you basically need to condition yourself to be at your best and not get fatigued at any point of the three phases.

Fitness for Safety

It cannot be denied that eventing—particularly the cross-country phase—involves risk, but there are things that you can do to make yourself and your horse safer. You wear a helmet and a body protector, you learn correct riding techniques and horsemanship, and you walk your courses and prepare yourself for each phase of the event.

Fitness is just another aspect of being safe and prepared: Fatigue can lead to a weak position and slower reflexes. A fit rider is able to react quickly to help the horse perform at his best and to make corrections when things aren't going right.

A weekend at an event is a busy time from start to finish: You'll likely haul your horse some distance and set up his stabling area to make him comfortable. You have to ride your horse more than once before the competition starts to prepare him, and you have to walk the cross-country and show jumping courses, not to mention walking around the grounds to pick up your competitor's packet, mucking stalls, and generally taking care of your horse. It's a full workout for the weekend, which is not to be taken lightly.

Better Riding Through Fitness

The biggest incentive for staying fit is so you can maintain your position in the saddle for a long period of time. In the dressage, core fitness will help you sit deep in the saddle and maintain your position so that your seat is effective and you look elegant.

Particularly on the cross-country, you need to be able to maintain a galloping position while riding effectively over varied terrain, sometimes on a horse that is excited and pulling to go faster. A Four-Star cross-country lasts for up to 12½ minutes, and a One-Star is about seven minutes. This doesn't sound like a very long time, but remember that you need to constantly think about how you will ride the next "question" on course, adjust your position to meet your horse's needs, and stay strong and effective for that full length of time while your horse is galloping, so you can keep him connected and in control.

When in the galloping position you need to be aware of which parts of your body you need to work on. Your lower leg is the stabilizing part of your galloping position: You must sink down in your heel and hold your lower leg in place. Your core—stomach area—needs to be strong and in shape to maintain your position, and your back muscles and hips need to be strong and flexible to be able to sit down into the horse. Your arms and shoulders need to have the strength to guide and control your horse from the beginning to the end of the course.

In show jumping you need to keep your seat light, your aids effective, and react quickly in order to navigate the course. Usually, this is the last phase of the event, and you don't want to be tired or sore by this point, which could also affect your position and reaction time and hinder your horse's performance. You have asked a lot of your horse and you owe it to him to be at your best.

Mental Fitness

Eventing is very much a mental as well as physical test. Preparation through training and physical fitness will help you to be confident and ride your best, but everyone has to deal with nerves at some time or another. Whether you read books, visualize your performance, meditate, talk to your trainer, or go to a sports psychologist, mental fitness can be the key to maximizing your performance (see chapter 10, "Mental Preparation for Rider and Horse").

Cross-Training

Although you don't need incredible respiratory or anaerobic fitness, riding can get your heart rate up, so you do need to have a certain amount of cardio and respiratory fitness as well as strength. If you are too tired to maintain your position effectively by the end of a lesson, or your muscles are very sore after a long ride, it's time to get in shape. Especially when you work at a desk job, you need to do some physical training to be fit enough to ride. It's a good idea to customize your fitness program to work on any weaknesses that you may have.

Any healthy person should be doing 30 to 60 minutes of exercise, six days a week. In addition to riding, at least 30 minutes of exercise a day will help you reach an optimum level of fitness. Just because riding in an event only takes a few minutes of effort doesn't mean you should train less. For example, a swimmer who competes in a two-minute race might train for two to three hours a day. Your horse is not the only one who can benefit from interval training: You can gradually build up your routine to go farther and faster.

To achieve optimum health, you need to address the three components of good fitness: cardio, strength, and flexibility.

- Cardio: Activities like running, bike riding, and swimming are good for a cardiovascular workout. Machines like the StairMaster are also useful for cross-training (figs. 5.3 A & B).

- Flexibility: Stretching helps muscles bend and flex and prevents cramping and injury. Yoga and Pilates are two great ways to work on flexibility and strength (figs. 5.4 A & B).

- Strength: Moderate weight training can be helpful for building strength. On that note, I think too much bulk in your muscles is not ideal; you want long, stretchy muscles rather than big, bulked up muscles in order to sit correctly in the saddle.

Horse & Rider Fitness 5

5.3 A & B Cycling is one form of cross-training that improves cardiovascular fitness. Running helps build your fitness for riding.

If you only have 30 minutes to work out, try to achieve something from each of these three areas. For example, do a 10-minute warm-up, 10 minutes of strength training, then 10 minutes of stretching. You don't have to join an expensive gym–there are plenty of effective exercises you can do at home.

A few ideas:

- Walk for 30 minutes and every five minutes, stop and do 10 push-ups, 10 crunches, and 10 lunges. This adds some variety to your workout and makes it more effective than just walking.

- Adding 10, 10-second sprints at the end of a 30-minute walk can improve your wind fitness and build overall strength.

- Exercises like lunges and squats can help build muscle strength and keep your legs from feeling like jello at the end of a jumping round.

5.4 A & B Stretching helps keep you limber and prevents cramping and injury (A). Yoga stretches and strengthens muscles for riding (B).

Diet

Daily Diet

Your body weight is important—it's harder for you to maintain your position if you are heavy, and it goes without saying that it will tire your horse when he has to carry around excessive weight. Keep in mind that in handicapped horse races, the jockey has to carry lead to add extra weight to slow the horse down!

Remember that your own health and fitness is just as important as the health and fitness of your equine partner. While he is the one galloping and jumping, he needs you to be at your best and able to help, not hinder, his performance.

On a day-to-day basis your food intake and exercise is going to be key for getting in shape. From my experience, staying at the right weight is pretty much based on what I eat and drink. I don't have a set diet plan, but I do try to eat all different kinds of foods in moderation. Big portions of food are not helpful in keeping your weight down, but everybody is going to have a different ideal personal diet. One of the issues I'm up against is the traveling I do. When you eat out a lot you have to pick and choose while trying to estimate what your calorie intake is going to be. The US Olympic Committee (USOC) has been helpful in this regard and they have nutrition advisors who have given us good guidance: For a man, the typical calorie intake needs to be around 2,000 calories a day, and it's too easy to get up to that! And the FDA recommends an average calorie intake of 1,800 to 2,300 calories daily for women.

You can fill up on a big salad with the dressing on the side; have steak, chicken, or pasta at night, but try to get less than the amount they often serve in a restaurant (smaller portions are key). Breakfast is important, too. There have been studies showing that people who go without breakfast tend to eat more later.

Keep in mind that some of the protein bars or energy bars contain 200 or even 250 calories and are designed to replace a whole meal. Their protein is helpful in stopping you from being hungry but you have to be careful not to eat two full bars as a snack because you will be gaining a full meal's worth of calories! Overusing these products can deter weight-loss goals as well as replace more nutritional whole foods. Probably, my favorite food snack that is low in calories (and high in fiber) is an orange—it fills you up and gives you plenty of energy. The chewy sports candies, like Clif SHOT Bloks® or Jelly Belly Sport Beans®, are mainly sugar-based and can give you a quick burst of energy in some cases.

As you get older it's easy to put on weight, so exercise is even more important. Pay attention to little things, too: Alcohol, and the cream and sugar you put in your coffee are all "empty" calories that can add up quickly.

Eating on "Game Day"

You need a commonsense approach to fitness and diet. I try to have a good meal in the morning and make sure that I eat about two hours before I ride at a major competition. If you eat too close to your ride time you tend to feel more bloated and not as effective. I also try to eat healthful foods like fruit and granola snack bars (as opposed to high-calorie energy bars) that can be digested easily throughout the day. If you get nervous find something that is palatable and easy on your stomach so that you still have energy for the physical demands of riding in competition.

Drinking plenty of fluids is obviously important since dehydration will cause your muscles to tire a lot quicker. Especially in hot weather, keep an eye on your liquid intake. Water is the best, though I find it hard to drink a lot of water because there's not much taste to it and sports drinks are too sugary. Instead, the night before, I mix about a quarter of a sports drink such as Gatorade to three-quarters of water, which tastes good and is hydrating. Take it easy on sugary and caffeinated beverages. I do tend to drink a cup of coffee about an hour before my ride to help stay alert and sharp, but the downside of coffee is that it tends to be dehydrating, so watch your intake, especially in hot weather.

PART 2
SCHOOLING and TRAINING

CHAPTER 6

Basic Dressage:
Teaching Your Horse Correctly

A thorough understanding of the basics of dressage is essential in the sport of eventing. Understanding the basics of dressage plays a crucial role in the development of your horse's strength, suppleness, balance, and submission. Whether you are riding the greenest horse or an experienced, advanced veteran, your aim should always be to train your horse correctly.

Good training is built block by block onto a strong, solid foundation. When you rush through the basics, it is likely to catch up with you down the road. But if you take your time and establish a correct foundation, it helps you in all three phases, not just dressage.

Remember that horses are creatures of habit: They gain comfort and security from doing the same thing every day, so having a routine is good. I try to focus the training of my horses with this philosophy in mind.

THE CORRECT HORSE

There are a few basics to correct training:

- Forward: First, you want the horse to go nicely forward, in front of your leg. This is a feeling of the horse having a *desire* to take you forward

6.1 A–C Student Kate Brown is riding young horse Melody, in a dressage lesson, schooling in a forward, calm, and straight outline.

with contained energy in all the movements. Even when you slow down, you want the feeling of being able to go forward at any time. You create this feeling by getting your horse to understand and accept the use of the lower leg (figs. 6.1 A–C).

- Straight: "Straight" means that if you were able to look down from above at your horse as he travels, you should be able to draw a line from between his ears, along his back to the top of his tail. And, when he is going "straight" on a circle his entire body, through his neck and back, should bend evenly around the circle—not with a shoulder or hip popping to the outside or falling to the inside.

- Accepting the bit: This is your connection to the power that you create in your horse. Ideally, you want your horse to take the contact from your hand to his mouth softly and evenly forward. The contact in both reins should feel similar, and you should be able to give aids with your hands to control the speed and direction of the horse.

- Roundness: You want your horse to use his *whole body* as he moves. First, he must bring his back legs through and underneath his body, which, in turn, gets his back "swinging" as he moves. This impulsion (or energy collection) brings about movement in the horse where he has "air time" or suspension in his movement. There should be enough power in each step that allows for this cadence. When the horse is using his whole body, his neck moves forward with each stride and the rider's hand must allow the horse to take the bit forward.

- Suppleness: A correct horse will always be relaxed and supple in his work. Through his training the rider develops a feeling of the horse having a slight suppleness or bend around the inside leg as he travels. The principle of "inside leg to outside rein" (see "Circles," p. 87) will always apply, even when riding in a straight line.

- Collection: You ultimately want your horse to have the ability to shift his balance to his hind legs and take more weight in his hind end, lightening the forehand so that he is more elevated ("uphill") with the front part of his body (legs, shoulders, head, and neck).

Once you understand your goals, you need to be able to teach your horse how to carry himself correctly. Every horse is an individual and has different requirements to reach his full potential as an athlete. I use a series of movements and exercises, which I will explain in a systematic and methodical way, to develop each horse's strength, suppleness, and balance. Just practicing movements mindlessly will not develop your horse correctly; the key is to incorporate them into his training so that he develops progressively over time.

As riders and trainers we have to be able to judge the right time to move on in the horse's training. Progressing too fast will result in a tense, confused, resistant horse that loses confidence and trust in his rider. However, a horse ridden in a low, novice frame each day will never develop the muscling that is necessary in order to become better balanced, more collected, and engaged from behind.

Warming Up

Like any athlete, your horse needs a good warm-up to get his blood flowing and his muscles loose before you ask him for more demanding work (figs. 6.2 A & B). When you warm up your horse each day, start with basic suppling exercises such as transitions and circles and gradually make the exercises more challenging. In the warm-up there are a few things that I keep in mind:

- I am always looking for suppleness, so starting out I want my horse to go forward and to stretch.

- His muscles need to be warmed up before I ask him to do anything more collected.

6.2 A & B Here I'm riding Fernhill Fugitive at the trot (A). As you begin to warm up, trot the horse forward in a long and relaxed, stretching outline. Move on to cantering on a circle, still in a long and stretching outline to warm up (B).

- I try not to sit too heavily in the saddle, sticking to rising trot and cantering with a light seat.

- I encourage the horse to move forward and reach down in front, allowing his back to get loose and swing.

- The speed (tempo) should not be fast but the horse should be forward enough to stay "in front of the leg" in a relaxed way.

Circles

We all know the age-old basic of the rider's "inside leg to outside rein." Your inside leg creates the energy, while your outside rein regulates it. This part of riding and training is so important that I hold true to this basic technique right through the three phases, not just in dressage. The goal is to encourage the horse to travel with his body softly bent around your inside leg. (When I talk about your leg, I am referring to your leg from the knee down: calf, heel, and when applicable, spur.)

Exercise

1 When you are on a circle to the left, your left *inside* leg, will be on the girth or close to that area, while your right *outside* leg, will be a little behind the girth.

2 The right *outside* rein is more of the "control" rein, keeping the horse coming around the circle instead of falling out of the circle with his shoulder. I sometimes refer to the outside rein as "the wall." The outside contact should be firm, with the feeling of the horse pulling you along.

3 You can use contact on your left *inside* rein to create some flexion to the inside of the circle. To achieve this, softly move the bit in the horse's mouth by opening and closing your fingers on the rein, encouraging him to relax his jaw. Think of it as a "softening" rein.

Change of Direction

There are many ways to change direction: you can go across the diagonal; ride a figure eight; or make a half circle back to the track, for example. As you change direction your inside leg becomes your new outside leg, and you change the horse's flexion to the new inside, using your new inside leg at the girth and the outside leg a little behind the girth. The same goes for the reins: The inside rein becomes the new outside contact or "the wall," and the outside rein, now the the new inside rein, begins to soften the contact as needed. Keep in mind that it is usually easier for a horse to work on a circle than in a straight line, so starting out on a circle will make it easier for him to learn to do what you are asking.

Exercise

The amount of bend and flexion in the horse's body should match the size of the circle or the turn (see notes on straightness on p. 84). When you are riding on a larger turn or circle, you will need less bend, and when on a smaller one, for example, 10 meters in diameter, you need quite a lot of bend.

Even when you are riding in a straight line on the long side of the arena you have an inside-leg-to-outside-rein connection. The bend, while not as pronounced as on a circle, becomes more of a feeling of having the horse bent slightly to the inside.

These simple basics can be mastered first at the walk to develop your horse's understanding. Once the connection and bend are established in the walk, go to trot, then when trot is mastered, you can go to canter. If the horse is struggling, I tend to back down a gait until the horse understands the exercise. For example, if it is not working in the trot, try to get it much better at the walk.

Transitions

A transition is a change of pace. This can be from one gait to the next, for example, walk to trot or trot to walk; or within the gait, from collected to medium trot, and so on. If you ride transitions correctly they will develop your horse's strength in his hindquarters, which will go a long way in helping to develop and train him.

I always start on the circle and work on the quality of each transition, making sure I have the correct connection from inside leg to outside rein and that my horse is accepting the bit. This requires strength from your horse, so his muscles must be built up gradually to do this correctly and comfortably. Eventually, as your horse becomes better trained, you can practice making transitions on a straight line rather than on the circle, but it is important to master the basics before you try something harder.

Over time, correctly ridden transitions will really improve your horse's balance as he gradually learns and becomes coordinated enough to carry more weight behind. An incorrectly ridden transition, on the other hand, doesn't really help your horse's training at all. Not only do poorly ridden transitions waste time as you struggle to change the horse's gait, they develop the wrong habits in your horse.

Riding and Executing Transitions

There are many different transitions but they all fit into two categories: *upward* and *downward* transitions. The principles of riding an upward transition apply through all upward transitions and vice versa. Begin with walk-trot, then trot-walk, and when that feels comfortable, move up to trot-canter-trot.

1 Prepare for the transitions by pushing your horse into the outside rein with your inside leg while the outside leg maintains the bend.

2 Pay attention to how responsive your horse is. Focus on maintaining the rhythm, a steady contact and correct bend throughout the exercise.

3 During the transition you must aim for the horse to stay supple and light in his mouth, not become heavy in the hand or bear down on his forehand. At no time should the horse resist against the bit.

4 In a correctly ridden transition the horse will step a little farther under his body with one or both hind legs, thereby increasing the level of engagement from his hindquarters.

All up and down transitions should be ridden in a similar fashion, allowing for some adaptation in intensity depending on which transition you are asking for. The more difficult the transition, for example, canter to walk, the more the horse needs to step under his body to execute the transition correctly.

I find that even the simplest of transitions are difficult for the green horse; patience and attention to correct use of your aids is important to help the horse learn the correct basics. Young or weak horses will need more distance to execute a transition correctly, but as they become stronger and more educated, the transition will be accomplished in a shorter distance.

The Half-Halt

Before the transition comes the *preparation*: The *half-halt*. A correctly ridden transition requires the horse to take more weight on his hind legs. In preparation you should let your horse know that a transition is coming up by closing your leg and your hand, asking the horse to step under with his hind legs more (fig. 6.3).

Exercise

To accomplish this, position your lower legs just behind the girth, depending on the sensitivity of your horse, and use light taps with the lower leg to ask for more engagement with the hind legs. Keep a nice, firm contact on the outside rein and gently give and take on the inside rein. Using these aids, ask the horse to step under himself and halt. Once the horse halts, take both legs off his sides, which should encourage him to relax and stand still.

Keep in mind:

- Before every transition, whether up or down, you need to use the half-halt to ask the horse to collect his step. This will help

6.3 Half-halts help to keep the horse balanced and "up" in front.

the horse prepare for the transition and help keep him in front of your leg.

- Through repetition and keeping your aids consistent, your horse will gradually be able to accomplish more difficult transitions with ease, thus improving his balance and strength.

- The use of a pulling or holding hand, or contact, during the half-halt only encourages the horse to lean on the rein and resist the contact. When doing this he stops "coming through" with the hind legs and the preparation and subsequent transition are incorrect.

Halt to Walk

The halt to walk is an elementary, upward transition, meaning the horse is increasing in speed. The horse should go smoothly and obediently from a square, even halt into a forward, relaxed walk while remaining on the aids. Mastering the walk to halt will help prepare the horse for more challenging transitions.

Exercise

To prepare for this transition, you need to get the horse's attention by taking a slight feel of the *inside* rein to move the bit in his mouth as you close your legs lightly on his sides. When you feel him react, close both lower legs firmly to urge him into walk.

Keep in mind:

- The preparation for this transition is arguably the most important part.

Trot to Canter

Included even in the most basic dressage tests, the key to successful trot-to-canter transitions is preparation: Use your half-halt before the transition to balance the horse and get his attention.

Exercise

- To ride the transition your inside leg is at the girth, encouraging the horse to bend around the inside leg.

- This inside leg also helps stop the horse from falling in.

- The outside leg is positioned a little behind the girth, which helps encourage the horse to bend through his body and stops him from falling out with his hindquarters.

- The contact is such that you are trying to get the horse to soften and reach a little forward, so that he is not against your hand in the transition.

- His trot needs to shorten from behind, not get faster before he canters. It is a little like down-shifting in a car.

- As he shortens and steps under, use a softening hand with the inside rein to encourage the horse's neck forward.

- Now your legs ensure that he stays on the line (straight) without falling in or out, all the time asking the horse to maintain the trot rhythm—not get faster or longer in his stride and just running into the canter.

- When your horse feels prepared, simply ask with your inside leg for the horse to step under his body and move forward into canter.

Canter to Trot

I find that teaching this on a circle makes things easier because the circle naturally helps to establish the bend in the horse. You can then get the horse's attention with the contact, asking him to come under from behind and shorten his stride.

Exercise
- Use the inside leg at the girth to keep him from falling in, or dropping his shoulder to the inside.

- The outside leg will keep him from falling out, or moving his hindquarters off the circle.

- With your hand, gently give and take the inside rein to half-halt in preparation for the transition.

- Gripping somewhat with your knee and thigh will also encourage the horse to "sit" behind and stay steady.

- All the time you are encouraging the horse to stay soft in the neck and mouth.

Getting Your Horse "Round"

I have just talked about the positioning of the horse from your inside leg to your outside rein. We also want the horse to stretch through his back and accept the bit, rounding his neck as he takes the contact. The horse should carry the bit forward in a responsive way, not "locked" onto it, or leaning against your hand, making the contact feel very heavy. He also should not hide "behind the bit," with his nose tucked in toward his chest to evade the contact, in which case you will have a very light feeling in your hand.

Each horse's contact is a little different, but we are after the same general feel with each

Responsiveness to the Leg

One of the most basic and essential parts of early training is to teach your horse to move off your leg. Obedience and responsiveness to your leg is crucial to making progress with your horse. To begin, at the walk place both your legs slightly behind the girth. Putting pressure on the horse's sides, ask him to move forward. If he does not respond, close the legs more firmly; if he still does not respond, then you can back up your leg aid with the spur and/or a tap from your dressage whip. You want the horse to be responsive to your leg aid—not dull—so do not just keep squeezing with your legs without getting a reaction. He needs to respect your aids but not get scared or tense from the touch of your leg.

As it becomes easier to send the horse forward in walk, progress to trot and canter using the same principles, then practice yielding away from each leg (see p. 94), again in walk, then trot, then canter. Spending time practicing and repeating these basic exercises will go a long way toward getting your horse to react correctly.

6.4 Ask the horse to flex in his neck and to bend around the inside leg. The horse is overbent here as he learns to accept the bend.

one. When a horse has accepted the bit, you have the feeling that he is taking the bit forward from you, but not dragging it away. Once you have this feeling, you can begin to ask for roundness. My goal is for the horse to keep moving forward, round, and softly accepting the contact with the bit. He should be using his whole body, stepping underneath himself with his hind legs and with the energy (impulsion) coming from behind.

Exercise

- For most horses, I start with a small circle.

- To begin asking for roundness, I close my leg and ask my horse to walk forward while applying some pressure on his mouth by squeezing my fingers on the reins to move the bit in his mouth (fig. 6.4).

- The whole horse should become round: His neck rounds a little in shape and his back lifts up as his hindquarters come under his body more, his hind legs reaching forward. He begins to use his entire body and accepts the contact with his mouth to come "on the bit."

- By gently giving and taking on the inside rein I keep my horse flexed to the inside, which helps to encourage this connection. I keep asking for this until I feel softness in his mouth.

If his neck is bent and his head is down, but he is frozen on the bit, he is not truly round. I always use my leg to encourage my horse to move forward and encourage him to go round. Once I am able to keep my horse round, I work on a circle in both directions, and then expand the circle until I can keep the roundness going around the whole arena. If I feel that I am losing the connection when I use the whole arena, I will go back to a circle until my horse comes round again, and then I expand the circle. Again, I start at the walk, then trot and finally canter.

Lateral Movements and Exercises

I will talk about some of the movements that I use in training my horses to develop obedience and suppleness, balance, and strength. In introducing your horse to these exercises, the emphasis is on him "thinking forward" at all times. I would rather introduce a lateral movement with only a little angle, with the horse thinking forward. Over time I aim for more angle, but in the beginning I prefer to focus on going forward in order to avoid getting resistance from the horse and having to deal with him backing off.

All these training exercises will get your horse more physically ready and mentally accepting of the increased demands that will be placed on him as you develop your training and move up the levels.

Leg-Yielding

Once I have established that the horse understands going forward from my leg, I introduce *leg-yielding* (figs. 6.5 A & B). Riding the leg-yield is exactly how it sounds: The horse yields to pressure from the leg and responds

6.5 A & B Leg-yielding in trot.

by moving both forward and sideways away from the leg. This can be performed at walk, trot, and canter. I find that with some horses it can really help develop suppleness and their understanding the leg-to-hand connection.

Leg-yielding at the walk is the first exercise I do on any new horse that is ready for basic dressage work. The correct aids for leg-yielding are: Apply your inside leg at the girth, pushing the horse in the direction you are going, to the outside rein, which is keeping the horse straight. The horse is bent slightly *away* from the direction he is going. The correct leg-yield should encompass the following key points:

- The horse's body should be straight with a natural flexion in the poll.

- Flexion through the body should be around the rider's inside leg, or *away* from the direction the horse is traveling.

- The horse should move forward and sideways easily and in balance.

Basic Dressage: Teaching Your Horse Correctly 6

Exercise

1 I usually introduce the leg-yield in walk.

2 I keep the horse straight in the neck by maintaining a nice contact with the outside rein.

3 I then supple the inside with the inside hand and push the horse across with the inside leg.

4 My outside leg remains in place.

5 In the beginning, I sometimes need to move the inside leg back slightly to get a reaction and to get the horse's hindquarters to move across.

6 My aim is to get the horse to move across parallel to the track where the leg-yield starts. This principle for staying parallel will always apply in the leg-yield. It is very important that the horse keeps going forward, not just sideways. I don't want the shoulder to fall out or the horse to fall sideways.

To establish the bend correctly, I put the horse on a circle and then yield him out of the circle with my inside leg. To prevent the horse overbending through his neck and falling out with his outside shoulder, maintain a steady contact on the outside rein. You do not want his hindquarters to move out first. If he does this, he is not going forward and is behind your leg. He must stay pretty straight, slightly leading with his shoulder and with a slight flexion around your inside leg.

Keeping the Horse's Nose in Front of the Vertical

If the horse's nose is not at least slightly in front of the vertical, most judges will mark you down in the test. The general feeling is that when the horse is behind the vertical, he has been trained somewhat incorrectly and is, therefore, hiding *behind* the bit rather than taking it forward correctly. I think it is important to be aware of where the horse's nose is and what the feeling is. A very light feeling in your hand is not correct because the horse is probably not in front of your leg or taking the bit forward. However, when I am starting out my warm-up and first suppling the horse, I feel that it is okay to not have the horse completely in front of the vertical as long as you have the ability to let the nose go forward at any time (fig. 6.6).

6.6 Riding the horse slightly behind the vertical for a while when starting warm-up: I feel that it is okay to not have the horse completely in front of the vertical as long as you have the ability to let the nose go forward at any time. In competition, however, this will lose you valuable points in your dressage test.

Once you have established this at the walk and he understands the exercise, you can try it at the trot. Again, use the same routine starting with the circle and then down a centerline. This is also a great exercise in the canter. The aim is to reinforce the understanding and communication from your leg to your hand: You want your horse to respond to the leg, moving nicely forward as well as away from your leg.

Shoulder-In

The *shoulder-in* is a great way to supple and train your horse and help him increase collection in his gaits. It can be performed in walk, trot, and canter; however, the most benefit will be gained in the trot. When ridden correctly, shoulder-in at the trot can really improve the quality of your horse's gait over time. Through the horse building correct muscling and improving his balance, the trot will develop more elevation and suspension.

I like to use shoulder-in for a few steps before each turn or transition to balance the horse and help prepare for the next movement. And although this movement is not asked for in a dressage test at the canter, I think shoulder-in at canter is a great exercise and training tool.

The horse is slightly bent through his whole body around your inside leg—for example, when traveling to the left the horse is bent around the left leg. The horse's inside front leg should pass and cross in front of the outside front leg. When observing a horse in shoulder-in from a place in front or behind, you see the horse on three tracks (6.7 A). The back legs still push forward on a straight line, unlike in leg-yielding where they are moving across and forward.

Exercise

1. To introduce a horse to shoulder-in I begin with small circles of 8 to 10 meters in diameter. The bend that you have for this small circle is the same bend that you want to maintain going down the long side in shoulder-in.

2. Once you have established a consistent bend and balance on the circle, progress down the track. As the horse's front end comes off the wall, send him off your inside leg and forward with his front end slightly to the inside.

3. Use your *inside* leg to push the horse's *front legs and body* forward and down the track, with the *outside* leg behind the girth to keep the horse's *hind legs* pushing him forward and down the track.

4. The inside rein is used for general suppling and softening the poll and the jaw, while the outside rein prevents the horse from overbending in his neck.

Troubleshooting

- In walk especially, you have to be careful that the horse keeps going forward and not just sideways.

- If the horse begins to move only sideways, send him forward and straight or make another circle before you ask him to go sideways again.

- What you don't want is just bending in the shoulder and neck; once you bend the neck the shoulder falls to the outside. You need to use the outside rein to maintain the same bend in the neck that is in the horse's body. It is important to understand that the bend comes from the horse's *whole body* bending through to the outside rein, and that you don't hold the horse on the bend with the inside rein.

- Also be careful not to let your inside leg go too far back and push the hind legs out, which will create more of a leg-yield and thus no added benefit to your horse's training. You want the horse to step forward, not just sideways (fig. 6.7 B).

6.7 A & B Correct shoulder-in on three tracks (A), and an incorrect shoulder-in: on four tracks (B).

Travers (Haunches-In)

In eventing competition, travers is introduced at Intermediate Level, but it can be used in training long before the horse gets to that level. It can be ridden in walk, trot, and canter. The main benefit is in the trot, which helps to supple and strengthen the horse.

In travers the horse's shoulders remain on the track and the hindquarters move to the inside. He moves in the direction of the bend and looks in the direction he is traveling. For green horses, a lesser angle on three tracks is better (fig. 6.8 A); when ridden on an educated horse, travers can be ridden on four tracks (fig. 6.8 B). At all times, the horse needs to stay forward and in a consistent rhythm.

Exercise

1. Like shoulder-in, travers can be introduced off a circle where the horse is bent around the inside leg already. As you go down the track, maintain the same bend you had on the circle.

6.8 A & B Travers on three tracks (A) and on four tracks (B).

2 Before the horse finishes the circle, with his front end on the track and his haunches just to the inside, send him forward along the long side with your outside leg, maintaining the bend with your inside leg to outside hand.

3 The horse's flexion is around the rider's inside leg. Contact on the outside rein keeps the horse's shoulders and front end traveling straight down the track while the outside leg can then encourage the horse's hind legs to come forward as the horse travels bent around the inside leg.

Troubleshooting

- You want the horse to stay soft in front and thinking forward, willing to move off your leg.

- Think about bending the horse through his body while keeping the quality of the gait, not just the angle.

Half-Pass

In *half-pass*, the horse moves forward and sideways across the arena on the diagonal, with his body almost parallel to the long side. The bend or flexion is around the rider's inside leg and the horse's body bent in the direction he is traveling. Half-pass can be ridden at walk, trot, and canter and is great for educating the horse at all gaits (fig. 6.9).

Exercise

1 As with the shoulder-in, establish the bend around the inside leg as the horse is moving forward across the diagonal of the arena.

2 Once again the inside rein can be used to soften the horse, while the outside hand stays close to the withers to help bring the horse across.

3 You don't want to get so caught up with getting the horse to move sideways that you lose the forward movement; if this happens, the stride will also become uneven.

4 The inside leg, at the girth, keeps the horse going forward and maintains the bend while the outside leg, behind the girth, drives the horse over, across the diagonal.

Troubleshooting

- When you are starting to school half-pass it is important to always keep the emphasis on the horse going *forward and across*, not simply moving sideways away from your leg.

- You want the horse's shoulders slightly leading the hindquarters; when the quarters lead your horse is going sideways too much and not forward enough.

Collecting and Extending the Trot

Some horses are born with a natural ability and strength to extend the trot, while others must be trained. For the horse to extend correctly, he must first be able to engage his hindquarters. If this doesn't happen he will fall on his forehand and be "wide behind," meaning that rather than flexing his hocks and lifting his legs up and forward to extend, he tries to extend by "pushing" his hind legs out and back behind his body.

6.9 Half-pass in trot.

Basic Dressage: Teaching Your Horse Correctly 6

Collecting

Collecting consists of a series of half-halts. It is like asking the horse to engage and prepare for the transition to halt, but as soon as he sits and balances, the rider closes the leg and keeps the forward motion. Over time your horse will understand that he needs to get quicker with his hind legs as he slows down the forward momentum, taking more weight on his hind end and developing more power and energy.

Lengthening and Extending

The key to creating a good lengthened or extended trot is to first develop a good *collected* trot, then release some of that energy as you send the horse forward (fig. 6.10). *Lengthening* the stride, a precursor to extending, is when the horse takes longer steps and begins to push forward with his hindquarters, reaching forward with his front legs. When he *extends*, the impulsion from behind is greater, the horse covers more ground, and there should be a moment of suspension in the gait where all four feet are off the ground. (See fig. 11.7 on p. 186 for an example of an extended trot.)

6.10 Lengthening the stride at trot.

Exercise

1 Sit with both legs slightly behind the girth and touching both sides of the horse.

2 When the horse wants to run forward, stay back with the upper body and close the hand and leg to encourage him to keep pushing but not just run.

3 Once you feel the horse pushing from behind, allow him to carry that energy forward by maintaining the leg contact and softening the hand slightly so that the horse can extend his neck forward.

Troubleshooting

If the trot starts to get low and flat, half-halt and repeat the exercise for a few steps. Over time the medium and extended trot will last longer; I find that in a lot of cases rising trot is a better way to teach horses to extend because it is easier for many riders and also allows the horse's back more freedom.

The Halt

It is important to train your horse to make a good correct halt. Not only does this help your dressage score, but a good halt is essential to the complete training of the horse. This means that the horse can step under himself as he goes into the halt and stay on the bit, which means not standing there with a hollow back and his head up. He should stand squarely, and be soft and submissive in his neck, back, and jaw (fig. 6.12).

I always begin training the horse to halt in the walk. As in most exercises, preparation is crucial. From a medium walk, start to shorten the walk steps, using a half-halt to make his back legs quicker off the ground and his steps shorter, without losing the feeling of going forward. The horse should stay soft in the contact to his mouth.

Success Through Repetition

Horses learn through repetition. If things don't go as you would like, reprimanding a horse generally doesn't get through to him. Instead, to get the result you want, use an exercise that he already understands.

For example, when I ask for a trot-canter transition and the horse rushes into the canter, reprimanding him with a hard hand to bring him back to trot or slow him down will not make him understand that I don't want him to rush through the transition or hollow his back.

A better approach, which would set the horse up to succeed, is to put him on a small circle and encourage him to bend more and respond to the leg with a lot of transitions. The circle will make it hard for him to rush, so he will learn to maintain a consistent pace somewhat on his own (fig. 6.11). Always remember to be patient and considerate of the horse in your training.

6.11 When a horse rushes into the canter, put him on a small circle encouraging bend and a response to your leg using transitions.

Once he understands what you are asking, you can close your leg, sit deeper in the saddle and ride him forward into a closed hand to ask him to halt, without stopping abruptly. Try to feel the back legs being the last to step as he comes to a stop. Your aim is to halt without resistance in the contact. In the halt, you want to have the feeling that your horse can step forward at any time. You don't want him to halt, then brace and be on the verge of going backward.

Next you can practice trot to halt. Again, prepare by creating shorter, active steps. You need a light feel in the contact, not heavy or one that is dragging you forward. Use a half-halt riding from your leg and seat to a closed hand to collect his stride and lighten his front end in preparation for a transition from trot to walk. Keep the walk active with short, quick

6.12 The horse is not quite square in this halt, but he is relaxed and accepting the contact. My heel has come up as I begin to ask him for the rein-back.

steps–not slow, lazy steps. Once this is correct, the trot to halt requires the same aids, but keep the closed hand and a half-halt through to halt. All the time, the horse should be still "thinking" forward and light in the contact.

Lastly, you can school canter to halt. However, this movement is not required in eventing dressage until the Intermediate Level, so there is not a lot to be gained by working on it early in the horse's education. Until he can collect his canter and really "sit" and properly prepare for the halt, you will probably just overface him by working on this movement, resulting in tension and resistance.

When he is ready, begin with canter to collected trot work, then canter to walk. Finally, keep the collected canter really "uphill" and ride from canter to halt. In the beginning, a couple of steps of walk before the horse halts is actually desirable, to keep the horse *thinking* forward.

If your horse anticipates and wants to stop too abruptly, mix it up from canter to trot, and canter to walk to keep him in front of your leg and prepare to halt, then ride forward without halting.

Exercise

You can practice getting the horse to stand square in front and behind, either by checking in the ring's mirror if one is available, or leaning slightly to the side and glancing down once he has halted to see how his legs are placed. Softly ask with your lower leg if the horse needs to move a leg forward. Never ask a horse to step back with a leg to square him up as this would be riding him backward. It takes some trial and error, as well as plenty of patience, to get the horse to step up squarely.

It is also important for your horse to stand quietly, relaxed, and "round" or on the bit once he is in the halt. You can squeeze the reins gently with your fingers to move them in the horse's mouth to encourage him to stay round and soft. Keep your lower legs securely on his sides to prevent him from backing up.

Troubleshooting

The horse:

- *Is on his forehand.*

Most horses that are on the forehand are leaning on the contact for balance and are not coming under from behind. Encourage your horse to be active behind from your lower leg. Ideally, you are aiming to have him working uphill, which means having him moving forward and "carrying himself" so that his withers are a little higher than his rump; and his head and neck are working forward and out in front of the horse. This kind of horse needs to be able to be prepared in a really "uphill" frame and sometimes even slightly above the bit.

- *Does not stay round in halt.*

Generally, this is more a submission issue than a balance issue as the horse starts to think backward in the halt. He backs off and stops thinking forward to the contact, then "hollows out" his topline in the halt. To correct this you need to have your horse always thinking forward, so instead of trying to stand still in the halt, start to halt, then trot on. A series of these transitions will teach the horse to always be ready for your forward aid. As he improves, you can allow him to stay longer in the halt, always having the feeling that you can easily move forward.

- *Halts but then looks around.*

Try to think of keeping the connection in the halt and the horse staying focused on his job, not his surroundings. Move the bit in his mouth so that the connection from your hand doesn't harden and lose the soft, even contact. Also have your lower leg on your horse and do not allow him to back up. Keeping your horse "on your aids" ensures that you can always move forward and encourages the horse to keep reaching forward for the bit.

- *Moves in the halt.*

This can be a frustrating habit to break. In the beginning I work on establishing the halt, then moving on so the horse is thinking forward, not stepping back or sideways. Over time as you maintain the halt for longer stretches of time, the horse will learn to stand still.

- *Does not stand square.*

Sometimes a horse will consistently leave one leg behind and won't square up. Each time you halt you should softly but firmly ask the horse to bring up the leg that is left behind, again, *always* by asking him to step *forward*. If it is usually the same leg, using a little more lower leg pressure on that side of the horse should encourage him to step under and square up.

The Rein-Back

The *rein-back* is introduced for the first time at Preliminary Level. Begin teaching your horse the rein-back before you are competing at that level, however. Once he is ready to easily go on the bit and is adjustable forward and back in all gaits, he is more than educated to begin learning to rein-back. However, when your horse is so green that it's still a struggle to put him on the bit or hard to get him going forward, introducing the rein-back would be a shock to him and could potentially cause problems like rearing because he would just be confused as he is not skilled and coordinated enough yet.

Some horses naturally back up very easily; if this is the case, not a lot of practice is required. Others are confused about it and become quite rigid; you may need somebody on the ground to put a hand on the horse's chest and gently encourage him to step backward.

Exercise

1 First, establish a good, square halt.

2 From the halt, lighten your seat slightly to allow the horse's back to move.

3 With your leg ask the horse to create energy and then with your contact in the reins, use that energy to ask him to step back rather than move forward (fig. 6.13). Softly moving the bit in his mouth will be helpful so that he can't get set against your hand.

4 In the beginning, one step of rein-back is good; reward him by moving forward or

6.13 As I close my leg and lighten my seat to create energy, I close my hand to encourage the horse to step back.

patting him before you halt and do the exercise again.

Troubleshooting

- It is best to teach the rein-back over a long period of time. Dwelling on this exercise on one day will make your horse a bit "backward," so slowly introduce rein-back a little at a time over weeks and months. The first day, it is sufficient if you get one or two steps each time you ask.

- Asking for rein-back is not something you should do straight out of the stable, either. Your horse needs to be engaged, warmed up properly, and going forward before you work on this. Ideally, he should accept the aids softly and obediently and back up without resistance and not rushing, instead taking deliberate, even steps. At any stage you should be able to send him forward again.

- Straightness in the rein-back is important. Some horses go either left or right: When the horse always gets crooked to the left, for example, line up against a wall or a fence and back up with the wall on your left side to help keep him straight.

- Another correction: When the horse goes right, just use your left leg to ask for the rein-back (and vice versa)—this also helps to keep him straight.

Counter-Canter

The *counter-canter* is introduced in eventing at Preliminary Level and above. I find it a great training, balancing, and educational exercise. Once your horse is able to canter easily and in balance on a 15-meter circle in the *true* canter, he is ready to counter-canter. Some horses are very strong in canter and can counter-canter early, while others need more time being educated in true canter or they will lose the quality of the canter or switch leads in the counter-canter.

Counter-canter requires the horse to go in the opposite direction of the lead the horse is cantering on (leading leg). The horse must be able to keep his balance easily.

In the regular canter on the correct lead, alter the bend in the horse, so rather than having the horse bent around the inside leg, he straightens toward the outside of the circle. This teaches the horse that while straightening him or bending him to the outside he needs to stay strong on his true canter lead.

At all times during the counter-canter, your leg position and aids stay the same: The *inside* leg—now on the *outside* of the circle—is on the girth, and the outside leg (now inside the circle) is behind the girth "holding" the hindquarters. (Remember, the leg that is called your "inside" leg is always the leg on the *inside* of the horse's bend, no matter which direction he is traveling.) While your legs must maintain this positioning, you can change the positioning of the horse's head and neck slightly in order to straighten the horse. Flexion does not always have to be toward the leading leg.

Exercise

An easy exercise is to canter down the long side of the arena and make a small loop 2 to 3 meters toward the center, then back to the track while staying on the same lead. Focus on your horse maintaining a steady canter, not losing his balance and falling on his forehand, and staying powerful in the counter-canter. As this exercise becomes easier for the horse over time, you can increase the difficulty: The loop becomes bigger and, ultimately, the horse should be able to hold the counter-canter on a 20-meter circle.

Troubleshooting

- The priority in counter-canter is that the horse stays on the original canter lead. The quality of the canter, with the horse round and "jumping" forward, does not change when you go from *true* canter to counter-canter.

- You shouldn't be holding the counter-canter just by flexing the horse to the lead and holding him there with your hand. Your horse needs to be on your aids correctly and stay in counter-canter from your leg position. You should feel at any stage in the counter-canter that you can send the horse forward from your leg and lengthen his stride if you need to.

- If your horse switches leads, make the counter-canter quite simple: Go back to that small loop off the rail, and emphasize your inside leg *on* the girth and outside leg *behind* the girth. The horse needs time to develop strength, coordination, and understanding, so keep it simple in the beginning.

Flying Changes

The *flying change* is introduced into the dressage at Advanced Level, but the horse and rider's understanding of flying changes earlier than this is very important, in particular, for the show jumping and cross-country phases. It is interesting that horses at a young age do flying changes very well. I've broken in a lot of horses and have never found one, when I first ride him, that won't do a flying change. In some cases, as you progress in your training, the natural "forwardness" and "feel" of the horse goes away, and getting a flying change on command is not as easy as it was on the green horse (for more on flying changes, see "Flying Changes" (p. 155).

I think from an eventing point of view we have two different types of flying changes. In the show jumping ring or out on cross-country, the attention to having a "clean" flying change–the hind leg coming through and the front leg changing together–is not as important. When we're jumping we just want a smooth change as we change direction; generally, if the horse is forward, in a nice balance, and straight as you change direction, he will usually change leads automatically.

If you're on the right lead and plan to change to the left lead, your left leg holds the horse so he stays in balance. Moving your new outside (right) leg behind the girth will control the horse's hindquarters as the new inside leg (left) asks for the lead change. If the horse is unresponsive to this leg, a light tap of the dressage whip behind the leg will help encourage him to change to the correct lead rather than go in counter-canter on the new circle.

I usually start to introduce the flying change at the Novice Level in a jumping situation. When flying changes don't come naturally, put a couple of poles on the ground in your arena, space them well apart, and in the canter ask for the change of lead as the horse steps over the pole. In most cases, the lead change comes quite naturally to him.

Wait to introduce flying changes in dressage when your horse is very adjustable in the canter. It makes sense that unless you can really collect your horse and create some power in his canter, it's going to be difficult for him to do a flying change in a dressage-arena setting.

Exercise

1 In this exercise, start by cantering on the left lead. As you know, the correct way for the horse to canter is to be softly bent around the rider's inside leg. in this case, your *left* leg at the girth and your outside, *right* leg just behind the girth. Your inside leg is then connected to your outside (right) rein.

2 To prepare for the flying change to the right lead, the horse's body needs to change its bend: For the right hind leg to come through, he needs to be bent a little bit around your right leg, with the connection coming through to the left rein. He needs to be able to do this while keeping the power in the canter so that he has the energy (power) to switch his leads.

3 In a lot of cases, when you can collect the horse enough and keep working on the collection as he prepares for the change, it's actually easier for the horse to change than it is for him to stay on that lead.

Troubleshooting

- Your body should stay in the center of the horse and not move to the side to "help" the change.

- The change should be executed from your leg rather than movement of the upper body.

- The change to the new lead should not be done by the new inside rein–you don't want the horse to change just because you change the bend. The horse first has to accept the change of bend without changing lead (counter-canter), then change lead from your leg.

- The horse must be able to collect and stay "powerful" during the preparation and accept the change in his bend without tension.

There are different ways of positioning your horse in preparation for the change: Going across the diagonal gives you a good feel for keeping the horse straight as you prepare him for the new canter lead. Some horses find it helpful to be asked to change while in half-pass—as you are pushing and engaging the horse already you can softly change the bend and ask for the flying change.

Flying changes cannot be taught in one day but rather should be learned over months of gradual training. Especially in the beginning, when you do a change or two it's important to go back and finish with counter-canter so that the horse is not anticipating changing leads every time you change direction of bend.

CHAPTER 7

Riding Cross-Country: No Jumping

The joy and exhilaration of galloping and jumping across country can hardly be compared to any other equestrian sport and is one of the main reasons many people decide to event. One of the keys to successful cross-country riding is to feel at ease traveling over varied terrain on horseback. This is the first skill you will need to establish before you start jumping cross-country fences, and you cannot expect to improve this part of your riding by simply getting a lesson in an enclosed area. You have to get out and get firsthand experience.

I was fortunate in this respect to have grown up on a farm in Australia where I spent a lot of my early years in the saddle helping on the farm, herding sheep and cattle, and chasing kangaroos, emus, and pigs around for fun! When you are in the saddle for a large part of the day cantering, galloping, or just trotting across fields or through forests, eventually the feeling of sitting on a horse becomes second nature. Cantering up and down steep hills, swimming horses across small streams, jumping fallen trees, and chasing runaway steers were part of our daily chores growing up in the Outback. In many ways, these were great training exercises for my later career as an event rider.

GETTING OUT OF THE ARENA

There are many ways to get experience riding in the open. You can go trail riding, take part in a hunter-pace event, or for more extreme training, participate in an endurance riding event. It is important to plan this part of your training as you would any other aspect: You need to practice in order to master the technique for riding out in the open.

A common way for riders in some parts of the world to become at ease riding across country is to go fox hunting. A lot of the heroes of eventing have spent many days in the saddle hunting through woods and fields. Although I had never fox hunted before I came to the United States, I can really appreciate the benefits of spending hours in the saddle and learning to trust your horse's instincts without having any real idea of where the hunt will take you and what type of land you will have to ride over.

The aim is for you and your horse to be able to walk, trot, canter and, where appropriate, gallop across all sorts of terrain—while staying in balance. If you can get access to land that includes trails, hills, shallow streams, steep uphills and downhills for your training, it is great practice before starting to jump cross-country.

Position

It doesn't matter what type of obstacle or terrain the horse is negotiating, most of the great cross-country riders of the world have an instinctive feel for staying in the center of their horse, relying on their legs and seat for a base of support, and always thinking and looking ahead.

I will talk about different riding positions in depth later (see p. 117). Riding cross-country is not so much about style and looks but about building the confidence and balance necessary to stay with your horse and trust his instincts.

Style aside, it is crucial to be able do all of this without hanging onto the reins and pulling your horse in the mouth to keep your balance. Your horse needs to be able to use his head and neck for his own balance, and he needs to gain confidence that he will not get yanked in the mouth unexpectedly as he navigates uneven ground and jumps.

Maintaining Pace

One of the parts of cross-country riding that riders have to work on is the gallop. It is important for the horse to understand that whatever speed you ride him, he should maintain that pace until you ask him to change. You shouldn't have to hold the horse back or kick him forward all the way around the course.

- When riding cross-country, it is most efficient to maintain a steady pace; constantly adjusting it wastes time.

- Some Thoroughbreds have been trained for racing and want to go faster and faster. You have to teach this type of horse that he is not in a race and that he has to settle at the speed you want and not get too strong or too fast.

- At the other end of the spectrum is the lazy horse that the rider has to encourage

Handling a Strong Horse

There is a real skill in being able to get a horse to settle and not just lean against your hand and get stronger and stronger when galloping. The horse needs to be taught to come back to you; it is not just about strength and the rider's build—consider that quite light jockeys can rate their Thoroughbreds in during a race—it is about training, the rider's skill, and communication with the horse.

If you happen to have a horse that gets strong when galloping, you can develop the ability to rate his speed. Start your training with a slow canter and gradually, over days, weeks, or maybe months, build up to doing faster work while maintaining the quality of softness and responsiveness that you had when starting out at a slower pace.

You can practice in an open field, in your galloping position:

1 Get the horse up to speed and teach him to stay at that speed and not go faster when you soften the reins.

2 As you start off at a slower speed you can move the bit in the horse's mouth so that he doesn't lock onto the bit.

3 If the horse speeds up, ask him to slow down and then give again. Constantly give to the horse and teach him not to go faster.

4 It is better to not use both hands at the same time to pull back on the horse. Using both hands encourages the horse to just brace against them.

You want this control to carry over onto the cross-country course when you are competing. With some horses it is possible to maintain the required speed on cross-country every time you go to a competition. However, some horses will just get stronger and stronger. In my experience, with a horse like Woodburn, I could only go fast every third or fourth competition or he would get very excited and quite strong, and had the potential to have problems on cross-country. What I would do is school him and go around at a slower speed at Horse Trials in preparation for the run that really counted—at the Three-Day Event.

The Runaway Horse

For the horse that runs away, a stronger bit will probably be necessary (see p. 44). I have talked about the idea that you ultimately want to be lighter with your hands: The key is not letting it get to the stage of struggling to hold the horse. When this has become a problem you need to address it at home rather than go to a competition where the horse is likely to get even stronger.

If you do have a situation where the horse gets out of control, you need to do whatever it takes—whether that means circling or stopping or doing whatever you need until the horse is obedient. The competition comes second to your (and your horse's) safety.

I find that standing up in a galloping position, trying to think about moving the bit and getting the horse to wait works better than leaning back and "skiing" against the horse. You want to stay with him in a gallop and in a lot of cases "round" the horse as you try to steady him. You don't want the horse to hollow out and brace against you because then he's in a much stronger position to fight against you.

USEF Rules

According to the USEF 2012 Rule Book, different cross-country speeds, distances, and jumping efforts found in Horse Trials (not FEI recognized events) are:

BEGINNER NOVICE
Speed: Allowed 300–350/420 mpm (meters per minute)
Length of Course: Allowed 1400–2000m
Number of Jumping Efforts: Allowed 14–18

NOVICE
Speed: Allowed 350–400/450 mpm
Length of Course: Allowed 1800–2200m
Number of Efforts: Allowed 18–20

TRAINING
Speed: Allowed 420–470 mpm
Length of Course: Allowed 2000–2800m
Number of Efforts: Allowed 20–24

PRELIMINARY
Speed: 520 mpm
Length of Course: Allowed 2200–3300m
Number of Efforts: Allowed 22–30

INTERMEDIATE
Speed: 550 mpm
Length of Course: Allowed 2800–3800m
Number of Efforts: Allowed 28–34

ADVANCED
Speed: 570 mpm
Length of Course: Allowed 3200–4400
Number of Efforts: Allowed 32–40

to go forward. This kind of horse, once he is fit enough, needs to get out often and be encouraged to go forward and gallop between the jumps.

Self-Carriage

The cross-country horse must be capable of staying in "self-carriage" between the jumps and be rideable in the open. What I mean when I refer to the galloping form of self-carriage is a horse that is not being controlled every stride. It goes back to flatwork where you can ride around the arena in a relaxed self-carriage and canter around the arena in a two-point position with the horse not necessarily on a loose rein, but starting to settle at the speed you've requested.

Exercise

In the arena, once your horse has learned to carry himself you can then start to vary the speed: Go once around asking him to go more forward, then shorten the stride and go around again maintaining that pace. You can mix it up on each lead—for instance, ride in a short-strided canter on the short side of the arena and then ease the horse into lengthening his stride on the long side. This helps the horse learn to adjust while staying relaxed and understanding what you are asking him to do.

After you have mastered this exercise in the arena, introduce your horse to cantering and galloping out in a field or on a cross-country course. The same method that you used in the arena applies: Start off slowly and let the horse canter around in a relaxed way. You don't have to go anywhere, just let the horse relax and canter around—but be sure that you have the control to turn and stop whenever you need to! If at any stage your horse takes over and wants to gallop too fast or run away, you need to make a circle and come back to a controlled situation.

Adding Speed

Once your horse is cantering steadily around the field, balanced and listening to you, you can start to go faster and add speed to your gallops. You should feel that at any time you can bring him back to a slower speed or make a turn. Training the horse to maintain a steady pace in self-carriage is not necessarily an overnight process. With some horses these steps will take months and months, while others may pick it up within days. It depends on your horse's previous training, breeding and general makeup. You shouldn't try to cram all this into a couple of training sessions, in any case. With correct and patient schooling the horse should eventually understand that he can go out in the open and stay relaxed at any pace.

Practicing Pace

Learning what correct pace feels like is essential. To practice feeling what different speeds feel like, it's quite easy to get a car or motorbike speedometer and map out an exact distance where you can canter in specific increments of time. It's great when it's on a straightaway, but it can loop around

7.1 Learn to check your watch when you ride cross-country so that you can practice maintaining a steady pace.

if you are short on space. In addition, you will need a stopwatch (fig. 7.1).

Exercise

Let's say, for example, that you're going to do Training Level at 475 mpm.

1 Map out 950 meters (it will take you two minutes to canter the distance) by setting out cones, buckets, or other easily identifiable markers.

2 Start your canter or gallop well before your first marker–you want to have the pace established already so that you can hit your stopwatch as you pass the marker.

3 You want the horse to settle into the speed so you're not changing the pace all the time, and learn to judge the speed yourself. Every horse's stride will be different so it takes some judgment and experience to settle your horse into the correct pace and get within a few seconds of where you need to be on your time trial.

4 Canter the allotted distance, and stop your watch as you pass your finish marker. Your aim is to canter the 950 meters in as close to two minutes as possible, while maintaining a steady pace.

Note: If you find it too difficult to check your watch while you are riding, in the beginning, have someone on the ground time you. Eventually, though, learn to check your watch while you gallop since that is what you will need to do during a competition.

Bear in mind that on your cross-country course during an event this is the average speed: A lot of jumps will require that you come in slower, or you'll have to turn sharply and won't be able to maintain the optimum speed. So if you want to make time, the speed you'll need to go between fences will have to be a little bit faster in order to average it out.

- You can change the measurements to whatever level you are aiming for or want to practice.

- You shouldn't practice this too frequently, because it will become taxing on your horse.

- Be sure to take into account the ground conditions and try to find good footing for practicing galloping.

Notes on Good Footing

Good footing is where a horse can get some grip so he doesn't slip—that is, not too wet, slippery, nor hard. Very hard ground can be just as slippery as wet ground, and can be quite concussive to the horse. The ground should be pretty consistently even, not changing from hard to soft, so the horse does not have to keep finding his footing and rebalancing. Studs can be helpful to improve the horse's confidence when galloping and give him more grip. (See chapter 17, "Hoofcare and Shoeing.")

Galloping Position

As for the rider's galloping position, to me it is very important when your horse is galloping that you should be able to get in the most comfortable position for your horse (figs. 7.2 A–C). Generally, that is over his withers, but note that this is for traveling cross-country efficiently and comfortably, not when you are approaching a jump. Here you need to bring your shoulders back with your seat closer to the saddle in order to stay balanced and safe.

- The base, or foundation, of the rider's seat comes from the knee down. This is what I call your "safety belt," where you have a really strong lower leg and are still secure in the tack, even when the horse stumbles, spooks, or turns sharply.

- In the galloping position situated up over the horse's withers, you are not touching the seat of the saddle. If you analyze a jockey in a race, where the difference between winning and losing is crucial and can come down to saving a second or two, jockeys are always positioned well over the horse's withers.

- Endurance doesn't play as big a part at the lower levels, but if you are fortunate enough to get to an FEI (One-Star Level or above) Three-Day Event where the courses are longer and the endurance factor greater, it will be very important in helping your horse perform efficiently. (Lower-level Three-Day Events are also a good test of endurance and a good training opportunity, but the test of fitness plays a much greater role at the upper levels.)

- At any level it is harder for the horse to carry you around if you are bouncing on his back. If you are sitting efficiently he will not be as fatigued after cross-country and he will possibly show jump better for you the next day.

Stirrup Length

A good starting point for determining stirrup length for show jumping: The bottom of the stirrup iron should touch your ankle bone when your feet are hanging down, out of the stirrups. Most people then raise their stirrups a hole or two for cross-country so that they can come off the horse's back for galloping.

- Your stirrup length needs to be such that you are able to get up out of the saddle and into a galloping position, but not so short that you can't come back into your jumping approach position easily and in a balanced way.

- Every stirrup length will be a little different depending on your body type; someone with short legs and a more compact body will not need to ride with stirrups as relatively short as a tall, long-legged person needs to in order to keep her leg on the horse.

- Stirrup length can also vary depending on the horse: On a skinny horse you can ride a bit shorter, while on a more robust horse you ride a little bit longer to get your leg around him.

7.2 A–C Jennie Brannigan, who has worked for me since 2008 and competed numerous horses successfully at the Three-Star Level, illustrates the correct rider position for galloping cross-country.

Rein Contact

As far as your rein contact, it takes a little bit of balancing to ride in a galloping position. It's fine to use a neck strap, grab a little mane, or use the neck in order to keep your balance when you're learning to gallop. I would rather see my students, in training, use a neck strap than hang on the horse's mouth or bounce on his back. Ultimately, you want an *independent* seat, but I'll admit that I still hold onto the mane occasionally. Doing so is not going to restrict the horse in any way.

Introducing the Green Horse

You are not the only one who needs to learn how to ride over varied terrain: To a degree, it is the same for a horse. Before you can expect him to do much jumping cross-country it makes sense to help him understand how to travel over uneven ground. In all of this work you are trying to develop your horse's confidence about negotiating unfamiliar terrain and gain his trust, which needs to be built up over time through positive experiences.

Exercise

1. Start in an open field and walk, trot, and canter. Work on keeping the horse relaxed and controlled.

2. Every horse reacts differently to being ridden in the open. Some are hesitant and need to be encouraged forward, while others want to race ahead and get too strong.

3. Add various natural elements to the terrain. Practice going from light to dark, up and down hills, and negotiating even steeper climbs.

I do this in small steps. First, I gradually introduce my horse to new and different places to ride without jumping. I don't mind if my green horse is a bit cautious, but I will always make sure that he eventually goes willingly where I ask him. It is important for the horse to move forward off the rider's leg, even when he is wary of where you are asking him to go. He has to be more respectful of your commands than whatever "dragon in the woods" is scaring him.

With your horse's potential reluctance to respond to your leg in mind, it is important to carry a whip at all times. You can pat your horse on the neck and reassure him, but if he is not responding to your leg aids by moving forward when approaching something new or intimidating, then using your whip behind your leg to encourage him forward is appropriate. I wouldn't categorize this as punishment but as a reinforcement of your leg aid.

Getting a Lead

Another way to get your horse started across country is to follow a confident, more experienced horse. At some stage your horse needs to be the leader, but as I said before, aim to gradually build up his trust. An experienced horse that forges ahead through whatever obstacles lie in his path can give your less experienced horse the confidence he needs to try new things by following the lead horse's example.

7.3 It is important to give the young horse a positive introduction to water. The water should have good footing, it should not be too deep, and shouldn't have a strong current.

Water

The next stage in my horse's education is to walk through water (fig. 7.3). This is an ideal scenario for using a confident and experienced lead horse. Once he is confident following another, your horse should be willing to walk in and out of the water on his own. The next step is trotting and ultimately cantering in and out of the water.

It is extremely important that you are certain the footing and depth of the water is safe before introducing your horse. Remember, you are gaining your horse's trust every day. If you take a horse into water that is more than 8 inches deep or with footing that is too soft to hold his weight, you will likely jeopardize this trust by scaring him.

Before Jumping

When I school in the arena and out in the open, here are a few guidelines I try to keep in mind as I prepare my young horses for cross-country jumping.

- Looking ahead: It is most important that the horse understands he needs to jump whatever I present to him. An event horse has to learn to jump the first time he is asked.

- He needs to develop trust that whatever you ask him to do will be okay. So, when schooling him in preparation for jumping, only present him with challenges that he is capable of handling and ones that increase his confidence.

- Before you tackle solid obstacles when schooling over show jumps in the arena, make sure your horse understands he must always go forward to the jump rather than back off or try to get out of it. Again, carrying a whip is very important so if the need arises you can encourage him to move forward.

CHAPTER 8

Introducing Cross-Country Jumping

Once you are comfortable riding in the open, it is fair to introduce your horse to low logs or similar natural obstacles. Always think forward and aim for the jump to "hold the horse."

What I mean by the jump "holding the horse" is when the rider, with seat and rein contact, focuses the horse on the upcoming jump. Then, through his training, the horse is "thinking" forward but "waits" for the jump, listening to the rider, and doesn't rush or panic on the approach. The horse is respectful of the jump without hesitating or dropping behind the rider's leg. When the horse has been educated to understand the *close* distance, there is no need to pull back on the reins on the last strides to the jump because the jump is "holding the horse."

Start with small, simple fences and work your way up. It is important that the horse "pick up on" or focus on the jump while maintaining a rhythm, rather than getting flat and rushing to it. Generally, cross-country jumps help here because most horses are a bit wary of them and tend to back off a bit. For safety, you want to teach the horse to jump the jumps slowly before you attempt to go fast. The horse must understand that there is no need to rush at cross-country jumps. You want a horse that is respectful of the jump but not thinking about stopping.

Cross-country schooling is about getting—and keeping—your horse

8.1 A & B Ryan Wood jumping a small cross-country jump on Davinci, a green horse. When the horse is comfortable cantering back and forth over a single fence he'll put a few jumps together.

confident. I would much rather keep the day's training a bit easy and come back another time than overface my horse by testing how difficult a jump or new challenge he can handle. It is very hard to regain a horse's confidence and trust after a bad cross-country schooling session or a problem at a particular type of jump. Generally, the only way to remedy this is to go back to a much easier obstacle that asks the same question, for instance, a smaller ditch or a lower jump, and by repetition gain his trust again. If this happens, it makes the process of his education much slower (and more time-consuming for the rider and trainer).

Venue

Finding the appropriate cross-country schooling area for your horse is essential, especially for your first time out with him. I usually start a cross-country schooling session with very small logs on the ground, 8 inches or lower in height, that are quite long (giving the jump a wide face to approach). These give the inexperienced horse plenty of room for error. When the jumps are low, the horse should be able to trot over them easily and the wide face makes it easier to keep the horse going toward the log without running out at the end. Starting simply will build up the horse's confidence.

Getting Started

Exercise

1 Begin by trotting the same jump in both directions at least six times to get the horse confident and in a rhythm. It is ideal to trot the jump and then immediately canter away. This reinforces the goal of encouraging the horse not to rush at or flatten to the jump on the approach, stay in front of your leg as he jumps, then move away from the jump in a nice canter.

2 Next, I find another log or similar jump of about the same height or a little bit bigger (fig. 8.1 A). Trot this jump as well, then if you have two jumps close to each other, trot the first jump and continue in canter to the next one (fig. 8.1 B).

3 If this goes well, find a third jump and link the three. I jump these three logs or small fences a few times until the horse is confident and enjoying himself. Again, repetition of a positive experience will build your horse's confidence and earn you his trust.

4 Depending upon how he copes with this basic experience, your horse should be able to handle jumping a course of 8 to 10 straightforward, log-type jumps in a row. If he breaks into trot on the approach to a jump, this is okay as long as he is committed to keep going. When he stays relaxed as he trots and gets deep (close to the jump) for takeoff, this is a good habit to encourage. Eventually, you want your horse to be able to canter around the entire course quietly and in a steady rhythm.

5 Keep the jumps small and straightforward in case you encounter resistance (fig. 8.2).

Holding Your Line

A good cross-country horse will stay forward and straight on the line that the rider chooses when approaching the fence. It takes some time for your horse to develop the level of understanding needed to trust you and jump the jumps this way. Again, making things simple and building up slowly will help keep the horse confident. As the "questions" get more challenging—say the jump is on an angled approach in which you jump from left to right or right to left across the fence—the temptation is for the horse to run past the jump rather than jump over it.

Exercise

To introduce your horse to *angles*, I approach the introductory jump on a slight angle. For example, instead of coming to the jump on a 90-degree straight approach, angle slightly to 70 degrees and then eventually 45 degrees.

You not only want to angle your approach, but also the departure so that the horse maintains a straight line on the entire approach, take-off, landing, and getaway over a single fence.

This can first be practiced in trot and then at the canter once the horse has developed confidence. Finally, you can make a straight line between two or three jumps at an angle (figs. 8.3 A & B).

Cantering Jumps

You want the horse to understand where he is going, so stick to a shorter, powerful canter stride—not flat and fast on the approach to a jump. This way, he has more time to analyze the question rather than rushing at it and letting the momentum carry him over the fence. Riding a controlled canter is safer than running flat out at a solid obstacle.

Rider Position

The last stride or two to the fence are crucial. You need to be firm and clear with your aids so the horse knows his job is to jump the fence in front of him. Your legs encourage

8.2 Keep the jumps small and straightforward in case you encounter resistance. Ryan stays calm and focused as Davinci has second thoughts about jumping this small log. By sitting close to the horse and keeping his leg on, he encourages the horse forward as he uses an opening right rein to straighten the horse who is drifting left.

8.3 A & B Here, Jennie and Dreamboat are jumping an in-and-out on an angle.

the horse forward, your seat sinks closer to the saddle, your shoulders are up and back, the rein contact is steady so that you can quickly correct any deviation from the line, and your eyes are up and looking where you want the horse to go.

Galloping and Jumping Out of Stride
Teaching your horse to jump out of stride will help you maintain a steady rhythm around a course. In most cases, the course is made up of about 70 percent "forward-riding" jumps, which, ridden properly, are a great way to get your horse *thinking* forward—confidently and bravely.

On a well-designed cross-country course in competition, the course will start off with forward-riding jumps, then after each technical section the designer will include more forward-riding jumps to get the horse and rider forward and confident again. It's important to be able to ride these jumps in a positive and correct way so you can really take advantage of the opportunity to get the horse forward and confident.

What I call a "forward-riding" jump is usually a maximum-dimension jump with a nice, direct approach so you don't have to shorten the horse's stride but can go forward positively to the fence: You don't need to collect the stride or substantially slow down for the approach.

Exercise

1 I practice this in the arena where the jumps can fall down. This is not just for figuring out on the cross-country course. In the arena, I position a jump like a triple bar or a sloping oxer where you have a good long forward approach to it, with the idea that the jump is going to "hold the horse" (see p. 123) so you can come to the fence on a strong, forward stride without having to hold back on the reins.

2 Once the horse understands, he'll use his instinct, and if he needs to, shorten his stride on his own. Rather than keeping the horse on a contained, short stride you can let him come forward in a free and open stride.

Rider Position
Approaching the jump, decide on the stride that you want and be a little more forward with your position—not sitting back in a defensive position deep in the tack, but lifting your shoulders slightly and bringing your seat a little closer to the saddle. As you get in close to the jump, keep increasing the impulsion without going faster. Use your leg to keep the horse's back legs moving and powering through to your hand so if your horse gets close to the jump and needs to shorten his stride, he has energy to do that.

On the approach to the jump you need to have the horse in the length of stride and pace that you want and feel like you're riding both forward and up, with the horse balanced—*not* down on his forehand and long. Being in the correct balance helps the horse either to shorten his stride or move up to the fence, lengthening (or "opening up") his stride to meet the jump at a correct takeoff distance.

Various Types of Fences

Galloping Fences

A big percentage of the cross-country course is made up of forward-riding (galloping) fences. Jumping at a gallop is the basis of cross-country riding so it is important to learn to ride these types of fences (generally ascending oxers, tables, and the like) and use them to keep the horse confident and in front of your leg.

Galloping-type jumps require a forward, positive gallop or canter stride. Whether you are leaving the start box or approaching the jump, you must develop a forward, connected gallop. On the approach let your seat come back into the saddle, close your lower leg and keep a feel of the horse's mouth to connect him and create more power, rather than allowing him to go faster. Again, you come from a galloping position back into the saddle without slowing down, but with a feeling of the horse becoming more connected and powerful. As you are approaching the jump, it is important to keep the horse's head up so that he sees the jump.

Rider Position

You will go from standing up in the irons to putting your seat back in the saddle. This gives you strength and connection from your seat and leg to the connection of the bit. You should then keep pushing and holding and containing the stride. On an aggressive horse this can be a gentle feel of the lower legs; on a cold or lazy horse this can be quite a strong and aggressive ride to get the horse's gallop more elevated.

As the jump gets closer, aim to get the horse more elevated ("up in front") without slowing too much. You will also lower yourself down deeper into the saddle and close your lower legs to hold the power to the jump. On the last few strides, use your judgment and the horse's instinct to shorten or lengthen slightly for a good takeoff stride. Because the horse is so powerful in the approach, if an adjustment of stride is needed it can be done easily without becoming a "backward" ride where you pull on the horse to shorten his stride, or a weak "move-up" ride where you lengthen the stride to meet the fence at a good distance but lose the impulsion necessary to clear the fence.

Over time, the horse should start to look for the jump while you develop enough power in the canter approach so, if needed, the horse can adjust his stride to meet the jump at a good takeoff distance, slightly shortening or lengthening to the jump as necessary. You should stay with the horse's motion without getting too forward, and as the horse jumps, let the reins slip through your fingers.

When you are jumping at speed it all happens quickly—the horse can stumble or hit the jump, and by slipping your reins and staying a fraction behind the motion you will be in a safer position. Upon landing, shorten your reins and stand up in your irons again as you return to your galloping position.

A Small Ditch

Once your horse is cantering over logs quietly and in good balance, I would introduce him to a small ditch. I stress the word "small" here! Ideally, you want a ditch that is quite narrow so your horse can easily step over it. A size less than 15 inches wide and 6 inches deep will be

8.4 A & B Ryan is introducing Davinci to a small ditch—then a bigger ditch.

enough of a challenge but small enough that if he is worried you can still encourage him over it without a big battle.

Exercise

1 Once your horse has popped over the ditch, have him *trot* over it in both directions a few times (figs. 8.4 A & B).

2 When first introduced to a ditch, it is quite common for horses to hesitate slightly, then jump. A slap with your whip behind your leg on the last trot step before the ditch will reinforce your leg aid, asking him to leave the ground more confidently.

3 Once he is confident here and if you are in the same vicinity as your 8 to 10 cross-country jumps, then you can incorporate the ditch into your course.

Note: The next time you school your horse expect him to jump over the baby ditch and then move on to a slightly larger and wider ditch. I really like the idea of trotting the approach to ditches when schooling because it reinforces that you don't have to go fast to jump these. This is not necessarily how you should ride a ditch in competition, but taking it slowly in training is a good way for your horse to learn and thoroughly understand the question.

Rider Position

On the approach to a ditch you need to be strong with the horse at the last stride in case he hesitates when he sees it. I am usually in

Introducing Cross-Country Jumping 8

8.5 A–D Jennie jumping a more experienced horse over the ditch and rails. Note how she stays balanced and in the middle of the horse on the approach, over the fence and on landing.

a bit of a defensive, behind-the-horse position with the plan of being quite aggressive on the last stride to encourage the horse to stay "forward-thinking" as he jumps (figs. 8. 5 A–D).

As the horse jumps it might be necessary to let the reins slip through your fingers so that you don't pull on his mouth.

The Water Jump

It is essential for event horses to be comfortable with water. Most courses have at least one water crossing or jump, even at the lowest levels. At the major Four-Star events, the "Head of the Lake" or another named main water complex, is usually the most exciting part of the course for the spectators.

I have already touched on exposing my green horses to water (fig. 8.6). I even like to get my advanced horses' feet wet whenever I have the opportunity. When you are riding in the open and want to take some time to school through the water, keep in mind that

8.6 Now Ryan is introducing Davinci to water at the walk.

natural streams and creeks are not always ideal. If you're not sure what the footing on the bottom is like, you have to be a little wary about going through streams that are muddy and slippery because the horse could lose confidence should he slip. If the stream has a good firm base of gravel or something similar, it is a good place for gaining your horse's trust. Also note the depth of the water and how fast the current is flowing.

I think it is quite reasonable when schooling a water jump on a cross-country course to walk your horse into the water before you start jumping it so he is confident the water is not too deep and the footing is good. Most horses will instinctively come out of water better than going into it, so to begin, I usually find an approach to the water jump where I can enter without jumping, just trot my horse in and through the water, then if there is a raised edge or small bank, I will jump the horse out. Once I have trotted in and jumped out a few times I will reverse the direction and trot off a ledge or small bank into the water, and trot or canter away through the water (figs. 8.7 A & B).

As with the ditch, if the horse hesitates you want to be quick with your whip behind your leg to encourage his commitment, riding forward away from the fence on landing.

No two horses are the same and you will need to adapt your riding and training to each individual. Some horses will want to race out of the water; this is not a great habit to have because once you move up the levels there will be another jump shortly—either in the water itself, or leaving the water—so your aim

Introducing Cross-Country Jumping 8

here is to jump in confidently, land balanced, and canter away without rushing.

Rider Position

Be prepared with your riding approach! You need a secure position: Both your heels should be down and firmly in the stirrups. Your upper body should be a little defensive, leaning back with a longer than usual contact on the rein. Should your horse hesitate abruptly, your body unexpectedly goes forward; since you need to be effective when this happens, a longer rein contact will allow you to sit back more and have more flexibility. I prefer that he stays steady and committed on the approach and not hesitate when he jumps. Not many horses will

8.7 A & B Trotting in over a small drop and cantering away through the water.

just launch into water; some may rush on the approach and then on the last stride, back off and jump cautiously.

Once your horse is jumping off a small bank or ledge into the water confidently then you can progress to a small jump into the water, such as a log. This requires more trust in the rider from the horse. Keep in mind, a horse that is rushing will steady on the last stride before the water. Make sure your position is a bit defensive and sit back so that you can absorb any sudden slowing or hesitation. You want to maintain your position to be

effective in encouraging the horse to move forward. If you are struggling to maintain your position, you cannot ride effectively so you should spend more time working on developing your strength and technique in the saddle on the flat.

Cantering a Jump into Water

To canter into water, the horse needs to learn to deal with the distraction of the splash while staying focused on the jump. Usually, the first few times the horse will, what I call, "Hang in the air," or hesitate once he starts to jump. If he's a little green he might be concerned about landing in the water. As a general rule you want to be quite positive and keep the horse going forward to the jump and in the air (figs. 8. 8 A & B).

I like to keep the schooling in water pretty straightforward so the horse stays confident. Doing short amounts is better than trying to rush things; if it's not going well, coming back another day is better than trying to make it harder and harder the first time you introduce water. Even with an experienced horse, I will often just walk around in water to reassure the horse, keep him exposed to the water, and confident. I don't always make him jump into the water.

8.8 A & B Jennie's horse is hesitant to jump into the water but she sits deep in the saddle and closes her leg, allowing him forward with her hand until he takes the leap.

8.9 A & B Jumping into the water and confidently cantering away.

Rider Position

Once your horse is jumping in, your rein contact should be slightly longer than usual. You want to think of guiding your horse with your hands rather than holding him. The longer reins will also allow the horse freedom of his head and neck as he jumps. The aim is for the horse to jump in committed and "forward," then land and canter away on the first stride (figs. 8.9 A & B).

A large percentage of horses will hesitate when first introduced to water. You can build a lot of trust here by keeping a good position and quickly encouraging the horse forward and straight when and if he hesitates at the jump. You want to give him a good experience by allowing him to stretch and "round" into the jump without holding back on his mouth.

Types of Bank

There are a few varieties of bank jumps. For example, you might canter in, jump up, take a stride or two on top of the bank and then drop off. It takes the same type of preparation as the jump up and the jump down (see pp. 136 and 137). The degree of difficulty can get harder: The top of the bank can be a one stride or a bounce and then off; or you can jump up and off, then up and jump off another bank and

8.10 Jumping up a bank.

back down. Schooling both up and down banks will be preparation for whatever type or combination of bank jumps you may encounter.

Jumping up a Bank

Schooling over banks is good practice and training for the rider's position and good for the horse's education. Jumping a bank teaches the horse to be clever with his feet and legs as he jumps up, lands—and learns to be safe when he jumps off. In general, horses naturally go *up* the bank in a more forward-thinking manner than they do when jumping off, so I start a green horse jumping up a small bank (fig. 8.10).

The jump could be something as simple as a step up rather than a full, man-made bank, so that the horse learns to go up and then forward. I start in trot and try to keep the stride short so the horse gets nice and close to the jump up. Keep him forward and positive but

Introducing Cross-Country Jumping

in control so you have steering and straightness and the horse doesn't take off too far away from the jump up.

Once the horse is confident about trotting up the step or bank, then you can proceed in canter with the same idea. Sometimes if the bank is too small the horse won't pay much attention to it in canter, so it's nice to have something big enough that the horse respects it but still small enough so it's easy for him to jump up and then go forward. You're looking for the horse to stay straight and listen to the rider on a short-strided canter approach, and then, when he lands, to go forward away from the jump.

Rider Position

Be a little more forward with your upper body here, because once the horse jumps there's a tendency for riders to get left behind. Even grabbing hold of some mane to keep the balance is not a bad idea. If you're more comfortable you can use a leather neck strap to help keep your balance and, more importantly, not pull on the horse's mouth as he jumps. Staying just slightly forward with your upper body will help you stay in motion with the horse as he jumps up.

Dropping off a Bank

Next you can reverse the direction you approached the bank, and turn it into a small drop fence. At this stage, *trotting* is a good way to introduce the horse to dropping down. It's okay for the horse to be cautious so I don't mind a green horse hesitating a bit, but always keep him "thinking" forward and realizing that he has to go off the drop. He is not going to learn by just rushing off the jump—it's good if he can take his time and jump carefully off. Again, the horse should stay straight and canter away from the little drop off. When he is confident, you can also canter the approach.

Rider Position

The rider's position going down the drop (figs. 8. 11 A & B) is the opposite of going up the bank (see fig. 8.10). As the horse drops down he'll lower his head and neck and you need to be able to follow this by allowing the reins to slip through your fingers. Also, keep your upper-body back a little bit. This is a good defensive position should something should go wrong with the jump or if the horse stumbles on landing.

Keep in mind that as the drops become bigger, gravity causes the rider to fall forward and over the front of the horse. At this point, focus on keeping your upper body back, still allowing the horse to jump by letting the reins slip through your fingers. On landing, as the horse is cantering away, shorten up the reins and get back to your galloping, more forward seat.

The next stage is *cantering* to the drop off. Again on the approach feel that you are "waiting" with the upper body. Try to get the horse to stay in a short canter without really holding him—most horses are going to back off and shorten their stride to the jump down, and it is not imperative the horse canters *all* the way to the drop. Let anticipation "hold" the horse so he slows down his canter or even breaks to trot before dropping off, letting the reins slip on the drop, then shortening them as you canter away.

8.11 A & B Jumping down a bank. Jennie's position is in balance with the horse: She is sitting up but not too far back and letting the reins slip through her fingers so the horse can use his neck as he drops down the bank.

It's a matter of preparation, keeping the horse straight, getting forward on the up, then getting back with the upper body in preparation for the drop, slipping the reins and then cantering away.

As the degree of difficulty gets harder the same principles apply: you want a short, powerful canter on the approach, a slightly forward position to stay with the horse, then a more defensive position on the "off," allowing the horse to take his time and be calculated about the jump off so he is clever and smart about it.

Jumps on top of the bank add difficulty to the question. Again, the important thing is for the horse to stay in front of your leg and look for the next jump.

Corners

A *corner (apex jump)* is usually introduced at a hard Training Level course or at Preliminary Level. I first show a corner jump to a horse in the jumping arena, not on cross-country. These are easily built with a barrel supporting both rails at one end, and with two small jump standards on the other end so the rails can fan out (fig. 8.12). First, keep the jump small so there's not much angle at all and then widen it as the horse becomes more confident.

Introducing Cross-Country Jumping 8

I usually build the jump so the horse approaches it at a right angle to the corner, or "square" to the front rail. If anything, the horse will want to run out to the "pointed" side of the fence, so keep that in mind as you bring the horse straight to the jump.

The biggest challenge is teaching a horse that he needs to go *straight* on the line of your approach.

The canter approach could be described as a "strong," show jumping style canter. You don't want the horse in a big "open" canter, but rather a more contained, strong stride. Once the horse is confident and jumping the corner

8.12 Introduce jumping a corner over a small fence.

8.13 Jennie is jumping a corner fence. The vertical poles in the photo are so that the horse gets used to jumping with flags as he would find on a competition cross-country course. If your horse tends to drift or run out you can add guide rails, using show jumping poles to help keep him straight and focused.

straight in both directions then you can make the jump wider, by opening the two standards. For a Prelimjnary Level horse, the fence can be 4 to 5 feet wide on the "open" side.

You should practice being able to ride to the corner on somewhat of an angled approach and keep the horse straight on his line as he jumps the jump. This is good training for both horse and rider later on because you will encounter fences where you're not able to approach the corner on a perfectly right-angled approach. There are other ways to train the corner—being able to approach it off a turn is important, as well.

Usually, I find that a corner is not a big jumping effort but more of a technical effort. It's important for the horse to understand the corner jump, go over it calmly and confidently, and not need an aggressive ride to the jump.

Once you have the horse confident in the arena you can start jumping corner fences in cross-country schooling (fig. 8.13). Here, I like to have some kind of wing (or rail) to help the horse because, should he get confused and start running out, it can be difficult to get him "straightened out" again. Once your horse is confident jumping a corner with a wing, you can remove it and get the horse to understand that he doesn't need a prop to stay *straight* as he jumps.

The same principles apply to the approach as they did in the arena: a show jumping canter speed; keep the horse in front of your leg; and no rushing. Without being hard with your hand keep the horse straight on the last stride and do not let him drift as he jumps.

Rider Position

The rider's position for jumping corners is a little bit more defensive. The last approach stride is really important because that's where the horse can drift or try to run out. Stay strong in your position to keep the horse straight.

Again, once you get more confident with your horse you can vary the approach line. Ultimately, you want the horse to come to this jump in a positive but controlled way and understand that he is to jump the jump on the same line as you approach the fence.

As courses get harder you will likely encounter a corner that's related to another jump or jumps. This can be a straightforward oxer to a corner or two corners in a row where the horse has to hold his line. These situations can be practiced in the arena, too: It all comes down to the training and the horse understanding what he needs to do. He must stay soft and listen to the rider about what is needed in the approach but still be thinking forward and straight.

Narrow Fences

Narrow fences are a big part of our sport, especially from Preliminary Level up. I start to introduce my horses to narrow fences pretty simply in the jumping arena with shorter jump poles, which can be cut to about 6 feet, or usually half the length of a standard jump pole. You can use barrels lying on their side with a "V" pole on each side acting as a way to help the horse understand he needs to stay straight to the narrow face.

Like the corner jump, a narrow jump is not usually a big jumping effort but it requires understanding by the horse and an accurate ride. I usually introduce the horse in trot, which allows me and the horse more time to "read" the jump and relax as I come in.

First, trot two or three different narrow fences in the arena in both directions until the horse is comfortable (8. 14 A). The next step is to canter to the narrow jump (8.14 B). Again, you can use "V" poles or another way to encourage the horse to stay straight. The canter needs to be short and organized and you don't want the horse strong in your hand–he needs to be light and engaged, waiting and looking for the jump. I find that it's really helpful to make the horse familiar with narrow jumps. Because they're not usually big jumping efforts, once the horse understands the question, narrow fences are relatively easy for him.

Once the horse is comfortable with them in the arena I introduce him to jumping narrow fences on cross-country (fig. 8.15). You don't want to be in an open, galloping stride—you need to be able to collect and make sure the horse is waiting, not rushing.

Narrow jumps vary a lot as you go through the levels, but the same principles always apply.

Rider Position

Remember when schooling narrow fences cross-country that you make sure the horse is properly prepared in his approach. Problems most likely occur when the rider gets too forward and aggressive, and the horse does not have time to see the fence, so he ends up rushing past it.

An emphasis must be placed on him not rushing but staying in front of your leg and *straight*. You need to be really conscious of this, especially in the last stride or two before the jump.

Combinations on Cross-Country

Combination fences consist of several elements. They are set up by the course designer at different places on the course to test the horse's willingness to come back into control, as well as test the rider's ability to comprehend the "question" the designer is asking, and ride it

8.14 A & B A narrow fence. When starting out it is a good idea to add guide rails to keep the horse straight (not shown here). The narrows can get higher as the horse becomes ready for the challenge.

Introducing Cross-Country Jumping

8.15 When a horse is comfortable with narrow fences in the arena, introduce him to one on cross-country.

appropriately. It is important when walking the course to completely understand what needs to be done when jumping the combination.

To me, the most important part of riding a combination is getting the canter approach correct and the first jump of the combination ridden well. In most cases, this involves coming back from galloping speed to a shorter, more controlled canter approach. When training, practice this so that you have the right judgment and sense of whether you are on the correct approach. This can vary from getting the horse back to a very collected "coffin canter" (see below) or a shorter (or longer) "show jumping stride," or a forward and balanced galloping approach.

Most combinations require you to approach in a different canter; I really like to get the first jump to "hold" the horse so you have a lot more control on the landing to be able to execute the rest of the combination. Mistakes are often made, first, when the horse and rider haven't come back to an organized canter, or second, the first part of the combination is ridden too aggressively or "open," so the rider needs to react and be hard on the horse to get him to come back for the last part of the combination.

Combinations also require the rider to think quickly, be aware of what needs to be done, and react promptly to the situation. Simple things like keeping your eyes up, being aware of the whole combination, and what needs to be done, next, are all very important.

Rider Position

The rider's position needs to vary depending on the question being asked, so it's hard to generalize. Having the horse organized and listening to you is important. Remember that most combinations only take a couple of seconds to get through, so every second counts once you're in the combination.

It's important to know your horse and anticipate what he's going to do in there; if it's a short-strided combination and your horse has a big stride, you need to get him to come back at the beginning. If your horse has a short stride you may need to ride into it more "forward" than somebody else does. It is important to be able to quickly react to the situation you're in so that you can make the appropriate correction. When the horse jumps in weak, you need to react with your leg to give him the power to get through the rest of the combination, and if he jumps in too boldly you need to quickly get him back and organized.

Coffin ("Ditch and Rails")

The coffin, consisting of an upright jump with one or more strides to a ditch and then another stride or more to another upright fence, is quite a big test for horse and rider. Bravery is required for the ditch, but because of the striding and the approach you are unable to come in fast and forward. The rider needs to be able to create energy and power on a short stride for the "coffin canter."

At home, practice keeping the horse on an 8- or 10-foot stride and still in front of your leg so you have power in the canter. Riding this type of combination requires that you go from a gallop for the previous jump to a short canter stride. You have to estimate, on the approach (depending on how long it takes you to produce this type of canter) just how far before the first fence of the combination you will start preparing for this jump.

Rider Position

Once you have obtained this canter, stay on the short canter stride (without a considerable amount of lengthening or shortening of the stride), to meet the first part of the jump. In the last stride before the jump be prepared with your position for your horse to set his eyes on the ditch and stall or hesitate. This means keeping your lower leg active and, if necessary, the spur. The horse should be in an uphill balance, "sitting down" behind, with your upper body slightly back in preparation for the moment in case he stalls or hesitates.

Once your horse jumps the first rail your job is to really urge him on over the ditch. This requires you to keep the horse dead straight, which can come from a nice, confident feel of his mouth on both reins to correct him if he wants to drift, as well as a strong lower leg and a feel for what the horse is doing underneath you. If the horse is going forward and not hesitating you don't have to be aggressive, but as soon as you get the slightest indication that the horse is backing off in front of the ditch, you need to give him some encouragement. Timing is everything: If you allow the horse to back off and do not correct him, a refusal or stop can result.

As the horse is jumping the ditch your position should be a bit defensive, that is, you should stay back with your upper body and not get in front of the movement so there will be a slight feeling of getting left behind. To me this is acceptable as long as you don't catch the horse in the mouth as he jumps: You must allow the reins to slip through your fingers as he bascules (rounds his body) over the jump.

On the landing you will be in a situation where you have your horse straight and going forward but your reins are long. It's fine to approach the last part of the combination with a longer rein as long as there is still a connection to the horse's mouth. If the first part of the combination is three or four strides from the ditch then you'll have time to shorten your reins, but if it's one or two strides to the ditch then it's better to negotiate the ditch and then jump out of the combination with a longer rein so that you are not constantly trying to reorganize. Your lower leg should stay in position to activate the horse as needed.

Sunken Road

The "sunken road" is similar to the coffin: It usually consists of a jump, a short distance to a drop down and then one or two strides to a bank back up, with a short distance to another jump. When done correctly, the sunken road is very much like a grid situation you can set up at home in your arena. Your approach will depend somewhat on the space between the fences. If it's a short distance, obviously you need to have the horse on a short canter stride–he can even trot off the edge of the drop so he has plenty of room to get through the combination (8.16 A & B).

Rider Position

Enter the combination after developing the desired canter for the approach, making sure

8.16 A & B Jennie jumps down in and up out of the sunken road.

the horse is dead straight, that you have a good feel of his mouth, and that your leg is on so he doesn't drift. Generally, there is not the same hesitation from the horse coming to a sunken road as to a coffin, so you can have a more forward body position, which makes it easier to steer the horse. A lot of the time, these jumps do not need to be ridden aggressively. Especially when the distances in the combination are short and the horse needs to have time to figure out where to put his feet and be a little clever, taking it a bit slow is the safer option.

The rider can actually go forward with the horse as he is dropping down. You don't want to be overly forward: You need to stay back with your shoulders, but stick with your horse so you're in a good balance coming out of the base of the sunken road combination.

Bounce Fence

A bounce on cross-country is a way for the course designer to make sure the horse will come "up" in his balance, sitting back on his hocks and with a more collected jump. How you ride a bounce depends on the distance between fences—if it's a forward-riding bounce you'll need a strong show jumping canter with power and energy. If the distance is shorter than 12 feet or less, a shorter canter stride is required.

The canter approach that you decide on will also somewhat depend on your horse. If he's very aggressive, you may have to "overdo" the collection and get through to him that he needs to be respectful of the jump and not rush. Other horses lose their confidence in a situation like this and need to be ridden more aggressively.

Rider Position

You want to keep the horse straight, so have a good contact from your leg to your hand and feel that the horse is on the aids. You definitely need to get the horse close to the first element, so keep him organized and not rushing that last stride. Allow the jump to "hold" the horse, and try to relax and not anticipate with your upper body; wait for the horse to jump the first element before you allow your upper body to go forward because if you get ahead of the horse, you will have less control and ability to act should anything go wrong in the middle of the bounce.

Personal Experience

One of my worst experiences in eventing was in a sunken road at Rolex Kentucky in 2004. Connaught was a brand new ride for me and was jumping through the course brilliantly. I felt that I got him back to the right length of canter stride but probably he was against my hand, so even though he was on a short stride he was a bit too ready to "explode." He jumped the first part of the combination well but then jumped way too hard across the bottom part, which caused us to get to the last part very close to the bank.

That year you had to come up a bank and then bounce out over a rail. Because we'd gone too powerfully in, when we got to the "out" bank, we didn't have enough power to jump up and then bounce over the rail, so we stopped at the rail. Unfortunately, there wasn't much room to stop so my poor friend and I fell into the bottom of the sunken road. Fortunately, Connaught was fine and later went on to jump through that sunken road many times, which is a true test of a horse's bravery and gutsiness.

CHAPTER 9

Show Jumping Training

There are many similarities and parallels in show jumping and cross-country, so when you school your horse for one phase, you are also educating him for the other. The main difference about show jumping is that the horse needs to be more "careful" than on cross-country, by which I mean that the horse must not even want to touch the jump–he wants to clear it and not have the rail down. On cross-country the emphasis is more on the horse's speed and bravery and less on his carefulness.

When teaching show jumping, you are trying to develop a horse that, first of all, is in front of your leg and forward enough to jump the show jumps confidently. He should do this without spooking and flying about, worrying about the colors and "fillers" on the course. Secondly, he must be very "ratable" (adjustable) to the jumps and you should have the ability to control him the whole way around the course. Usually, the horse is better able to perform well when he is in a relaxed state of mind, so you must practice until this is all second nature.

Developing the Stride

One of the first basic exercises for training the horse to jump is getting him to travel on an even stride, not accelerating to or backing off the fence.

9.1 Davinci's face can be in front of the vertical—he doesn't need to be "on the bit" for jumping because he should be looking for the jumps as he travels along.

Show Jumping Training 9

He should maintain the same rhythm as he approaches the jump, jumps it, and gets away.

You can accomplish a lot with poles on the ground and small cross-rails. Trot and canter on both leads and teach the horse to jump various configurations while keeping his stride regular as you go around. There are several essential things to focus on:

- The way the horse canters can vary depending on the individual horse and the way he goes. It is not as important to have the horse "on the bit" for show jumping as it is in dressage, in fact, you don't want the horse's face too vertical because you want him to see the jumps (fig. 9.1). That said, it is important that every horse is responsive and able to carry himself in an uphill balance.

- The horse's stride needs to be adjustable (fig. 9.2). To accomplish this you must be able to lengthen the horse's stride on command, also collect or compress the horse's stride whenever you need to. Practice lengthening

9.2 The stride should be adjustable, meaning you can easily shorten or lengthen the stride to meet the jumps on a correct takeoff distance and find the comfortable distance between fences.

and shortening the stride over poles on the ground or cross-rails before you introduce him to jumping a course.

- With the variety of courses your horse will be exposed to, his dressage training will come into play: He will need the ability to shorten his stride at the last moment; "add" strides on the course; and approach the jump out of a more "open" (forward) canter stride. Practice over low fences or poles on the ground before you introduce jumping an entire course.

Exercise

A good exercise to practice shortening and lengthening the stride is by placing two cross-rails 20 yards apart. Your horse should be able to canter down the line in four strides, in five strides, and, if he's going well, in six strides. Through this exercise what you will actually produce is a 12-foot, 10-foot and then an 8-foot canter stride.

As your horse becomes more educated you will expect him to stay in a consistent rhythm at whatever stride's length you need. With this 20-yard exercise, a normal or average show-jumping canter will have a stride length of about 12 feet.

1 First, the horse and rider need to be able to pick up a steady, even rhythm—all the time.

2 Next, to shorten this length of stride you need to activate the horse's hind legs. Do this by using your lower leg to make him go a bit quicker behind and without restricting him, ask him to collect by riding him up into the hand.

3 You ultimately want the horse to "lift up" in front. You don't just pull up the horse's head, which will result in him tightening his neck muscles; instead you want him to elevate his entire front end as you engage the hind end to collect him.

4 As the horse gains experience, strength, and confidence you can collect the stride for longer periods and develop more collection each day.

5 Once you feel that he understands the concept of "collection," then ride him forward and give him some release in order to give him a break.

6 As I've talked about before, the horse is a creature of habit and you have to slowly but surely introduce the right habits for *him*.

Remember:
- Once the desired length of stride has been established, it is important for the horse to understand that as he gets closer to the jump his canter should not change. If you want to approach those two cross-rails in any length canter stride, he should maintain the same rhythm through the entire exercise.

- In all different canters you must train the horse to be in self-carriage. During the 12-foot stride the horse should be relaxed

Show Jumping Training 9

and settled and not strong in your hands. The same goes for the more collected canter stride: When you activate the horse from behind and get him to become more powerful and collected, it doesn't mean he can be stronger or more aggressive in your contact.

- There will be some jumps that require an even more forward canter–possibly a 14-foot stride–say, approaching a big wide triple bar. The horse must still understand that he has to stay relaxed and not aggressive in the context of that one fence.

Take Your Time

While the time you put into getting your horse to be able to produce this kind of canter work may seem lengthy, you will be rewarded later on when you expose him to more jumping exercises and start jumping courses. Even when you have a horse that is an incredible athlete and makes a great shape over a jump, if he is hard to ride between fences or difficult to ride to the jump, you are going to be limited in how far you are able to go with him. Putting in the time to master the basics will be time well spent.

Remember that different horses have individual requirements.

- Generally the OTTB, in most cases, has been taught to gallop fast and with a strong contact on his mouth. To be fair to this kind of horse, spend plenty of time getting him to understand the basics and become confident about going in a shorter, slower, more relaxed way of cantering. (See page 113 for tips on stopping a runaway horse.)

- Alternately, the more sports-bred type horse like a Warmblood or Warmblood-cross will often need to become more powerful and learn to stay in front of your leg in canter.

Introducing Jumping

As in cross-country schooling, the horse must understand that the jump will "hold" him (the horse waits for the jump to come to him, rather than rushing at the fence). You don't want to have to hold him with your hand every step of the way or have a horse that just wants to get to the other side of the jump quickly with a flat or low jump. Teaching him to get to a deep distance (get close to the fence) so that he jumps up and over rather than flattening his body in

Training versus Bitting

Taking a shortcut by using a bigger, stronger bit or other devices generally does not help the horse's training in the long run. Training the horse to develop different types of canter in a snaffle will reap the best long-term results. From a safety point of view, there are some horses that call for a stronger bit or device to get through to them and encourage them to soften; however, I would try to use this as a temporary training tool so you can get back to a softer bit or a snaffle rather than thinking the horse has to go in the stronger bit for the rest of his career.

the air, is crucial to getting him to jump carefully in the show-jumping arena.

I start most of my horses jumping in trot. This is a good way of reinforcing that they need to wait for the jump and put the last trot step in close to the jump. It is also a good way for getting through to the horse that jumping is not about going fast. At the trot he can develop his confidence by staying in a slower speed approaching the jumps. Once he is comfortable approaching the fences at a trot, you can begin to take them in a calm, rhythmical canter (9. 3 A–D).

Trotting a small vertical in both directions, although very basic, is a great training tool for your horse. Once he understands how to trot in quietly and get a close distance to the jump, he should be able to nicely canter away. On the approach, the jump "holds" the horse, then on landing, you should close the leg and ask the horse to canter away in self-carriage, prepared to take the next jump on course.

Canter Leads

From the beginning, teach the horse to pick up either *canter lead* after a jump. This is a very basic training skill that helps you later on when you start riding courses.

Exercise

1 First, it is important to understand that the aids to pick up the left canter lead are as follows: Your inside leg on the girth and the outside leg just behind the girth.

2 I like to start on a circle, approaching a crossrail in trot. As the horse jumps, open the rein to the inside and encourage the horse forward with your outside leg. The opening rein should get the horse to take the lead in that direction. Once this lesson has been learned, try the other side—using the same principles.

3 The next step is to do a figure eight over the jump, giving the aids to turn *left* the first time, then *right* the next time.

9.3 A–D Jumping a grid is a simple way to build your horse's skill and confidence over fences. (See Appendix D, p. 316, for more jumping exercises.)

4 Once the horse understands turning in the air, trot in to the jump, stay straight over it, then turn left on landing.

5 You can use an *opening inside rein* to first teach your horse. It is important that your outside rein becomes the "wall" to prevent the horse's shoulder from falling out while you just bring the horse to the left with the inside rein.

6 On a green horse these aids will need to be quite exaggerated in order to get the horse to turn left and take the correct lead on landing. As his training becomes more finessed, that same aid, in a much subtler way, can encourage the horse to pick up the correct lead on landing without actually turning him. This means the horse needs to be attuned to the rider's leg aids to pick up each lead correctly. Because you are keeping him straight, you cannot use the opening rein to help pick up the lead.

Flying Changes

Long a part of the hunter/jumper's basic training, *flying changes* are now a very important part of the event horse's training, especially for the upper levels where they have been introduced into the dressage tests at the Four-Star Level. For the horse to be completely educated, the flying change is very important and should be taught at an early age (for more on flying changes, see p. 108).

When breaking in horses and riding them for the first time I haven't ever had a horse that, when first ridden, wouldn't do a flying change. Somewhere in between the beginning and further along in his education, many horses get confused and struggle with the flying change.

This usually arises out of a need for the horse to have enough power in the canter and not have to trot behind to switch leads. So, once you have some adjustability in the canter–being able to collect/shorten or lengthen the stride–you should introduce the flying change.

Having a pole on the ground is a helpful first step in teaching the horse to change leads. If you are not confident about teaching a change, have a more experienced rider or a professional introduce changes to your horse.

For a "show jumping" flying change:

1 Yield the horse toward the leading leg in preparation for the change.

2 As you're yielding, you're changing the bend in the horse so he will be bent toward the new leading leg.

3 As you yield across, ask with the new outside leg just behind the girth for the change of lead.

4 Keep thinking "forward" so the horse goes forward into the change.

5 The horse should learn to change leads without the rider turning or bending his neck. The change should come from behind, so when the horse is not changing you can use your crop behind the leg on the outside to encourage him to step through.

The flying lead change is essential to maintaining an even, consistent canter stride when you are navigating a jumping course. If you have to constantly bring your horse back to trot to change leads it disrupts his rhythm; makes him more difficult to ride; and usually results in a slower time around the course.

Seeing a Distance

To become a confident and safe rider, it is important to be able to understand the concept of "seeing a distance." This is not rocket science. All it means is the ability of the rider to judge which adjustments need to be made to get to the jump at what we call a "sweet takeoff distance." In other words, as you are approaching the jump you should be able to see whether you need to steady up to meet the fence nicely or just let your horse move up and softly lengthen to get to a comfortable takeoff position.

Just as in any sport, some people are going to be more gifted than others at making this judgment. However it is important that we all work at seeing a distance and developing this skill.

Exercise 1

1 I try to think about what I call "creating a distance." Rather than approaching a jump and waiting until I see what I have to do, I try to work on my horse's canter so that coming to the jump I have a lot of options whether it is to shorten, lengthen, or maintain the horse's stride.

2 Cantering a long way out, say 20 strides away, I put my eye on the jump and have a feel for the canter length of stride that I need: When it's an oxer with some width to it, I'll need to have some power in the stride. For a more upright fence, if I'm not sure what I need to do to get to a nice close distance, I collect and elevate the horse's canter more as I approach the jump.

3 As I get closer I add more power and collect the horse more until eventually, through this collection, I have actually created the distance that I want.

Exercise 2

1 Practice learning to see a distance using poles on the ground or small cross-rails, not just big fences.

2 Work on being able to approach the jump, then create your distance as you're approaching it.

3 Create your distance by adding more power and more elevation to your canter, as described above.

Adding Strides

One of the first ways to teach yourself the skill of creating your distance is by *adding strides*, which means approaching on a very short canter stride. Remember, in the horse's training, you ideally want to ride *forward* to the jump. However, it's very hard to ride *forward* when your horse sees the jump and rushes since your inclination is to try to slow him down. So, teaching the horse to add a stride is crucial in order for him to progress and become easy to ride.

- The first way to get that feeling and understanding of creating a distance is keeping your horse on a short canter. To do this, use your leg and close your hand to squeeze the horse and collect him more, asking him to quicken his hind legs as he shortens his stride.

- Although you don't want to be just waiting and adding strides all the time, adding strides is actually a good exercise for you to learn so that you understand how to wait for the jump.

- Once you have learned to shorten the stride, however, there is a danger of getting to the jump a little "backward" or "holding" too much, so you need to be able to do it out of a more forward canter.

Related Distances

Related distances are found in more than one fence set in a line—or on a turn—where you decide how many strides the horse should take in between the jumps. This becomes a necessary skill as you help your horse negotiate the course. Note: When jumping fences that are on a turn you can either approach the fences on a bending line; approach the fences straight; or canter straight through the line, angling the approach to the fences (figs. 9.4 A–D and see Exercise 4 in the Jumping Exercises in the Appendix, p. 318).

The typical horse's stride is about 12 feet. It's important to be able to set up different lines and be able to produce whatever number of canter strides you want. The horse needs to be able to compress the canter stride, quickening

9.4 A–D This related line can be approached a couple of ways. In photos A, B, and C, Jennie and Dreamboat opt to jump the first fence straight on, then make a bending line to the left before jumping the second fence straight on, then on landing, they make a bending line to the right before jumping the third and final fence. Jennie keeps her eye on the upcoming fence, uses her outside leg and rein as "the wall" to keep the horse from drifting to the outside, and bends the horse around her inside leg while guiding him in the correct direction with her inside rein.

In Photo D, they are approaching the same line of fences on a direct line, which means that they will jump each fence on an angle: The first fence from right to left, the middle fence from left to right, and the final fence from right to left. Jennie looks ahead down the line of fences and focuses on keeping Dreamboat straight between her leg and rein aids.

behind and shortening the length of the stride overall, or take a longer stride—again by being powerful from behind.

- You can usually make a decision, based on whether a line is short or long (the course designer did not leave much extra room or there is a little extra distance) about the best way for you to jump a line on your particular horse. So when jumping a four-stride line measuring 42 feet between fences and the line consists of a tall vertical to a wide oxer, it is wise after you jump the vertical to keep the horse powerful and forward so he has enough energy to get over the oxer in four strides.

- When you are jumping a vertical to a stile (a narrow jump), on the other hand, make the decision to jump the vertical quietly and compress the horse in a shorter more upright stride so he has more time to assess the stile and a greater chance of not knocking it down.

- The same applies as you go up in stride numbers—say, five or six strides. Once you get to seven or eight strides, in my opinion, it is a bit too far away to stick to a predetermined number. At eight and nine strides it is better to have more time to make some adjustments in stride if you need to, rather than be committed to one kind of ride.

- Again, coming to a line that is set at 42 feet or four strides, you could compress the horse and do five or even six strides with a more educated horse. Your horse should then be able to do it in four again and then five strides. Establishing this sort of cooperation gives you a lot more options when you are riding your show jumping round.

In your training you want your horse to stay relaxed at all times: He shouldn't get strong and "flat" when he lengthens, or aggressive and strong when you collect him. He should be responsive and soft when you add a stride.

Combinations

On a course you also have *combinations*, which can consist of A and B, or A, B, and C elements, where each jump is one or two strides apart. At Beginner Novice and Novice Level, combinations consist of two fences maximum—an "in-and-out." From Training Level up there can be three fences in a row—a "triple combination."

Distances in a combination can vary slightly so you need to hold your horse on a stride: Shorten slightly or lengthen slightly to jump the fences well. When the jumps are three strides apart or less, do not add an extra stride or your horse's canter will be too weak and "backward," which makes it difficult for him to jump the second and/or the third element.

In competition, be aware that when the jumps are numbered A, B, and C, and you have trouble at any element of the combination, you must negotiate the entire line again—for example, if the horse stops at C, you must jump A and B again before you reattempt C.

Riding Specific Types of Fences

Vertical

A *vertical* requires the horse to produce a steady, uphill canter. To achieve this you need to stay soft in your hand and consistent with your leg. You do not want to get strong and aggressive or the horse may rush and pull at the jump, running past the desired takeoff distance.

- When you can have him soft in the contact and focused on the fence rather than fighting against you, the approach will be easier. It is important to create this softness and "uphill" canter *in preparation* for the jump, not at the last moment.

- The length of the horse's stride can be a little bit shorter and more condensed than usual, to create a jump where the horse goes quite high in the air as opposed to jumping *across* the fence.

- Straightness is very important: When your horse drifts in one direction or the other, he will usually jump lower and is more likely to knock down the fence (see p. 165 for suggestions to correct this).

- While the horse should not stand off too far from the fence, it is ideal to have a takeoff distance where he leaves a little bit of room in front of the jump so he has time to get his front legs out of the way in order to clear the front rail.

Rider Position

You can be in a slightly forward position coming to a vertical, maintaining a short contact to get the horse in front of the leg. Once the horse takes off, think about following the motion with a slow upper-body movement, allowing the horse to come up before you go forward. Being too quick to move forward with your upper body will, in some cases, make the horse lower himself in front, causing rails to come down.

Oxer

The *oxer*—a spread fence—requires a little bit more power, which means a more forward canter to ensure the horse has enough energy to clear the back rail. In the canter, you still want softness, not an aggressive power; and you want the horse to listen and be responsive to your aids. As the horse jumps and stretches, follow with the contact and don't restrict the horse's bascule (roundness through his body) as he jumps. This gives his back legs freedom to clear the last part of the oxer.

- It is generally best to get your horse fairly close to the base of the fence to take off over an oxer. And keeping the horse straight to the fence is important because any angle will make the fence more difficult to jump.

- An *ascending oxer*, with the front rail lower than the back one, is somewhat easier for the horse to clear than a *square oxer* (see p. 161). You can have the horse on just a slightly more forward stride and get a little bit closer to the fence for takeoff with this type of oxer.

- A *square oxer* is a bit harder to jump than an *ascending oxer* because you have to get the horse to respect the front rail, and then clear the back rail as well. You want a canter that is in between the canter you need for a vertical and an ascending oxer. The horse needs to be a little bit away from the front rail to give his legs time to clear it, yet still have enough power to get over the back rail.

Rider Position

Sit slightly deeper in the seat to urge the horse forward. When the horse takes off it is important for you to be able to stretch across the horse as he bascules and jumps the wider jump. You have to "give" appropriately, however: When he is only jumping a small oxer there is not as much effort from the horse, so maintain your usual jumping position. As the jump gets higher you will have to stretch and go with him. It is important that no matter when the horse jumps, he has freedom and is never restricted in the air. He should be confident and able to trust his rider not to pull him in the mouth when he jumps.

Triple Bar

A *triple bar* has a high back rail with three rails sloping down to quite a low front rail. The main thing to think about when jumping a triple bar is whether the horse has enough power to get over the back rail. This requires him to approach the fence at a much faster speed and on a *long* canter stride. It is important to still try to get the horse close to the jump for takeoff so he doesn't have to jump quite as far to clear the back rail.

Rider Position

Again, remember to give the horse freedom in the air to clear the jump. Because you are coming in at a faster speed you can sit somewhat deeper in the saddle and be more aggressive in your position; as the horse jumps, do not restrict him, and on the last stride keep a little bit more forward so you can stay with the horse over the bigger jump.

Note: After a big effort like this it is important to rebalance and regroup your horse as quickly as possible to prepare for the next jump on course.

Swedish Oxer

A *Swedish oxer* is where the rails are sloping from high to low on opposite sides, so the front rail may be lower on the left and higher on the right and the back rail the opposite, sort of like an "X" hanging in the air.

- The key to riding this type of jump is to be able to jump the fence in the exact spot you choose. Usually, this means jumping to the side where the front rail is lower—that is, not in the middle of the fence but slightly off to one side.

- If your horse does not stay straight, or you allow him to jump where the front rail is higher, it becomes an "unfair" effort: Because the front rail is higher than the back rail, it's difficult for the horse to negotiate cleanly—chances are he will have the front rail down.

Rider Position

Ride a Swedish oxer in a manner similar to a normal oxer, but put more emphasis on the approach, keeping the horse straight and holding his line to the jump. This requires more emphasis on steering and preparation in order to get to the right takeoff point.

Plank

Plank fences are very upright and usually require the horse to be careful, soft and light in the approach. A lot of the time planks are set on flat cups, which means that if the horse touches them they are likely to come down. (Usually, jumps are set on 25 millimeter cups, which have a slight curve in the cup thus holding the rail in place more securely.) Ideally, the horse needs to settle and even slow down and relax on the last stride before the plank, which helps him to "come up" and spend more time in the air over the plank, rather than jumping flat and fast over it.

Rider Position

Your position is similar to the position for jumping a vertical. You need to prepare quite early in the approach and give the horse time to settle and soften, but still have him "uphill" and in a powerful canter while soft and light in the contact. You just need a nice, comfortable takeoff distance, not too deep or too long.

Stile (Narrow Fence)

One of the main issues, because of the narrow width of the jump, is that a stile is not imposing enough to some horses and a lot of times doesn't quite "hold" them, so they can get too aggressive coming into it. You need to prepare early so your horse focuses on the stile and understands what his job will be.

- The green horse will need even more clear direction to make sure he knows to jump the fence and not just run past it.

- You don't want to give a stile or any narrow fence an aggressive, fast ride; keep the horse on a short canter stride, allowing him to take the time to understand his job and jump cleanly.

Rider Position

It should be similar to when jumping a vertical, with a little more preparation and focus on maintaining a strong connection from leg to hand so the horse clearly understands that he is meant to jump the fence rather than run past it.

Liverpool

While not always found at eventing competitions, the Liverpool does need to be schooled at home so you are prepared, especially if your horse has a tendency to look down at the jump when he is clearing it or just before he jumps (fig. 9.5).

You can make a simple schooling Liverpool at home by placing a folded tarp, horse blanket, or other filler underneath a vertical. Be sure to use something heavy enough so it will not flap around, and use ground rails on either side to anchor it to the ground.

- It is imperative for the horse to pay attention to the *top rail* and not be concerned about the water tray beneath the jump.

Show Jumping Training 9

9.5 Ryan and his horse are schooling a Liverpool, or water tray. It is imperative that he pays attention to the top rail and is not concerned about the water tray beneath the jump.

- Generally, you want to ride to a Liverpool with a little bit more power, a little bit more weight in your hands, and keep the horse connected. Then you ride up to this connection from your leg to your hand. It is best to get to the Liverpool with a little bit more power so should the horse question the fence, you have plenty of power to jump it when you get there.

Rider Position

On the approach, you will be just a little bit more defensive, with the upper body position slightly farther back than normal, so that if the horse starts to hesitate you can be there and be strong for the horse. Your lower leg is ready to squeeze the horse and keep him in front of the leg all the way through to the last stride before takeoff. Slightly increased contact from your hand to the horse's mouth will help to keep the horse's head up on the last stride and prevent him from looking down into the water tray underneath.

PROBLEMS YOU MAY ENCOUNTER

Rushing

Generally a horse that rushes, I find, is worried about jumping and is not necessarily a bold horse that is doing his job because he loves it. A lot of the time when he sees the jump, he just goes tearing toward it. I think that with this in mind, working on the horse's confidence is important—not by overfacing him and making the jumps bigger, but by trying to get the horse to relax and jump in a soft way. Getting the horse to understand a deep takeoff distance is crucial; if the horse grabs the bit and rushes at the jump, we don't want him to leave out a stride and take off too far away from the jump, which could result in him not clearing the jump. If he adds a stride he'll be a much safer horse to jump.

- A series of canter poles or trot poles placed before and after the jump are helpful in many cases of rushing. These poles make the horse place his feet between them and put his focus on the fence. In some cases "V" poles placed at the front rail that open out on the approach side of the fence are enough to give this horse something to look at and slow down.

- Grid situations, where jumps are set up in a line, encourage the horse to think about where his feet are going and to think about his stride.

- Overall, the main things to work on are adjustability and connection in the horse's canter. When the horse becomes worried and wants to rush the jump, if his canter is adjustable, you can keep the connection and maintain the same canter stride from the leg to the hand.

Spooking

A lot of horses tend to get spooked or worry about colorful fences and the flowers and fillers underneath them. The event horse needs to be exposed to a lot of things so he becomes brave and realizes there is nothing to worry about. We also need to get the horse to focus on the top rail and not worry about what is underneath the jump.

- When the horse is starting out, lots of jumping over simple fences without fillers will give him confidence. But it is unfair to take him to a show if he's never been exposed to anything more interesting than plain fences. Put buckets, flowers, and other unusual (and safe) items under your schooling fences to help him get used to all kinds of such distractions.

- There is a flaw in your training when your horse spooks and drops behind your leg as he approaches a jump. You, therefore, have to be that much more aware of getting him in front of your leg. There may come a time when your horse ignores your leg and hesitates or looks down every time there is filler under the jump. Use your whip once, just behind your leg, as the horse takes off to encourage him to jump cleaner and more confidently at these fences.

- Getting the horse to go faster on the approach doesn't usually fix the problem; bringing the horse back to trot and letting him take his time to understand the question is usually a better way for him to learn that the jump is okay, and build his confidence.

Not Staying Straight (Drifting)

It is reasonably common for the horse to *get crooked* on the approach to a fence or in the air; this must be addressed before it becomes a habit. For a horse to be rideable and jump clear, he has to learn to stay straight.

The first thing to look at is his soundness. Often, when a horse is sore or lame on a front leg he will drift away from that leg. If it is hind-leg lameness he usually drifts toward that side. If you rule out a soundness problem you need to find ways to correct the habit.

Jumping then turning is one way to correct this. For example, when the horse wants to drift left, jump a small fence and keep him turning right on a circle. Or, as you are approaching a jump, hold with the right (turning) rein to keep him straight.

Some other methods:

- Using only one "V" pole—that is, put one end of a pole on the ground at the side and angle the other end to set it down on the middle of the jumping rail—is also a good way of keeping a horse straight to a jump. However, this method needs to be used at all jumps, or at least, every second jump to keep the horse "thinking straight."

- You can also set two poles at right angles to both sides of the jump on the landing so the horse has stay straight in order not to land on a pole.

- Another tool is to raise the jump rails higher on the side the horse drifts toward in order to encourage him to jump the lower side and stay straight.

Rider Position

- The main thing is to keep the horse straight with your leg on the side the horse is drifting toward: When he drifts right, really use your right leg or even the spur to keep him straight, and vice versa.

- Maintaining a correct position is important: Sit straight on the horse and stay in balance. Make sure you are not leaning to one side and *causing* the horse to drift.

- As the horse jumps, hold the rein in the direction that you want to straighten the horse. For example, when he drifts right, hold the left rein to keep him straight.

Refusing

Refusals are usually caused by a lack of confidence and the horse not staying in front of the rider's leg. One of the first things an event horse has to learn is that he has to go forward and get to the other side of the jump.

- To help the horse be confident, keep jumps set at a height he is comfortable jumping.

- You can also use the stick on the last stride before the jump to back up your leg aid if you feel the horse starting to "suck back."

- It is fair to say that riding a habitually "stopping" horse is not really good for your riding and tends to encourage the development of defensive habits. If your horse is refusing to jump, I would suggest the help of a professional before it becomes a serious problem for your horse and your riding.

Having Rails Down

This is a pretty broad topic: There are a lot of reasons for having rails down, from training to riding to surroundings.

- A lot of times a horse that lacks confidence will have rails down because he wants to get to the other side of the fence and land quickly. As he develops more confidence in you and in jumping he will spend more time in the air over the fence.

- Horses that rush need to spend more time on the approach and in the air. Slowing things down helps them to keep rails up.

- A horse's jumping technique will sometimes cause rails to fall: When he doesn't bascule properly or use his back he can come down early with his back legs.

- When a horse is not "tidy" with his front legs he will sometimes hit the top rail of the jump (or the front rail of an oxer) and knock it down because he is slow to lift up with his front legs. By nature, a horse is either careful or not and some horses just don't care as much whether or not they hit the jump!

It takes great skill or a lot of experience to get the horse to understand that in one phase of our sport—cross-country—we want him to go fast and not be so worried if he brushes a jump, while in another phase—show jumping—we want him to be more calculated and careful. Try to keep your jump training for these phases separate from one another so the horse has a chance to understand the difference between show jumping and cross-country training.

PART 3
COMPETING

10.1 Woodburn and I take part in the Victory Gallop at the Rolex Kentucky Three-Day Event in 2010. When you and your horse are well prepared mentally, as well as physically, you will find success.

CHAPTER 10

Mental Preparation for Rider and Horse

Before I discuss the actual competition, I want to say a few words about being ready because when you are well prepared in advance—physically and mentally—it helps you deal with nerves and allows you to relax more at the event.

I try to think about setting myself up for success (fig. 10.1). Being organized is the first step. It's the attention to all the little details that help make a competition smooth and rewarding. This starts with your entry: It's important to enter at a level where you and your horse are going to be confident and have a good chance to be successful. Don't think about the next level until you have totally mastered your current level in all three phases.

It's important to be prepared so that you can go through the competition smoothly. Everything from knowing the dressage test well, to getting a lot of practice in the lead up to it—especially the week before. This means being totally ready for cross-country and show jumping phases, with both horse and rider fit and ready.

When you pack for the event, check that all your tack and equipment is in place (see p. 315 for a packing list). When you have the luxury of having somebody to assist, go over exactly what needs to be done and at what times so you can be helped most effectively. All of this planning becomes even more essential when you are riding more than one horse.

MENTAL PREPARATION

Getting yourself mentally prepared is as important as your physical training. Once you feel that you and the horse are fully physically prepared, go over in your mind the phase that you are about to ride. Through experience you will discover what works best for you to get mentally prepared for an event. Some people need more time for this while others get nervous when they have too much time on their hands.

- If you are nervous about the dressage phase, try to think in advance about nearly every possible scenario and how you would deal with each possibility.

- Prepare yourself mentally for the possibility that your horse could be more uptight and nervous at the event than he is at home. To improve your chance of success, plan to arrive on the early side and as you ride him, pay attention to his physical and mental state. This will help you to take out as many unknown variables as you can, exposing your horse to the environment at the event and getting him and yourself used to the grounds.

- To prepare to ride cross-country, walk the course as many times as it takes for you to feel comfortable so your energy isn't focused on where you are going on course, but rather on riding a safe, confident, and successful round (see chapter 12 for tips on walking the cross-country course).

- With show jumping you may or may not have a chance to spend a lot of time walking the course (see chapter 14 on walking and riding the show jumping). When you can watch other riders do it well, it will give you more confidence and security about what you need to do to ride a clear round.

A few ideas for mental preparation and relaxation include:

- Go over your test or course on paper.

- Sit quietly and visualize your ride.

- Listen to music to relax you and help block outside interference.

- Talk through your plan with a coach or another good listener.

- Have confidence in your skills and preparation for the event.

- Set aside any distractions from your personal life and focus on the competition.

- Finalize and commit to your game plan or strategy.

- Spend some time alone before your ride to get yourself mentally prepared and "in the zone."

Mental Preparation for Rider and Horse 10

Dealing with Nerves/Being in the Moment

Try to create an ability to be in the moment (be "within" yourself), which means being able to react to your horse and the competition environment on the day.

Being nervous before an event is completely normal. I don't know of an event rider who doesn't have nerves and apprehension like everybody does at a sporting event. It's how you handle these nerves that is important. I think the biggest part is that you don't want to let nervousness detract from all the time, training, and hard work that you've put in. I try to let the nerves help me compete better by giving me a little competitive edge, without letting them overwhelm me and take away from the experience.

Everybody tends to deal with nerves or the pressure of the event differently. There are lots of ways to educate yourself on this: Some of the psychology books on training your mind can be helpful, and there are also simple exercises that can help you relax and concentrate better.

A very simple exercise that anyone can do at any time is to take deeper, slower breaths. This always helps me get my mind clearer and prepared for the competition. This is also something that is very simple to do while you are on your horse, preparing to go into the start box for cross-country or arena for dressage or show jumping.

There are going to be times when things haven't been going your way. This could mean that you have had a bad dressage ride or that you have not had a very good preparation leading up to the event; maybe your horse was a little sore, you had bad weather to contend with, or you had trouble on course with another horse and your confidence is shaken. It is important not to let any or all of these factors affect your next ride. You have to believe in yourself and your horse and the training that you put in leading up to the event. Go out there and make sure that you get the best out of your horse and yourself and do not let negative thoughts get in your way!

Staying Focused in Warm-Up

The warm-up area for all three phases can be a chaotic place. It is important that you not get sidetracked by what other horses and riders are doing.

- While it can be beneficial to talk to a rider you trust and respect about what to expect on course, this is not something that you should rely on. You have to stick to your plan and, again, trust all the training and hard work that you put in leading up to this competition.

- Remember to focus on your horse and yourself and what you need to perform your best.

- If somebody else in the dressage warm-up is doing a lot of fancy looking extended trot, this is not a reason for you to do extended trot too; you have to be fair to your horse.

- If you are warming up for show jumping and there is a jump on course that is not riding well, certainly advice from your coach can

10.2 The atmosphere at a competition can be distracting to your horse. Give him time to settle in before your ride.

be helpful but also going over in your mind how you are going to accomplish that jump will help you stick to your plan.

Introducing Your Horse to the Competition Environment

Most horses behave a little differently at a show than at home. It's good to be mentally prepared and not be too surprised or put off if yours has a last-minute personality change.

The atmosphere of the horse show is exciting: There are lots more horses, the loudspeaker, golf carts, dogs, and so many more distractions than your horse has at home. As he becomes more experienced and gains mileage, his behavior should improve; however, even the most seasoned horse can experience nervousness and change his behavior at a show.

A few ways his behavior can change:

- Generally the Thoroughbred, especially an OTTB, becomes nervous, anxious, and shorter in his stride, possibly thinking he's back at the track.

- Other breeds don't want to go as "forward" as they do at home.

- Some horses become very inattentive and it's hard to get them to focus on the work you want them to do.

The Green Horse
The best way to educate a really green horse that's never been to a show before is to slowly introduce him to small changes of environment from his home base. This can be as simple as taking him to a friend's place and riding around, going to another schooling facility, or attending a local schooling show. I encourage a lot of different venues before you actually send off the entry form for his first Horse Trials.

You should aim for your horse's first event to be a low-key, smaller show without the hustle and bustle that goes along with a bigger event (fig. 10.2). You want a quieter atmosphere so there is not a lot of pressure on your horse his first time out.

Because the horse is going to be exposed to so many new experiences, it is best to have him pretty established in his training first. Some people would argue that taking him to a show early on is a great way for your horse to learn, but I feel it's better to make it an easy experience, so I try to have my young horses well trained before their first outing. This sets them up positively for their future career as event horses.

That means that your horse should be used to:

- Going in a dressage arena.

- Flowers around the arena.

- Many typical show items, such as golf carts, dogs, tractors, crowds of people.

- Jumping around a course with "fillers" in and around the jumps.

- Being confident on cross-country.

You need to be prepared for a lot of different scenarios when you are at the show all day: Can you tie him to the trailer? Will he stand in the trailer and not panic? You need to get to know your horse because you have the responsibility to make it the best and safest possible experience for him. This can also mean taking an older, more experienced horse along to babysit your youngster.

Having somebody there at the show to lend a hand when needed is also important–whether this means holding the horse while you walk the course, hand-walking the horse if he's nervous, or helping you drive to and from the competition. We always hope our horses will be well-behaved en route and when we get there, but it is better to be prepared for anything, just in case.

10.3 During your first warm-up ride, keep the horse forward, relaxed, and stretching down as he gets accustomed to his new environment.

Mental Preparation for Rider and Horse 10

Your First Ride

When you're riding your horse at the show, he needs to remember all the training he learned at home. There's not much point putting all that time into his education if you get to the show and find he forgets—or ignores—all you've taught him. When you first get on, your goal is to reinforce the leg-to-hand connection, get your horse's attention, and make sure you go over the basics of what he has learned. By the time you get to the dressage test there should be harmony between you.

Depending on the event and timing, most horses will benefit from two rides: The first, when you arrive at the show to get communication going and the early excitement of being at a show out of his system. During this ride, be sure to send him forward, making sure he stretches and reaches, yields, and takes the contact easily (fig. 10.3). For most horses this means a lot of transitions forward and back to get them really listening and working with you. It is not that important to do movements from the test, but more to get them controlled, "adjustable" and correct in their movement so that you can ride the test later. This first ride should:

- Last 20 to 25 minutes.

- Fit into your day so you have plenty of time to cool your horse down, then have him polished and ready for the dressage test.

- Take place at least one and one-half hours before you need to get on and warm up for your actual test.

Keep in mind your type of horse: How fit is he? Does he have a lot of nervous energy? Is he a lazy horse? If the latter, your task on that first ride is to keep him *thinking forward*, but be sure that you don't overdo it and wear him out. You want to have something left in the tank when you ride in front of the judge.

CHAPTER 11

Warming Up and Riding Your Dressage Test

WARMING UP

It is important to know the horse show's procedures. First off, know where your warm-up area is. If you start to ride in the wrong place, it can waste a lot of time finding out where you should be, not to mention taking your mind off your preparation.

Watch a few tests, find out where the "bit check" takes place and be fully in control of your warm-up. The "bit check" is an area in or near the dressage warm-up where a volunteer will check to make sure that your bit, spurs and whip are legal within the competition rules.

Most of the time it is preferable when you have the opportunity to warm up close to where you actually have to compete, because horses take time to settle into a new environment (figs. 11.1 A & B).

A general rule is to get on your horse about 30 minutes before your actual dressage test. Start out pretty much as you always do so that everything is the same as your training at home. The last thing you need to do is to have your training influenced by competition nerves. You need to make everything very deliberate and similar to your regular training routine.

11.1 A & B The dressage warm-up arena can be a crowded place. Take time to relax and watch other horses during your warm up.

Warming Up and Riding the Dressage Test

11.2 During a walk break, remove your horse's boots; have your bit checked; and wipe away any dirt and sweat. However, do not take so much time that it detracts from your routine.

When there is room at the grounds, I try to find a quiet area where I can start off my warm-up not being interrupted by horses and other distractions. Once you have communication going, move to a larger area with more things going on.

Remember, if your horse has boots on they need to be taken off at some stage during the warm-up: The walk break is a good time and you can wipe sweat off and deal with anything that detracts from your overall look (fig. 11.2). However, this needs to be planned beforehand. Don't waste too much time or take away from your ridden preparation. And, don't forget to have you're your horse's bit checked by an official before you enter the competition ring.

A typical warm-up routine:

1 Start in walk on a 20-meter circle if the warm-up area is large enough. Introduce "inside leg to outside rein." I usually start on the left rein, because most horses go better to the left and it starts them off well–mentally. Get the horse walking nicely forward, slightly bent around your inside leg, and encourage him to reach softly down and forward.

2 Use some leg-yielding exercises to reaffirm your training and get the horse listening to your leg in both directions, left and right. Once you have his attention at walk go to rising trot on a circle, making sure the horse

11.3 Boyd Martin's Neville Bardos is stretching nicely in the trot before his test at the 2010 Alltech FEI World Equestrian Games (WEG).

is correct. The first walk should take about three to five minutes, then you are into trot. Rather than thinking about the test, focus more on the correctness of the horse: You want him reaching for the bit softly; obedient to inside leg to outside rein; and with flexion to inside (fig. 11.3). Do the same work on the right rein, then introduce smaller trot circles, like 15- and 10-meter circles, depending on your level. The horse should stay focused and balanced.

3 Do lots of changes of direction and transitions within the trot—forward and back—to keep your horse's attention and prevent him from getting "stuck" in the one exercise. This should take about 5 to 10 minutes.

4 By now, the horse's back should be supple and loose enough to introduce sitting trot (fig. 11.4). I do a little bit of sitting trot—left and right—then ask for the canter on the left lead.

5 Be reasonably firm about the horse listening to you. You have to get him to understand you want him to concentrate and not play around. Because the horse is a creature of habit you must instill the rule that he always listens to you and not to what is going on outside the work area.

11.4 Annie Jones' Young Man is coming up nicely in the trot before our dressage test at Jersey Fresh.

11.5 Young Man and I are focused and riding forward in the canter as we prepare to perform our winning test at Jersey Fresh in 2011.

6 At this stage, you are still focusing on the correctness of the canter: softness in front, the ability to reach forward and down, and flexion around your inside leg. You should be able to softly move the horse forward and then collect him in the canter (fig. 11.5).

7 I do probably three or four canter-trot-canter transitions on each rein. Canter-trot is a great way of testing how well the horse is on the aids. I don't want him to run or hollow out, and he should stay obedient through the transition. The canter work should also take three to five minutes.

8 After you have cantered in both directions, take a small break at walk. This is not for him to "stick his head in the air," but to be on a softer contact and still in touch with the leg and hand. Don't allow him to "lose the plot"; remember you're about to start work again.

9 With about 10 minutes to go, I work on the actual movements. When there is not an actual dressage arena to warm up in, I make up an imaginary one in the warm-up area. There may be a fence on one side.

10 I take parts of the test to work on, for example, trot down the centerline; halt; then trot on and turn left at C. You might overdo the bend around your inside leg so that when you are riding your test and you ride past the judge's box, your horse will stay focused and forward through the turn. Or ride through the trot work from the test and mix things up a little so he doesn't anticipate the test movements later. Do this a few times and get a feel for how your horse is going and what he might do in the test.

11 Do the same exercises with the canter work–not necessarily in the same order of the test. In fact, some horses really anticipate movements so doing them out of order is better training. Going through the canter work again to get some last-minute practice will help you figure out what you need to do to get the best out of your horse.

12 When there is one horse to go before your test, go back and work on your horse's correctness–getting him in tune with your aids. Do lots of transitions–every half a circle or few seconds I go trot to walk; walk to trot; canter; back to halt; medium trot; keeping the horse listening and thinking. Also spend some time varying the horse's frame, so you can ride him in a longer, lower and softer outline if you need to, or ask him to collect more and elevate his front end.

13 This last part of the warm-up is really to reinforce his attention to you; you're preparing him so that when it's your turn, he is listening to you. I like to keep an eye on the competitor's horse right before me and note where he is in the test, because after

11.6 Woodburn and I are saying hello to the judges at the 2010 WEG. This is a good opportunity to connect with the judges as well as expose your horse to the goings-on around the dressage arena so that he will not have any surprises when you go down the centerline.

he is finished, those previous minutes when you are allowed to ride around the whole of the outside of the arena can be a huge bonus. Watch for him going down the centerline for his final halt: You can gain a few more seconds when you are ready to circle the arena immediately he is finished.

Circling the Arena

Usually the judge takes a minute or so to go over and make comments on the previous rider's test; you want to utilize all this time to ride around the arena:

- Your horse may be easily distracted, so it's a good opportunity to get it out of his system and listening to you. With a green horse, rising trot is preferable so you can keep him going forward, maybe in a lower and more reaching-down frame than in your test.

- Most dressage arenas are going to have some kind of flowers or ornaments around them. Especially, if your horse is a spooky type, bend him away from whatever is getting his attention.

- Once the judge is ready for you, ride past making sure your number is visible. Acknowledge the judge with a nice smile and appear ready and prepared to show off your horse and do a good test (fig. 11.6).

- You have 45 seconds after the judge blows the whistle in which to enter the ring. Even if your horse spooks or does something unexpected, you still should have time to make a circle and get his attention back again.

- In this preparation around the arena it's good to notice how the arena is situated and how you're going to approach A and the centerline. Sometimes it's better to come off one rein or the other. If the test requires me to turn left at C, I will approach off a left-hand circle outside the arena (or vice versa) so my horse starts off bent in the correct direction.

RIDING THE TEST

You want to begin your test with a good impression, so it is important the horse stays straight down the centerline. The best way to keep him straight is to make him go forward.

Generally, if a horse is wavering down the centerline he is not really committed to going forward; especially when on a green horse, I push him to go forward down the centerline. After that you can turn it down a notch and let him relax, but really "think forward" on that first centerline.

At the lower levels there is not usually a halt and salute; from Preliminary and upward, you need to halt and salute the judge, so once the horse is going down the centerline you need the aids and communication to ride the halt. The judge is looking for softness and does not want the halt to be abrupt and hard. Usually a halt with one or two walk steps scores better than an abrupt halt ridden from too much hand.

As you move forward and start riding the test it is important to be "in the moment": Be able to evaluate what the horse is doing as you go along and react by making subtle adjustments when the horse needs them, throughout the test.

- If the horse starts getting resistant, putting him in a softer, lower frame can help counteract the resistance.

- If the horse is reacting by getting too forward, use a corner to bring him back so the whole test doesn't become rushed.

- When you need to get him more forward and in front of the leg you can also use the turn to create more energy and impulsion for the next movement.

- The greener horse is especially apt to change throughout the test: At the beginning, he can back off and act spooky, and by the end be rushing and getting too aggressive. Keep evaluating and adjusting your horse as you go through the test, improving as you go.

Keep in mind that there is a mark judged for each movement—it's not a case of just cantering at the letter, but how the horse executes the canter transition. Say the test requires you to pick up the canter lead at C: In the corner before C, prepare the horse so that at C he is ready to pick up the canter and it won't be a surprise.

If you know that your horse is especially capable in a particular movement, take advantage of the opportunity to let him shine (fig. 11.7). This is a chance to earn a few extra points that could mean the difference between winning and

11.7 Woodburn is doing an extended trot at the 2010 WEG. Focus on your horse and your riding, not the atmosphere or other distractions.

Warming Up and Riding the Dressage Test 11

11.8 Lengthen your reins as you leave the arena, and praise your horse for a job well done as I am doing at Rolex Kentucky in 2008.

placing. At the same time, a nice steady ride can earn more points than "going for it" and then blowing it! You can base your decision on whether to ride for extra points or keep things more conservative on how your horse is responding to your aids and reacting to the environment around him.

Most tests have a hiccup or two. Again, remember that each movement is scored individually so if you have a bad movement, try to regroup and not let that affect the rest of the test. Always think ahead to the next movement: At the end of the test the judge gives you an "overall impression" mark, and you can still get a really good score even when you've had one or two movements that are not your best.

At the greener levels, judges are not expecting a perfect test. They are looking for the horse that is on the road to being a well-trained, confident horse.

As you come down the centerline to finish, it is your last chance to impress the judge. Try to make it deliberate and polished. Ride forward into a square halt, give a clear salute and smile at the judge as an act of acknowledgement.

Leave the arena on a loose rein and let the horse stretch. I like to do a circle before I walk out so the horse understands he can't just duck and rush out of the gate. Don't be in a hurry to leave the arena (fig. 11.8).

When you are very disappointed with your horse's performance, you can go back to the warm-up arena and spend a few minutes schooling to improve your horse's way of going before you take him back to the barn. Be considerate of your horse and other competitors and keep this session brief.

Getting Extra Points in the Ring

- The corners of the arena are important and should be regarded as your "friends." In each corner, spend a second to regroup and improve the way the horse is going.

- Really know the test well and prepare the horse before every movement.

- It's also important to execute the movements exactly as the test asks for them. This shows the judge that you have a well-trained horse and you are professional about how you ride the test.

- An accurately ridden test will always score better: When the test requires a 10-meter circle, you shouldn't ride a 12-meter circle—or one with 6 meters on one side and 4 meters on the other. It should be well formed and well executed.

- When we talk about executing a movement *at the letter*, the horse's withers (shoulder) should be at the letter, not the tip of his nose nor the point of his hip. Accuracy can earn extra points.

- At the bottom of the paper, the judge has four boxes on the test for the "collective marks," which evaluate *submission, gaits, impulsion,* and the *rider's position and seat*. It is important, throughout the test, to convey to the judge that you are proud of your horse; that you sit well in the saddle; and you conduct yourself well. Be firm but sympathetic to the horse during your ride.

- Your overall impression to the judge is important. How the horse is groomed and how you look gives the judge an impression of a well-educated, well turned-out horse and rider enjoying the sport.

You want to set yourself up to succeed. This means making sure the work that you have done at home is more advanced than what the test requires. When you have the horse educated to a higher level at home, and the test at the competition is easy for him, chances are he will have a good experience.

Recognized events, in particular, are not the place to retrain your horse or give him a school. It is also not the place to show bad sportsmanship or horsemanship, or to get in an argument with your horse. Try to set yourself up so you are there to have a successful ride.

That said, it is a part of sports that things don't always go right; having respect for your horse, the judge, and your fellow competitors is important, and remember there is always another competition.

The schedule of the three phases from one event to another varies somewhat; you might have two or even all three phases in one day, so give your horse time for a rest and yourself time to prepare for the next phase.

CHAPTER 12

Walking the Cross-Country Course

DEVELOPING A PLAN

Walking the cross-country course is nearly as important as actually riding it, because the course walk is your opportunity to develop a plan that gives you the best opportunity for a successful ride. I don't think that there is a magic number for how many times you should walk the course; basically, you need to be really comfortable with the course, and you can walk it as many times as you feel necessary to learn your way around. Some people with less experience need to walk it more times. Give yourself plenty of time to make sure you have a good understanding of where to go, what the footing is like, and how you plan to ride each fence.

Going around the course should feel a little instinctual, like driving home from the barn or work. When you're on course and galloping at speed, the course comes up a lot faster than when you're walking on foot! It is not a great idea to be out riding cross-country and trying to remember where to go. With the course firmly set in your mind, you can concentrate on your riding and your horse.

Walking the Course

Walk for Success

Here are a few things to keep in mind as you walk your cross-country course:

1. Your first priority is to get your bearings and learn the order of fences and the route you have to ride. The organizers will provide you with a map, which may be very detailed, with pictures and descriptions of each jump, or very basic, with lines and numbers showing the fences, and maybe a few directional arrows. Make sure you know exactly where to go and don't be afraid to ask an official to clarify any questions about the course.

2. Consider the terrain. You will likely be going up and down hills and through the woods, and you need to have a good sense of direction, since because of these hills, trees, or other natural or man-made obstructions, you may not be able to see out very far.

3. Familiarize yourself with the conditions and what the footing is going to be like when you

12.1 When you begin your course walk to plan your ride, think about how your horse will come out of the box.

ride it. Knowing how hard or slippery the ground is can help you decide which kind of studs you might use (see sidebar, p. 281).

4 If you are going to ride for time, figure out where you can open up your horse's stride to make up a few seconds.

I usually start walking from inside the start box, since that is where you begin. As you walk out of the box, try to get an idea where you're aiming for to get to the first fence. Try to visualize how you'll come out of the box and what kind of start you'll have (fig. 12.1). Notice whether you are going away from the stables or past an area with a lot of activity, which can be a distraction and make the horse resistant to going forward.

At the beginning of the course, if I had to generalize, it's more about getting the horse moving forward and in front of your leg, while at the end of the course it's about keeping him thinking and being smart and not too bold and aggressive. Every horse is different, though. If your horse starts aggressively out of the box you'll want to get him settled. A lot of times by the end of the course you're dealing with a stronger, more aggressive horse. The other extreme, of course, is when the horse is starting to tire from the exertion of cross-country and you are dealing with a very different horse than you had at the beginning when he was fresh and alert.

I usually use the first two or three fences to get into the horse's mind that I want to have a positive, forward round. These first few fences are usually uncomplicated, forward-riding jumps, and it's important to utilize them to ride in a very positive and confident way that will set the tone for the rest of the round.

Mapping Out Your Course

- The start of the course is a good time to quickly evaluate how your horse feels and whether you need to get him more in front of your leg if he seems cautious, or maybe get him to settle and think about jumping rather than rushing at the fences. Try to make the most of this opportunity.

- Generally, after fence three you will be presented with the first question of some difficulty. It's important to understand what the question is—for instance, is it a control, turning, or bravery question? When you ride, you will need to keep this in mind as you develop your horse's canter in the approach to that jump.

- Be sure to consider the terrain as you walk. Because of the nature of cross-country riding the course is often spread throughout fields where you can't see the next jump, so as you walk the course you have to look for natural markers that you aim for to get to each jump. After Fence 3, for example, you might need to aim for a gate in the fence line or a big patch of trees because that's where Fence 4 is. It's not just about learning the course but getting a feel for the terrain and where you need to aim to get to each jump.

- Cantering up a hill is going to require a different balance than cantering down or across

Technology and Your Course Walk

Will the meter wheel one day be obsolete? As of publication, there are a number of smartphone applications that are helping to bring eventing into the twenty-first century. No doubt software developers will continue to improve on the existing technology, but at this time applications like CourseWalk use GPS technology to record and display your cross-country course. This enables riders to:

- Record the course track and distance in meters.
- Identify minute markers.
- Take photos of fences and waypoints.
- Retrace the entire course, displaying the fences as you go.
- Share your course online.
- Download courses onto your phone.
- Link to live scoring.
- View the terrain along the course with minute markers and fences.
- View terrain in different colors on a map.

There are "apps" for dressage tests, weather updates, directions to your event, and even an app to search FEI-approved drugs for your horse. The US Eventing Association Omnibus (Calendar of events) is available online; live scores from most events are available, and you can enter many competitions online. While some riders prefer to do things the old-fashioned way, with pen and paper, there is certainly plenty of room for technology in modern eventing.

a hill. Cantering down a hill will lengthen the stride and coming up a hill will shorten the stride. This is all information you need to store in your mind as you develop your plan before you set out riding the course.

- Different types of footing will determine how you ride: When the footing is good you can carry on as usual, but if it's rutted or muddy, it's best to slow down and not risk injuring your horse.

- You have to evaluate the turns you'll have to make, but remember it's much easier when you're walking the course to make turns than it is on a galloping horse. Some horses are better in one direction than the other and this is also something to take into account when you're planning which direction you will turn on your ride.

Specific Fences

As you walk around the course you also need to evaluate what you expect to be difficult for your horse and take this into account as you plan where to start your preparation for each jump. It means that at a certain point, whether it's near a fence post or a certain tree, you will start to steady up as you approach a fence. On my course walks, I try to think about what could happen at every jump—not in a negative way but to prepare myself for the unexpected by keeping in mind that the horse might drift in one direction or back off. I try to analyze every jump and have a plan for different scenarios (fig. 12.2).

When walking cross-country combination fences, it is important to understand that

Walking the Cross-Country Course 12

12.2 Jennie Brannigan considers a cross-country jump during her course walk at the Jersey Fresh CCI***.

because you are galloping cross-country, your horse's average canter stride is going to be a little bit longer than it would be in the show jumping ring. This will vary depending on what the jump is—for example, a big ditch under a jump may well back the horse off and shorten his stride, as will jumping into water.

I also try to think about what my riding position should be at various jumps. A big part of being a good cross-country rider is to be able to stay in position. At a drop fence I will talk to myself about slipping my reins and sitting back to keep my balance. The same goes for all different jumps—I make a mental note of what I need to do.

When you think about riding cross-country, galloping along and jumping out in the open is probably the first thing that comes to mind. In actuality, while the cross-country course is usually made up of some forward-riding jumps, many of the jumps on course require technical skills like a collected canter, turning or shortening the stride.

I try to utilize the forward-riding jumps to get the horse in front of my leg and confident. With the jumps that you might regard as straightforward, try to be sure that you make the most of them and ride forward and confidently to help your horse make the most of his round. Having a "miss" or a scary ride at these jumps will not help the rest of your round when you face more difficult questions.

Generally, the hardest part of the cross-country course is the water jump. Whether the water or another difficult section of the course is the most difficult, it is important to prepare before you get to each jump. For example, if your horse is a little cautious at water, it makes sense to plan to ride aggressively before the water and keep the horse in front of your leg as you approach the water complex.

If your horse is quite green it is probably prudent to slow down at a narrow fence or corner and make sure the jump prior to it is ridden in a controlled way so you can instill in your horse that you need control and accuracy at the next jump.

Riding for Time

Riding for time is a real skill that needs to be developed; it's not about going at a faster speed but rather improving the efficiency of your round and being able to average a good speed. As you walk your course, keep the following in mind:

- The easiest way to become fast on cross-country is to get away from the jumps quickly and efficiently, making up time on the landing side.

- Another way is to take the shortest possible distance: The wider you make turns, the farther the horse has to travel and, theoretically, the slower you will be. When you walk the course, pay attention to the line you will ride.

- The approach to the jump is also a place to save time but this takes more experience as you must be fully prepared and balanced for the jump. Less experienced horses and riders need more preparation.

- Carefully walk your lines to give your horse every opportunity to jump efficiently not wasting time, but safely, too.

- There are parts of the course where you will be able to make up time and then there are sections that are slower. Be prepared to take more time to get a clean round, making sure your horse jumps confidently over the harder sections, and make up time on other parts of the course safely and without scaring your horse.

Measuring the Course and Using a Watch

At the Beginner Novice and Novice Levels, speed is not really a factor–you just want to canter around at a show-jumping-type speed. At Training Level speed is somewhat more of a factor; in some cases, people ride too fast, so measuring the course is a way of helping them to understand the speed they want to achieve.

I don't usually start carrying a stopwatch until I'm at an FEI event, but I think practicing with a watch at the lower levels is a good way to help you judge your time and learn the speed you need to ride. It's good to learn to ride for time without a watch; however, using one will help you learn to get the feel for the right speed (see "Practicing Pace", p. 115). You will need a stopwatch and to either buy or borrow a meter wheel.

You need to measure the course and know where you need to be at every minute or half-minute to make the stopwatch useful. Measuring or wheeling a course is also something that I generally save for the CCI events, but even at the lower levels it can be good practice as you learn to get a feel for pace.

Measure the course with a meter wheel (fig. 12.3) and every minute (say 450 meters for Training Level), you pick a point where you need to be—say, a road crossing, a tree, or a point near a jump. Remember that these points are just a guide, because some minutes will ride "faster"—out in open fields, for example. Woods or a twisty section will naturally slow the horse down, so if you are a little behind your time, you can make it up on a more open part of the course.

It goes without saying that you can't just ride by your watch; you have to ride with feel and can only expect to get from your horse what he is capable of on that day. As I talked about earlier, it's important for the horse to learn to jump cross-country jumps slowly and confidently—before you add speed.

Terrain

Weather conditions and terrain play a big part in how hard or easy it is to make the time. If it's pouring with rain it's going to be a lot more difficult to see where you're going and be safe.

12.3 You can use a meter wheel to measure parts of the cross-country course and find markers at specific points on course in order to check your pace.

12.4 Consider the terrain, open vs. wooded areas and roping for galloping lanes as you walk your course.

A flat course makes it easier on time than one where you constantly have to readjust your horse to go up and down hills. A wooded course through lines of trees is usually harder, as well. Even roped-off galloping lanes slow you down because you tend to slow up to steer your horse a bit more than you would in an open field (fig. 12.4).

Some Three-Day Events throughout the world are known for being hard on time—Burghley, in England, is one because of its terrain. Although it's not extremely hilly, your horse is always going up and down. Then, if you add rainy conditions, sometimes ending up with 15 or 20 time faults is considered a fast round.

The Fair Hill Three-Day in Maryland is another event where making the time is difficult. Again, it's because of the terrain and the constant rebalancing needed by horse and rider. It's always harder for your horse to gallop at speed over undulating, hilly courses; this type of terrain rides slower even without jumps.

At the major events, a course designer sets out to make sure the more experienced horses can ride the course in the time allowed, while the less experienced ones cannot—especially at the higher levels of competition. He will build jumps where you have to slow down, like sunken roads, coffins and "narrow/turning questions," which always require the horse to approach the jump in the 200 to 300 mpm range. Since you have to average 570 mpm at these levels, a combination that slows you

Walking the Cross-Country Course 12

down that much means you need to go a lot faster between fences to finish in time.

It is important to remember that riding for time is a "feel" in itself and not something that you can just go out and do. It takes years of practice from the rider and the horse.

12.5 A & B Crowds, tents, and other distractions can make it challenging to keep your horse focused on course, like here at Millbrook Horse Trials in New York, 2010 (above) and at Rolex Kentucky in 2008 (below).

MODERN EVENTING WITH PHILLIP DUTTON 199

Distractions

Especially in the upper levels, at bigger events with tents and crowds of spectators, distractions on cross-country can cause issues, especially with horses that spook (figs. 12.5 A & B). To generalize, the well-trained horse should be in tune with you and go forward from your leg so if he sees something that concerns him, you should be able to squeeze with your leg and he'll disregard his spookiness. Obviously, in the real world, you are dealing with horses that are not so well trained. Here are a few suggestions for bringing your horse's attention back to you:

- Try to think about bending the horse away from the distraction. If you come around a turn and there is a problem on the left, bend the horse right to keep his focus off the distraction and continue to pay attention to you.

- I often become a bit firmer with my ride and sharper with my leg and spur and even give

Option Fences

All fences are numbered, but some "option" fences consisting of more than one element, will also have a letter for each part—A, B, C, and so on. Usually there are several option fences on course that allow you to choose your way through a combination. The easier option is always the longer way but if you have trouble at one of the fences—a refusal—the first time you attempt the combination, you can go back and take another route—that is, you don't have to re-present the horse to the jump that caused difficulty.

When your horse isn't jumping as well as you'd like, knowing (in advance) the easier options, gives you a better chance at having a good, confident, clear round rather than presenting him at a jump he isn't ready for that day.

So, on your course walk learn what the options are and have a Plan B ready.

- When you have trouble at a jump in a combination, if the fences are lettered A, B, C, you have the choice of *re*-presenting the horse to the *previous* fence(s) in the combination and jumping it again, or you can choose to skip the previous fence(s), and just *re*-present to the fence where you have encountered difficulty. For example, if you have trouble at Fence B you can jump A again first, but you do not have to.

- The "black flag option" gives you an alternate fence to jump. For example, you will see two fences numbered 6B—one with a black stripe across the number. This means you can choose which of these fences to jump. So, if your horse refuses the one you have initially chosen, you can approach the other Fence 6B on your second attempt.

There is a lot to understand and think about on your course walk. The rules for all levels change every year and it's important to keep abreast of them. When you're not clear about an option fence or how a combination is meant to be jumped, ask the technical delegate for an explanation.

him a little slap with the stick, or raise my voice to get the horse's attention away from the distraction.

- Most of the time—especially at the lower levels—distractions are more of an issue in the show jumping ring because it's more enclosed.

Riding the Finish

Typically, the last fence or two on course are not that difficult: The course designer wants you to have a nice ending. Make sure your horse jumps them confidently so he'll be happy to jump around another course the next time. Give these last jumps as much respect as the rest of the course; don't allow yourself or your horse to lose concentration until you've gone through the finish flags.

As you're walking the last part of the course keep in mind:

- Your horse may well be tired and not as easy to steer and adjust as he was at the beginning so plan for these fences with this in mind.

- After the last jump it's important to go *between* the finish flags, or you will be eliminated. Carefully note where these flags are located.

Mental Preparation

I like to walk the cross-country course several times to get a feel for the ground and the jumps. Once I'm prepared, the morning of the event, I take time before I get on and go over the course in my mind. I personally find it helpful to go off on my own in a quiet place, whether sitting in the car or a quiet room, where I can totally concentrate on what I've got coming up. Sometimes I shut my eyes and, starting at the beginning, I picture how it's going to feel riding up to each jump, and I try to think about what to expect in various circumstances.

Rather than thinking, "That jump is going to ride great!" I feel it is beneficial to expect the unexpected so you are mentally prepared when your ride does not go according to plan. I do not mean that you should go out on course thinking negatively, just that before you leave the starting box, consider all the options and how to react when something unexpected happens.

CHAPTER 13

Warming Up and Riding Cross-Country

WARMING UP

At a one-day Horse Trial you will have already performed your dressage test before cross-country, so your horse is somewhat warmed up. At a Horse Trial that takes place over several days, you need to give your horse a good preparatory warm-up ride before cross-country to get his mind and body ready for the challenge ahead. It is essential to give yourself plenty of time to loosen up your horse's muscles and school a few fences, and to get your horse and yourself in a forward-thinking, positive frame of mind before you set out on course.

Your cross-country warm-up should be calculated—you want to put some thought into it. When things go wrong, you must evaluate the situation. In general, the problem is probably caused by the horse being distracted in the competitive environment, and the fact that you haven't established the same communication that you have at home.

Take your time. If your horse is running away, try to slow down and get away from other horses; jump a jump on your own instead of right on another horse's heels. If he has backed off, get him in front of your leg and paying more attention to you. This all comes back to the connection

13.1 A & B Begin your warm-up with a forward trot and canter for 10 to 15 minutes. I'm warming up Young Man for the CCI** at the 2011 Fair Hill International Three-Day Event in Maryland.

from leg to hand and making sure you're getting the right reaction to your leg.

Be sure to tailor your warm-up to the horse you are riding. For example, some horses get excited before cross-country so jump some fences early so they can calm down and relax before heading to the start box.

1 First, get your horse adjustable on the flat with 10 to 15 minutes of stretching in trot and canter (figs. 13 A & B).

2 Work on his adjustability in the canter. It is important, by the end of this work and for a short amount of time, to get the horse up to

Warming Up and Riding Cross-Country

the speed that he'll actually have to go on cross-country.

3 Give him a short break before you start his short jumping warm-up. This is a good time to talk to other competitors about how the course is riding (fig. 13.2).

4 Generally in the cross-country warm-up area you will have some show jumps as well as some solid, cross-country jumps to school over. Begin with the show jumps and then jump a few solid fences.

5 Horses usually go out at two-minute intervals, so beginning your jumping when there are five to six horses to go before you are scheduled to start, will give you plenty of time to prepare for your ride.

6 When schooling the warm-up fences, remember to keep the red flag on the right and the white flag on the left—the same as on course.

7 Breathe!

13.2 I'm discussing the course with fellow riders Will Coleman (left), Jon Holling, and Boyd Martin (right, on Cold Harbor) at the Fair Hill International CCI**. You can find out valuable information about the course, footing, and how specific jumps are riding by talking with riders who have been watching the competition or have already been around the course.

13.3 A–C Warming up over a cross-rail, vertical, and ascending oxer.

Warm-Up Jumps

Start your cross-country jumping warm-up the same as your warm-ups at home by:

1 Getting to a good, deep takeoff distance by trotting small cross-rails (fig. 13.3 A).

2 Cantering a small oxer.

3 Cantering a vertical (fig. 13.3 B).

Next, start to raise the oxer with the back rail one or two holes higher than the front rail—an ascending oxer (fig. 13.3 C). In most cases, I don't square the oxer because you want your horse jumping in a nice shape, but not backing off as much as before the show jumping phase. A sloping or ascending oxer (one that has lower front rails and is higher at the back) is the best way to accomplish this.

As the jump gets higher, start to add more power to your horse's canter and ride more forward to your oxer. Once you have the jump set to the height of your competition level I would then set up a vertical at a similar height, jump the oxer and then the vertical. Mix this up so you get the feeling of the different ride you need from a wider jump to a vertical and vice versa.

Warming Up and Riding Cross-Country 13

Make sure you have the ability to turn and ride to each jump and that the horse is listening to you and steering well. It is important to then vary your canter approach to the oxer so you can approach it confidently out of a gallop, (the speed for your level on cross-country, not a flat-out gallop) and also approach it in a canter stride that is appropriate for a coffin or sunken road, or any other fence requiring a short canter approach.

Add Solid Fences

- Once your horse is jumping the show jumps well, canter some of the practice cross-country jumps and see how the horse is dealing with solid fences; this will give you a feel for how your horse is going and whether or not he is in front of your leg (fig. 13.4).

- Then approach either a cross-country jump or show jump at different angles so you instill

13.4 Jumping a solid warm-up fence.

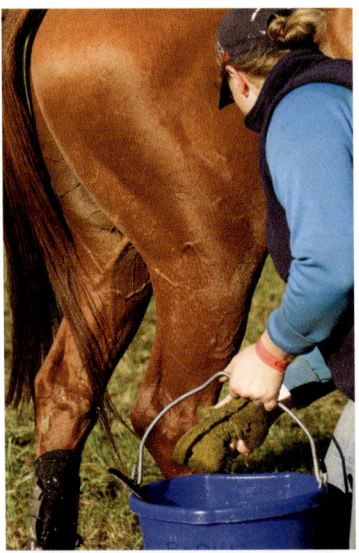

13.5 A–F During a short break before my ride, Emma sponges Young Man's neck and between his hind legs (A & B). Leelee scrapes off the water and sweat, and Evie takes Young Man for a short walk (C & D). I take a moment to have a drink of water and reflect on the course while my helpers tend to my horse (E). They dry off the reins before I remount so they are not slippery (F).

the idea of the horse staying straight on the line on which you approach the jump.

- It is also a good idea to work on getting away from the jump quickly, encouraging the horse to lengthen his stride and pick up speed when he lands after the practice fence.

- To finish off, when I'm on a strong horse I do one or two jumps at a very controlled canter; when on a lazy horse or one that lacks confidence, I gallop one or two jumps to get him going forward.

Walk and Get Focused

On most horses, I like to try to relax them before starting cross-country. Having the horse gallop a warm-up jump, then go straight to the start box is recipe for a "wound-up" horse. He's not going to forget how to jump if you give him a two-minute break! This is also a good chance to adjust any tack, wipe off any sweaty areas including your reins if slippery, and have a quick drink of water before you set out on course (figs. 13.5 A–F and figs. 13.6 A–C).

The Start Box

The start box can be a place where the horse, especially after some experience with the fun of cross-country, starts to anticipate what is coming up. Just being around or standing in the start box can get the horse excited, so especially at the lower levels, teach him to stay calm

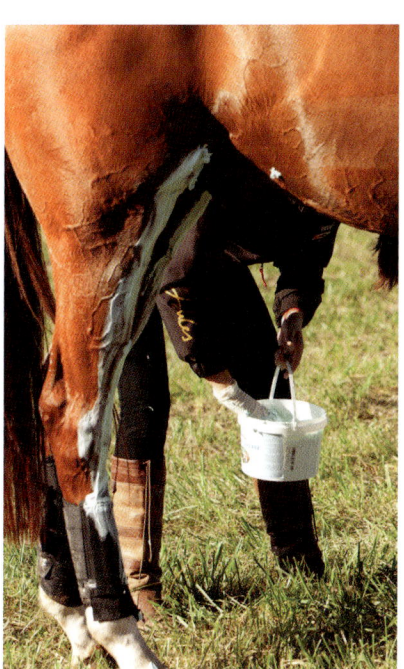

13.6 A–C Leelee greases Young Man's legs.

13.7 Walking the horse around the start box to settle him.

13.8 Canadian Jessica Phoenix checks her watch on the fly.

and not race out of the start box. He needs to understand that the box is an okay place to be, and he does not need to run away from it.

With an OTTB in particular, don't stand in the box too long, letting the horse get stressed, nervous, and anxious. It is better to take your time walking around and then go into the box—even get on course a couple seconds late rather than have to sort out an anxious horse before the first fence.

1 Walking around the outside of the box in a relaxed way is a good way to settle the horse before the start (fig. 13.7). Some horses I've ridden, like The Foreman, get very wound up; I couldn't walk him, so I trotted him around then walked the last step into the box.

2 You usually have a couple of minutes to get into the box. When you are riding a green or nervous horse have somebody lead the horse in or just walk him in and out of the box to reassure him before your countdown begins. If you can make the start box a positive place to be and an easy experience for your horse, it will help you later on in his career.

3 With a tense horse, judging time is crucial so that you only have to spend five seconds or less in the start box. You can then come out of the box riding positively, without having scared him.

4 To time things right, as the starter is beginning to count down from five seconds, I head to the box and hopefully get there with about two seconds to go, and then we're off. Again, I'd rather get in there a bit late than sit in the box trying to hold a horse that is getting really upset.

5 Do not give your horse a sudden kick or startle him into a gallop, but pick up a controlled and organized canter or gallop, keeping him focused and in control.

Note: As mentioned earlier, a stopwatch can be helpful on course, especially at the CCI events where we know where the minute markers are. I generally press the start button on my watch when the timer counts two seconds to go, so on course I am generally a second or two ahead of what the clock says. You can also get a watch that counts down 30 seconds before starting and then ask the starter to give you a 30-second warning before it's time to start your round (fig. 13.8).

RIDING THE COURSE

Set the Tone

- Use the first few fences to get the horse going positively forward while remaining respectful of the jumps.

- As mentioned, the first few fences are usually welcoming, straightforward jumps, and it is important to utilize these by riding forward, keeping your leg on, your shoulders back, and your eyes forward.

Riding for Time

13.9 The best place to save time is to make sure your horse gets away from the fences on landing, as I'm doing here.

13.10 Overall, maintaining a steady pace is the most effective way to make time.

- As I mentioned in the previous chapter, the first and easiest way to make up time on cross-country is on the landing stride of each jump, by getting into the habit of galloping away from the fences (fig. 13.9). When you can be efficient you can aim to save a second per jump. Over a course of 20 to 30 jumps this can really help your time.

- Saving time on the approach to the jump, by maintaining a steady rhythm to the fences and jumping out of stride, is more difficult and something to work on only after you and your horse have a really good partnership on the cross-country.

- By balancing for the fence—that is, slowing the horse down and preparing to jump when you are closer to the fence, rather than far away from it—you save a lot of time. That said, if you are not prepared for the fence early or well enough, you risk having trouble at the jump.

- Some courses ride faster than others. Hilly terrain, fence design, the way they are measured, and the use of wooded areas all affect their timing, as of course, does the weather.

- Timing other competitors before you go, or talking to fellow riders you respect, can also help you decide how hard it will be to make the time. Obviously, the higher up the levels you are competing, the faster you need to travel.

- The effort or skill that goes into making the time will vary from event to event because of different variables that I've already discussed. It's good to plan the speed you need to travel before setting out.

- Try to *average* your speed around the course; it's easier on your horse when you consistently go at the right speed rather than making him sprint and accelerate (fig. 13.10).

- Lastly, remember it's much more important to have a good jumping round than it is to make the time allowed. And, you don't make good time unless your horse jumps well. I always have that in my mind when I set off.

Warming Up and Riding Cross-Country

- Keep in mind the takeoff distance: You don't want to come to these jumps "holding back" to a deep distance, which just makes your horse defensive and hesitant. You want to ride forward to a deep distance, which keeps him in a more positive and determined frame of mind.

- When you have a big, strong horse that tends to pull, the first few fences are a good opportunity to let him settle and relax. If he is rushing being too bold and aggressive, he is not thinking enough, which often leads to him not jumping safely. Keep things quiet and relaxed to help him keep focused.

- A green or less bold horse needs to be encouraged to go forward at the first few fences to get his "heart into it." Keep in mind what kind of horse you have, how he feels on that day, then ride accordingly over the first few straightforward jumps.

Making Time

Depending on your horse, you may or may not plan to try to make the optimum time on course. When weather or footing are not ideal; you are riding a green horse that needs a slow confidence-making round; or it is your first time competing at a higher level, think about riding a little conservatively. Don't make crossing the finish line under the time allowed your first priority.

If you are setting out to make a fast time, get into the habit of really getting away from each fence and accelerating to a speed that is appropriate to your horse, the course, and making the time.

Generally after the first few jumps you will be presented with a jump that requires some adjustment of your horse's stride, whether it is a turning exercise that requires you to bring the horse back to a controlled canter and turn sharply; shortening the canter to a combination; or some other question. So once you've got those first few forward-riding jumps out of the way, start to test your horse or "feel his brakes" before you get to this first real question, making sure that he is going to be "adjustable" and listen to you when you ask him to alter his stride.

Make Adjustments as Necessary

Once you've negotiated that first big question, get back into a rhythm and focus on making the time, if this is your goal. Reevaluate how your horse is going and what you need to do to improve the round. This can be something as simple as taking a little bit more time before each jump to balance him if you're not meeting the takeoff distance as smoothly as you'd like, or it can mean a more aggressive ride at each jump to keep the horse more committed and "honest" to the fence. Really evaluate your round as you're going along, rather than let a small problem spiral into a big one.

A good cross-country rider also thinks ahead and knows what is coming up next and what kind of ride he's going to need at the upcoming jumps. For instance:

- If your horse is a little bit "sticky" about water, use your whip at the jump *before* the water to really have him at his best when he gets to the water jump.

- If your horse is hard to turn right or left, do a bending exercise, it is smart to really slow up and get him back and listening to you quite early before you approach one of these turning exercises.

13.11 When your horse makes an extraordinary jumping effort, like Connaught here at Rolex Kentucky 2008, a good secure riding position is essential.

Rider Position

In the training chapter I talked about the importance of rider position (see p. 117). When you walk the course, make note of any jump that is going to require you to have exceptionally good balance and a secure position so you can prepare yourself properly before it. And, as you ride, constantly go over how you can get yourself and your horse ready for each upcoming jump (fig. 13.11).

For instance:

- When there is a big drop fence start to prepare your contact so that the reins will slip through your fingers as you jump. This helps ensure your body is not "thrown" forward by gravity as the horse drops down off the edge of the fence (figs. 13.12 A–C).

- Conversely, when jumping some steps up, or over a big jump going up a hill, start to shorten your contact and be in a more forward position with your upper body.

The Aggressive Horse

Many horses will start to change the way they go as you are progressing around the cross-country course. It's ideal when the horse gains confidence as he goes around and becomes in sync with you for a nice forward, confident round. Sometimes, however, a not very confident horse will change to being quite aggressive the farther he goes. We have to be good enough to feel this and start to change *our* ride accordingly.

When he gets stronger and less respectful of the jumps, it is dangerous to allow him keep accelerating out of control (figs. 13.13 A–C). You need to slow him down and spend more time on the approach to the fences. Work on getting him lighter in his contact so that the jumps "hold" him and he doesn't keep accelerating on the approach. When he does this, instead of being "respectful" of the jump, the horse is showing no judgment: He doesn't shorten his stride and he gets too close to the jump on takeoff.

This means that on the approach you should:

1 Bring the horse's head up.

2 Sit deeper in the saddle and close your leg

13.12 A–C You need to be able to adjust your position and ride the horse that you have at the moment.

13.13 A–C The rider needs to react to how the horse is feeling and jumping. Woodburn nearing the end of the course at the 2010 WEG was still going strong after quite a long and challenging course.

to create a canter where he gets lighter and comes off your hand.

3 In some cases, this means that you have to be stronger with your hand, making fairly aggressive half-halts so that you can then let go or lighten up the contact.

4 Just constantly holding on is usually not a good answer: You need to create a "feel" so

the horse is not leaning against you on the approach to the jump.

The Nervous Horse

A different situation arises with a horse that has lost some confidence during the cross-country round and is now starting to question each jump. You need to be a little more aggressive with him, keeping your upper body slightly back and defensive, with your leg on and really encouraging him to be more committed and more forward at the jumps.

The Tired Horse

When a horse is starting to get fatigued, his reactions and skills are not as sharp as usual; the time he takes to come back to you is slower and his natural "cleverness" will not be as good.

In the big, major Four-Star events you can hear the phrase on the loudspeaker, "The rider is nursing the horse home," which means he is taking it slowly, keeping nice and balanced and not trying to jump quickly. Everything is very methodical, controlled, and slower to allow the horse time to evaluate the jumps and get home safely.

The "feel" of riding a tired horse is not something you experience when training; it usually only happens in competition and is more common in the CCI events where the courses are longer. Having this possibility stored in your mind is the first step to understanding when you have a tired horse on the course.

You need to be aware at all times how your horse is feeling. Every horse will become tired at some point, slowing his reaction times. And, there can come a time when your horse is so fatigued that you will need to slow down for him to catch his breath—or, in extreme cases, just pull up and call it a day.

Also, if at any stage you feel your horse has really "lost the plot" on cross-country and is being dangerous, it is appropriate to call it quits for that day. As you spend more time in the saddle, you will learn how to judge your horse's fitness and way of going.

Expect the Unexpected

An element of cross-country riding is your instinct or "being in the moment." You have to be able to react to what happens to you and your horse on that day. You can walk the course and plan as many times as you like, but the nature of the cross-country phase is that every horse, at some point on course, is going to react a little differently from another. To have a successful ride in spite of an unexpected turn of events:

- Be focused and sharp enough to feel the change in your horse and react when it happens.

- This can be something as simple as the horse slipping on a turn, knuckling over going into water, getting panicked and racing away, spooking, or making some other unpredictable move.

- Start this phase knowing that anything is possible; don't get put off when something happens unexpectedly. We riders have to be flexible and not get easily distracted in order to be able to deal with problems—and carry on.

A "Hold" On Course

Sometimes, your round can be interrupted because of a "hold" on course, which usually occurs because a rider ahead of you has had a problem. An official stops you in between jumps—or at a jump—and notes the time; you wait there until the course is open again.

13.14 You should have a calculated round right through to the finish line, paying attention to your pace, how your horse is galloping and jumping, and riding appropriately.

1 First thing, make sure the official writes down the time when you are stopped. Keep your horse alert so that he realizes that his cross-country round is not over.

2 You have the right to take plenty of time to warm up when you are told you can start again. You may take a practice jump if you wish. When you are stopped before a straightforward fence, the practice jump probably won't be necessary, but if you are held before a more difficult fence like a water complex, it is appropriate. An official will tell you which one you can jump.

When you are held for a very long time, you can get off your horse, but make sure you have time to get back on and warm up before you start out on course again. While outside help is usually considered unauthorized assistance and a cause for elimination, while you are being held you may receive help to care for your horse. In extreme heat, for example, you can get help cooling the horse off a bit, or if it's cold, someone can get you a quarter sheet or blanket so the horse's muscles stay warm.

Riding the Finish

As you approach the last part of the course it is important not to let the thrill of galloping at speed overtake your common sense and judgment. Keep a calm head all the way through the course and do not become overconfident about your abilities; you should really have a calculated round right through to the finish line (fig. 13.14).

TIPS: Dos and Don'ts

- Don't be aggressive by asking your horse to jump fences from too far away or at too fast a speed. This will likely catch up with you, and your horse—if not on this day then some time in the future.

- Remember to ride every fence, including the last one—it's not over until you cross that finish line!

- I don't think it shows great horsemanship to gallop flat-out for the finish line. Instead, let your horse "coast" through the finish flags and then gradually slow up. Allow him to trot, then walk before dismounting.

- Abruptly pulling up is not good for your horse, (the exception being if he has sustained an injury). With a very strong horse, pulling up gradually may be easier said than done, and you might have to strongly encourage him to slow down.

- No matter how your ride went, treat your horse with respect and spend time cooling him out, giving him a bath and a good grooming (see p. 304). Check his legs and body for injury and treat as necessary. Make sure that he is well cared for after the efforts of the day.

14.1 Woodburn is calm and steady in the show jumping at the 2010 WEG.

CHAPTER 14

Walking and Riding the Show Jumping Course

WALKING THE COURSE

Walking the show jumping course and coming up with a plan is crucial to a successful ride. This is your opportunity to assess not only the jumps but the terrain and footing, the surroundings, and get an overall impression of the course.

Before you begin:

1 Your first impression of the course—its layout, and position of the judge's box—can help you plan for how you'll enter the arena from the warm-up area.

2 Some horses are better if you enter at a strong canter, which signals to them that you want them to be forward and stay in front of your leg. Other horses are better when you arrive at a relaxed trot: These are usually the types that tend to get stronger in the ring, so entering the arena in a relaxed way gives them the idea that they should stay calm and quiet during the round (fig. 14.1).

3 Figure out where and how you're going to enter the arena so you can give your horse a little preview of what's to come: Think about which fences you want to walk and canter past. The rules state that you can't show your horse any fences, but when there is something "spooky," whether a Liverpool or a combination, it is not a bad idea to walk, trot, or canter past that jump to give your horse some confidence that it's going to be okay to jump it.

4 It is appropriate to halt or walk and salute the judge before you begin your round, so when you walk the course you should figure out where you will do that. After you salute, you have 45 seconds from the time the judge rings a bell or blows a whistle to go between the start flags. This is plenty of time, so don't rush.

Planning this part of your ride—how you will get to the start flags from where you salute the judge—is important as well. In these 45 seconds you have an ideal opportunity to establish the kind of canter approach you need for the rest of your round. If necessary, you should have time to make a second circle to be sure the horse is in front of your leg before you approach the first fence.

The positioning of the start flags and first fence may determine the lead you come in on, but in many show jumping courses you can approach on either lead. Most horses have a dominant lead so choose your horse's best one for the approach. When you have to turn left after the first fence and approach it on the right lead, the horse will take a left lead after the fence and vice versa—something to take into account as you develop your plan.

The first fence is very important. I always want to ride this fence confidently to set a precedent for how I want the round to go. Gauging how your horse reacts to the first fence and making appropriate adjustments will be essential to establishing the kind of ride you want—right from the start of the course.

As you walk the course, walking the line you plan to ride is important, rather than just wandering from jump to jump. Plan the lines to give your horse time to see each jump, but not with such "wide" turns that you are likely to get time faults. The judge—or technical delegate—usually measures the course where a good horse is able to hold the line between jumps. In most cases, the course is not measured very "wide," though you should not have to cut every turn either. You should be able to stay on a line between the jumps that is reasonably efficient. If you have a horse that tends to jump more cleanly on a shorter stride, take into account where you can cut the turns to save some time. Plan this in your course.

Of course, you need to know exactly where you will be going. Even before you walk, study the course map and have it memorized so when riding you don't have to put a lot of thought into where to go. Your mind should be directed toward creating the right balance and ride for your horse to jump cleanly.

Consider that as the course goes on, some horses tend to get stronger and start pulling against the rider as they get excited about jumping and galloping. If this is likely, make mental notes of where you can rebalance to settle your horse and get through the last part of the course.

Notice if there are parts where you will have time to regroup, usually where there is some time between the jumps (when they're not "related," see below). It is helpful to make a mental note that when you get to this point, you should quickly evaluate how your horse is going so that you can rebalance, get the horse more in front of your leg, or do whatever is needed to help with the rest of the course. Too often, we finish a round thinking, "I wish I'd got him in front of my leg," or "I wish I'd had him more organized," so it's important to have a feel for how the horse is going and make adjustments as necessary.

An overview of your course walk is not only to get to know the course well and remember the order of fences and direction you jump them, but also to make a plan for how to best prepare your horse for each jump.

Related Distances

When walking the course, a "related line" means that between each jump you can make a decision about how many strides you want your horse to put in between fences. When coming up with a plan, take into account whether your horse is long- or short-strided. This helps you plan for how to approach the first jump in a related line. Watching the first horses go on course is also a good way to help you devise a plan. Keep in mind that when they see two jumps in a row, some horses are more aggressive while others tend to back off.

- When the distance between two jumps is more than six strides, I suggest not getting too concerned about striding and just ride each fence separately. Once a line has more than six strides, the amount of change in the horse's stride length is such that you're better off not being set on the striding but rather riding the stride that you have at the time.

- When the related distance is three strides or fewer, in nearly all cases the striding is not very flexible since you will not have room to add a stride.

- When the distance is one, two, or three strides, be aware of whether it is going to be a "forward" or "holding" one, two or three-stride. (See p. 157 for more on distances.)

- If the first jump in a related line is an oxer, the line will ride *longer* than if the first fence is a vertical. Usually, the horse will land farther out from a vertical than an oxer. When there is "filler" under a jump or if it is a Liverpool, your horse will also land farther away from the jump.

- If a related line is set in four, five, or six strides, you have the option of keeping the same striding as the line walked or, if your horse feels hesitant, possibly adding an extra stride. The disadvantage of adding a stride is that it takes more time, and sometimes the horse will resist you more and lose some power when you add a stride. However, for others, adding a stride helps them to jump better because it helps set them up, rebalance, and it creates a canter so the horse doesn't jump as flat. Again, get to know your horse and the best ride for him.

Consider the type of jump you are approaching to help you determine whether to add a stride or keep riding in a forward, open stride. If you are approaching a big, wide Liverpool it does not make sense to add a stride because the horse needs to be going forward and be a little bit bold in order to clear the spread of the fence.

However, if you are approaching a small vertical or even two verticals on a short stride, or a plank fence or stile, it makes sense to rebalance your horse and shorten his stride so that you do not have a flat, forward stride when you approach the fence. In this situation, when you walk the course, come up with a plan for how to ride each of these related lines based on how your horse goes, what would be the best ride for him, and also taking the design of the course into account.

Combinations

Combination jumps are numbered as one jump with up to three efforts—A, B, C. If you have a refusal at any of the elements, you must go back and start jumping at A, even when you had a refusal at the B or C element. When you walk the course, notice the layout of the combination and where the arena's outside fence and the other jumps are located. This will help you figure out the best plan for re-approaching the combination should you have a problem.

When some horses see jumps in close proximity, they panic and want to rush through them, while others have the opposite response—they get cautioius and back off. How you jump the first fence in the combination affects how the rest of the combination is going to ride.

The type of fences also make a difference: An oxer to a vertical will likely require a more forward ride than a combination with the vertical jump first. As I talked about before, horses land farther away from a vertical than an oxer. When it's a scary jump in, you may need to ride more assertively over that first fence.

If your horse tends to drift when he jumps or doesn't stay straight, recognize and account for this in your approach. Drifting or jumping crooked shows up a lot more in a combination where you have one jump after another, as the problem tends to become compounded as you proceed down the line.

To correct this as your horse is jumping, think about holding him straight as he leaves the ground. Also, if the horse drifts left, go down the left side of the line, closer to the standards, which will act as sort of a "V" pole like you used in training. This may keep your horse straight and probably make him jump higher.

Watch Other Horses Go

Once you have walked the course, if you have the opportunity to watch other horses go around, it can help you decide things like how many strides your horse might take through the combination, or how to approach different fences. Make note of any horse on course that is somewhat similar to yours and how he is going. Conversely, if you are riding a short-striding

Walking and Riding the Show Jumping Course 14

horse, for example, and are watching a horse with a huge stride, keep in mind that you will need a different type of ride.

WARMING UP

Your show jumping warm-up is a cross between the dressage and cross-country warm-ups. Have your horse relaxed because he'll be more careful about his jump than an excited or nervous horse. You also need the horse to be responsive—the same as for cross-country, where he gallops forward and comes back to you on command.

Your flatwork encompasses everything you have to do on course without actually jumping: lengthening the stride, shortening the stride, and softly changing direction. So address the

14.2 I prefer allowing the horse to have a higher head carriage when approaching a jump—even above the bit is better than a low head carriage.

weaknesses of your horse in show jumping on the flat. If your horse is generally behind your leg or a bit lazy then getting him to be really eager to go forward is probably a good tactic. When your horse tends to rush the fences, warming up with a lot of transitions from trot to canter and back, keeps his mind on his job so he doesn't just rush off.

A typical warm-up for the jumping phase looks something like this:

- I usually allow 15 minutes for the flatwork section. This leaves time for some quiet, soft, stretching work in the trot and canter and then some work in the canter getting the horse adjustable, going forward off my leg easily and coming back when I ask, and turning both left and right easily and willingly. This canter is usually at show jumping speed, around 350 mpm.

- Vary your seat so that you can sit down in the saddle or slightly out of the saddle in a two-point position. In your show jumping flatwork, the emphasis is not so much on the "roundness" of the horse but getting him to react quickly. Having your horse round will not necessarily make him jump better, but having a good connection from your leg to your hand is important.

- You can have a horse with a higher head carriage on the approach to the jump as long as you don't have a lot of resistance from the horse. I think you will find that the horse doesn't jump as well if he is down on his forehand or has a really low head carriage, so having a horse what we call "up in front" and, in some cases, even "above the bit" is preferred (fig. 14.2).

- The flying change is important in show jumping so your horse can jump a course without a lot of resistance or interruption in his gait, and to maintain a steady rhythm. Practicing some changes before your ride is helpful; however, teaching your horse how to do a flying change in the warm-up ring is not a good idea! If your changes are not established, practicing how to hold the counter-canter would be more beneficial.

Jumping in Warm-Up

Your jumping warm-up should take around 10 to 12 minutes only. I usually wait for the fifth horse ahead of me in the jumping order to go into the ring before I start to jump. Jumping your horse early and then waiting around is not good because the horse loses his focus. And, if you jump him too much you end up wearing him out. There's a real knack to knowing how much or how little to jump in the warm-up ring, and a lot depends on the individual horse.

There is also a mental aspect to show jumping preparation. When I warm up a horse for cross-country, I push the horse a little more forward, since I want him to go out feeling brave. For show jumping, the horse needs to be responsive to me so I'll have a slower, more dressage-oriented warm-up. You want him to understand that there is a difference between the two phases, and with experience, he will begin to know one from another.

1 It is best to begin with a low jump like a cross-rail. Starting in trot gets through to the horse that you want him to stay relaxed in spite of the show environment. At home you have practiced waiting for the jump and getting to a deep distance, so trotting in and cantering away from a cross-rail is a good way to start.

2 Try cantering the cross-rail and really put an emphasis on keeping the horse in a steady, even rhythm, not rushing or dropping behind your leg in the approach or when cantering away.

3 Then I usually jump a small oxer. Working over an oxer is a good way of getting the jump to "hold" the horse and also to create a nice shape (bascule) when he jumps. I start with a couple of canter approaches, again working on the control and evenness of the canter and getting a deep distance to the jump.

4 Start to make the oxer bigger in an ascending way, that is, with the back rail higher than the front, probably by about two holes (fig. 14.3). This is the stage where you get the horse to really work and get into a nice jumping frame. The lower front rail allows him to gradually improve his jump. As each height becomes easier for him, it is appropriate to raise the front and back rails by one to two holes. At each height you can probably jump two, possibly three times before raising it.

5 As the jump gets higher the difficulty is increased, so you need to add more power in the canter on the approach. Keep in mind the principles of an even stride, close distance, straightness to the jump and a nice canter departure away from the jump. It is also important to approach the jump from both directions, and on each lead, in order to work both sides of the horse. Vary your approach between a big, long one and an approach off a tighter turn.

6 As you increase the height of the oxer, also increase the width, still with a lower front rail than back rail. Keep making this larger until you get the height you'll be jumping in the ring. At most events they have a mark on the warm-up fences indicating the maximum height you are allowed to jump. I usually recommend warming up to this height, though, very occasionally, when a horse lacks confidence I jump smaller fences.

7 Once you are jumping the maximum height, vary the approach so you can ride into the oxer with a more "open" stride as well as a "waiting" stride.

8 By this stage you are getting close to having your horse ready for the show jumping round. It is beneficial now to take a little break and evaluate how he's going and how

14.3 I'm jumping an ascending oxer in the warm-up ring.

he feels, and whether there is anything you need to fine tune.

9 The last few jumps are important. First, the clock is ticking and you don't have much time. Second, you want to finish your warm-up by giving your horse confidence before you go into the arena.

10 This is the time to square up the oxer: Ride your horse nice and forward to the oxer. If he hits the front rail, fine. This is a nice friendly reminder that you want him to really pick up his legs and be careful in the ring. If he jumps it well, you're in good shape! If he makes a small mistake he'll probably improve next time around.

11 When he has a bad jump, however, go around again and maybe even lower the fence so you finish on a confident note (figs.14 A & B).

12 The last jump I warm up over is a vertical. With many horses, these are more difficult to ride and require a more careful approach with a slightly shorter canter. This is a good, organized way to wrap things up before going into the ring.

13 I like to let the horse walk as I evaluate the course by watching the horse in front of me go.

If you finish your warm-up with time to spare, it's not advisable to do a lot more jumping, since you'll just wear the horse out. Instead, practice a few transitions forward and back in the canter to keep the horse sharp, then jump one final vertical before you go in the ring.

14.4 A & B Young Man knocking a rail down in the warm-up at Fair Hill.

RIDING YOUR SHOW JUMPING ROUND

1 Enter the ring at the trot or canter, depending on your horse. It is important to keep the horse really in front of your leg—not aggressively, but he should be thinking forward and understanding that you are in charge and that he has a job to do.

2 Before you begin your round make a circle around some of the jumps, maybe the Liverpool or a combination, so the horse has a chance to feel comfortable in there.

3 You also need to halt and salute the judge before you cross the starting line. After the judge rings the bell or blows a whistle you have 45 seconds to canter through the flags. This is plenty of time, so don't feel rushed. It's a great chance for you to get your horse in front of your leg and approach the first fence exactly how you want to ride it.

4 Often you'll have the option of approaching the first fence on either canter lead. Make this decision depending on which side he is strongest, or based on the course and what is the best approach to the fence. Be positive

14.5 A positive first fence sets up the horse for a good round.

14.6 A & B When the horse knocks a rail down keep riding forward to your next fence.

and forward to your first jump as it sets the tone for the rest of the course. This reminds your horse of what you have been practicing and sets you up for a nice round (fig. 14.5).

5 After the first fence it is important to evaluate the horse so you can make adjustments as needed. Nobody quite knows how their horse will react in the ring until he gets there. If your horse is getting really strong, find a way to help him settle down. On the other hand, if he is backing off and dropping behind your leg, you need to urge him forward.

6 Sometimes a horse will change his way of going at some point within the round: He might start out feeling like he is backing off but halfway get very strong. Be flexible and not just stuck on one plan—in other words, you need to ride the horse, not just the course. Get prepared for each jump and create the different types of canter needed for the various types of jumps.

14.7 Cutting corners can save valuable time on course.

14.8 As you jump the last fence, don't let your guard down; keep riding all the way through the finish flags, then give your horse a pat for a job well done!

7 If you have a fence down don't dwell on it (figs. 14.6 A & B). Ride on.

8 Time is important, so being aware of your turns and shaving or cutting time where possible is key (fig. 14.7). Don't take undue risks and cause your horse to have a fence down because you've rushed him at it.

9 Keep thinking ahead and riding all the way to the finish flags (fig. 14.8).

PART 4

CARE and MAINTENANCE

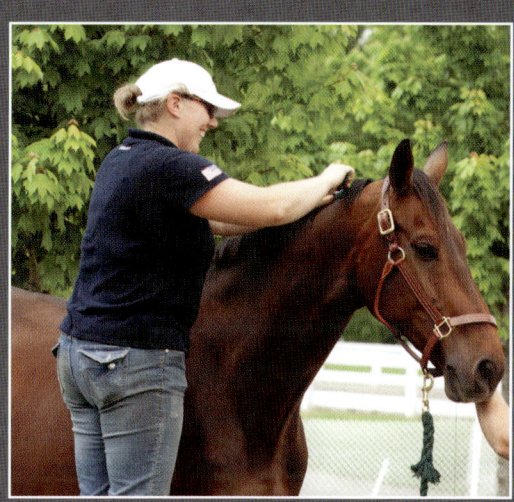

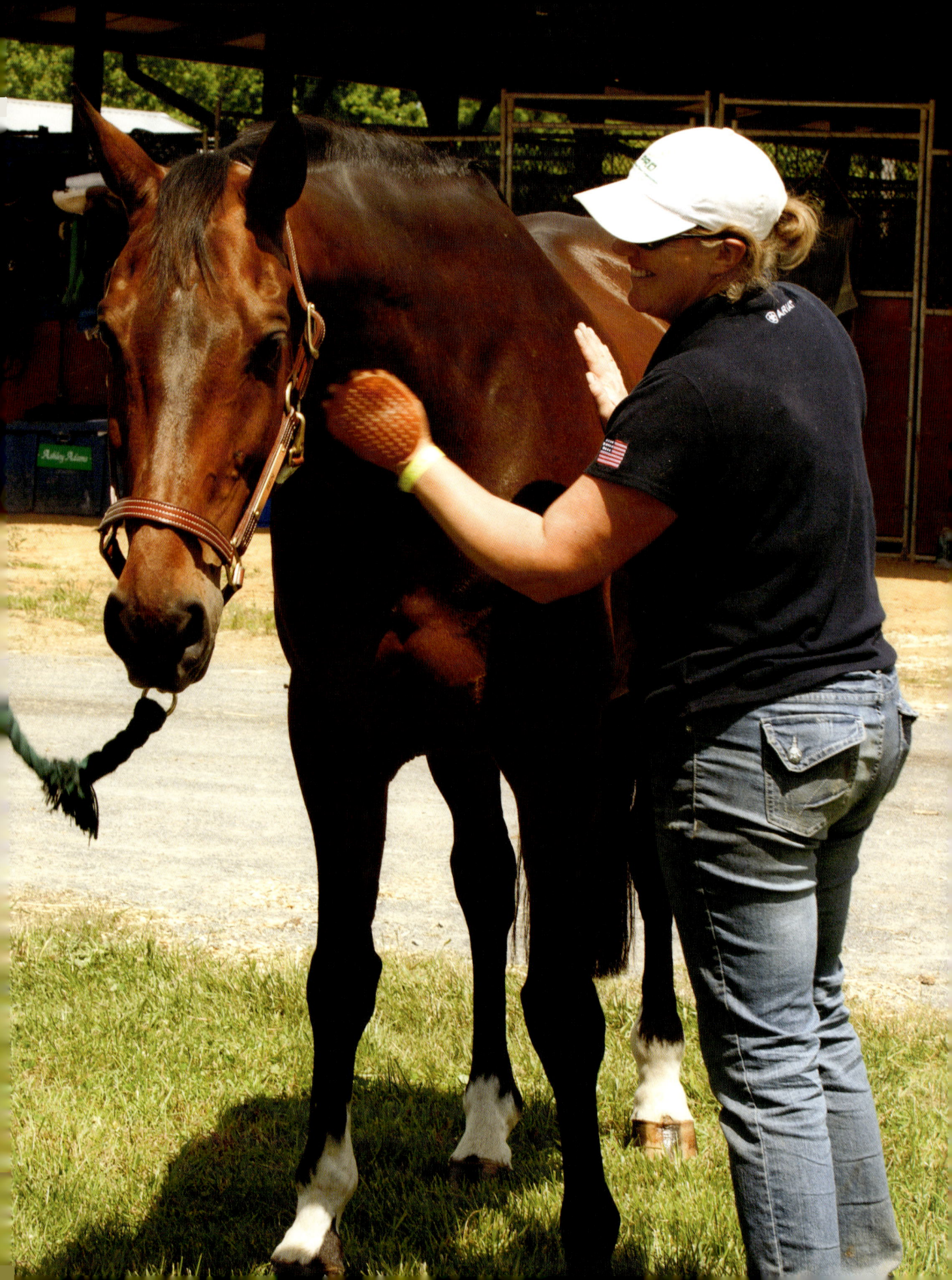

CHAPTER 15

Grooming

By Emma Ford
Former Head Girl at True Prospect Farm

Introduction to Emma

Getting to know your horse and his health and habits is really crucial to having a happy and successful partnership. If you are in a situation where you only have the one horse, really spending time with him and getting to know all of his personality traits goes a long way to creating a successful partnership. Simple knowledge like what your horse likes to eat and how much; whether he puts on weight easily; the way his legs look when he comes out of his stall and after he's been worked; what makes him happy in the barn; and whether he is happier with another horse for company or prefers to be on his own, these are all important pieces of the puzzle—and the list goes on and on. Getting to know your horse is part of being a true horseman.

In my situation, where I have a lot of horses, I employ what could be termed a "groom" to oversee things and manage my horses on a full-time basis. This job means catering to all their needs and spending nearly every day with this one thing in mind. Emma Ford was until very recently my Head Girl in charge, and I relied heavily on her to give me feedback. I trusted her to do everything for the horses to be healthy and happy.

Each morning Emma checked all the horses' legs, feet, and body for any abnormalities or changes, and she made sure that they were eating and passing manure normally. She oversaw their turnout and prepared them and tacked them up for their daily rides. She also did a proper cool down after riding, then at the end of the day, groomed them and gave medical attention when necessary before they were put away for the night.

In this chapter, beginning with "Maintenance" below, Emma describes what she looks for and what she does to keep the horses at their absolute best. I'm very privileged to have had somebody like Emma working for me, who is as good as anybody in the world at caring for horses.

About Emma

British native Emma Ford kept Phillip's barn organized and his horses looking their best from 2005 to 2012. She has traveled with the horses to Germany; England; the 2007 Pan-Am Games in Rio de Janeiro, Brazil; the 2008 Olympic Games in Hong Kong; the 2010 Alltech World Equestrian Games in Lexington, Kentucky; and the 2012 Olympic Games in London, England.

15.1 Emma Ford.

MAINTENANCE

I groom the horses every day, not only to keep their coats clean and shiny but to thoroughly check their well-being. To me the grooming process is about going over the horse's entire body, looking for any abnormalities—whether swelling and heat in the legs, a growth, or a skin condition like rain rot or fungus. Depending on what I find, I have various products to treat different conditions and issues (fig. 15.2). Obviously, when I find anything wrong with a horse's legs, I have the vet check him out before he is ridden.

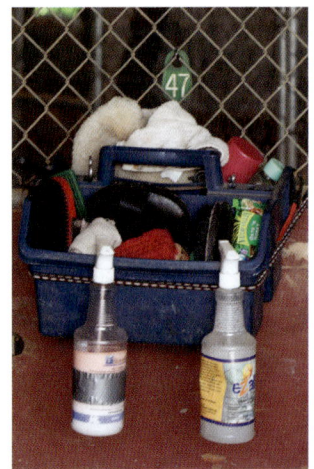

15.2 Emma's grooming kit.

Grooming 15

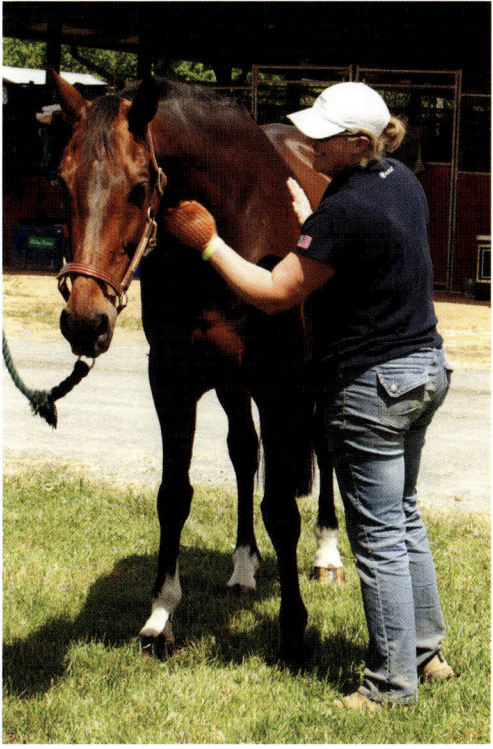

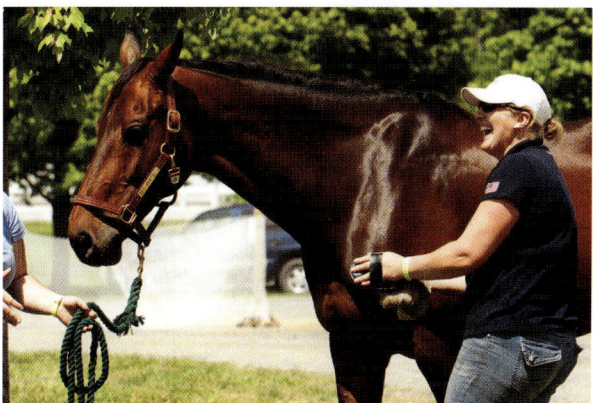

15.3 A-C Currying the horse with the jelly mitt and following with the body brush and damp towel.

Daily Grooming

For daily grooming I start with the feet, work on the coat and the mane and tail, then finish up with the feet again:

1. Picking feet: This is a good chance to check for thrush or any irregularities like a loose shoe. Use the hoof pick from heel to toe and clean out the dirt and manure caked in there, making sure to check for any small stones that can get wedged into the bottom of the hoof.

2. When I brush the horse's coat I start with a "jelly mitt" to curry the horse's entire body, including the face. One side is soft, so I use that on sensitive areas like the head and lower legs. When the horse is thin-skinned I use this soft side on the body as well, but with less sensitive horses I use the harder side on the body (fig. 15.3 A).

3. Next, I use a body brush and a damp towel to brush the horse from head to toe, wiping the brush on the towel every four to five strikes to remove dust (figs. 15.3 B & C). Finally, I spray coat conditioner on a towel and wipe it over the entire body.

MODERN EVENTING WITH PHILLIP DUTTON 237

15.4 A & B Spraying detangler and combing the tail.

4 Now I comb the mane over. If the mane doesn't lie flat, I wet it first to keep it tidy.

5 I spray detangler in the tail hair before brushing it, though, on a daily basis, I only run my fingers through the tail. I only use a comb or brush at a show, when the hair is really clean, because they tend to break and rip the hair out when overused (figs. 15.4 A & B).

6 I finish by applying hoof oil. I like Effol® Hoof Oil from Schweizer-Effax GmbH for soles, heels and hoof wall.

Treats

I'm definitely not against the use of treats! Carrots are number one and Mrs. Pastures Cookies for Horses are a close second. I use treats for horses that are tricky around their heads so that they eventually understand that brushing their head can be a positive experience and learn to lower their head willingly. This takes time but, after a while, most horses come around and enjoy it.

Bath Time

Providing the horse has no skin issues I tend, on a daily basis, to just hose him off with plain water after he is ridden, according to how hard he has worked (figs. 15.5 A–D).

Should a horse develop hives, there are various products available. Before using harsh, medicated shampoo I try washing him with apple cider vinegar, putting about a pint of vinegar into a 5-gallon bucket of water. Let that mixture sit on the coat for at least five minutes before scraping off the excess, then dry with a towel.

Grooming 15

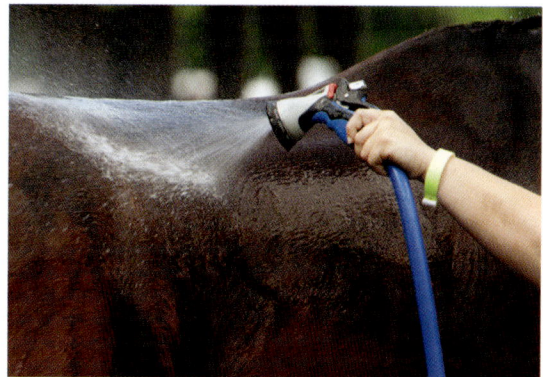

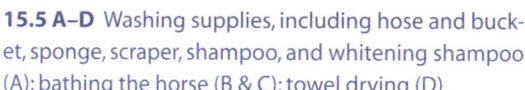
15.5 A–D Washing supplies, including hose and bucket, sponge, scraper, shampoo, and whitening shampoo (A); bathing the horse (B & C); towel drying (D).

The day before a competition, each horse gets a "show bath." At the competitions, the horses are bathed with shampoo every day. It is very important to thoroughly towel-dry them once they have been scraped off, prioritizing areas such as the head, ears, and lower legs to prevent skin issues. In an ideal situation, horses can be hand-grazed outdoors to dry. This helps to prevent future skin irritation as they tend to dry quicker and more thoroughly outdoors

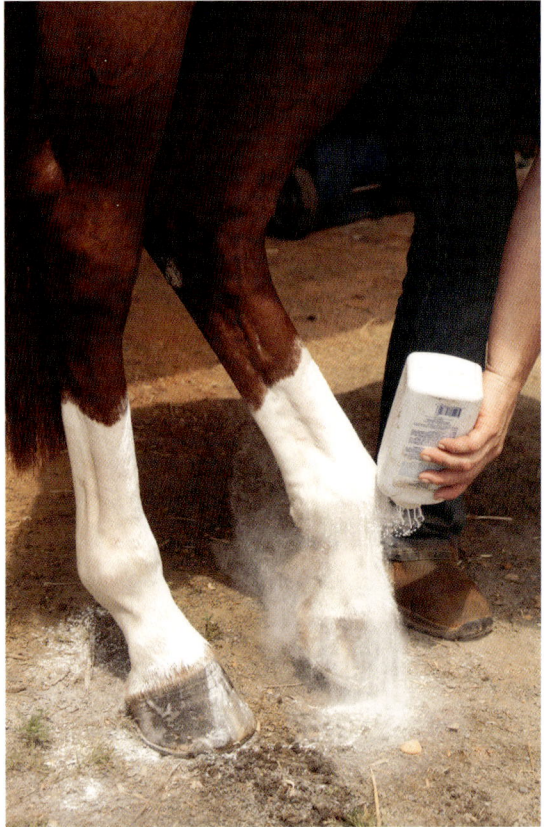
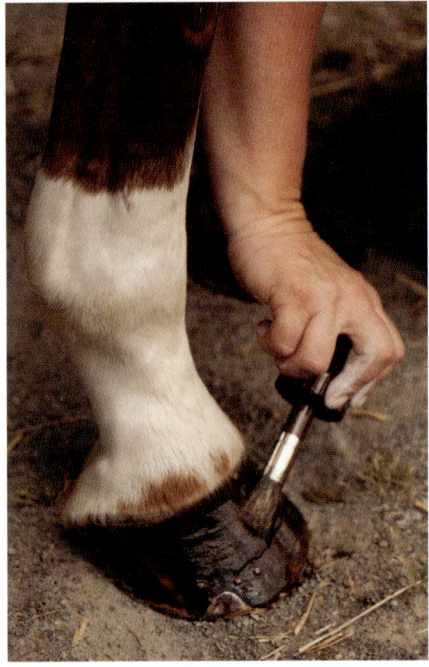
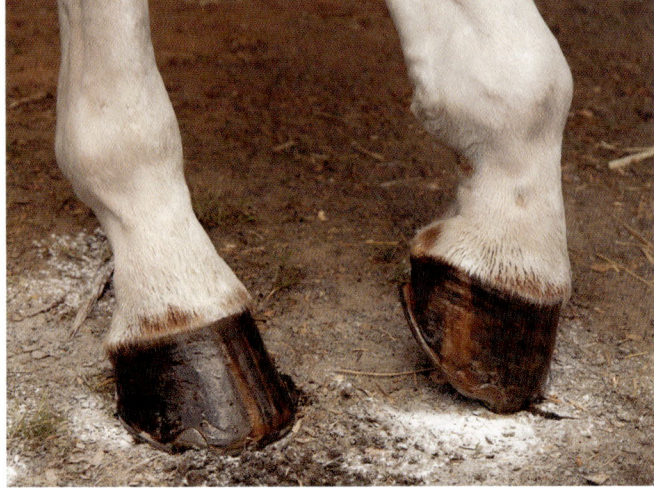

15.6 A–D Washing socks (A). Baby powder helps socks look brighter (B). Apply hoof polish after baby powder (C). Ready for the show ring (D).

than they do standing around in their stalls. I do not believe in daily bathing of horses, which strips their coat of its natural oils making it dull.

Keeping Whites *White*

To truly maintain a horse's white areas you need to take care of them on a regular basis (fig. 15. 6 A). The key ingredient is elbow grease!

- Heavily stained hair is nearly impossible to get clean; purple/bluing (for example Quic Silver™) shampoo is most effective but, on occasion, I also use Tide® detergent, which really gets stains out. This should not be done daily as it dries out the horse's skin.

- For white tails, I leave the bluing shampoo on and braid the tail overnight–it may leave a slightly bluish cast, but that looks better than yellow. If left in for too long, however, it can leave the tail very blue! For initial cleaning I put the shampoo on for two hours and then wash it out thoroughly with regular shampoo or soap: Ivory® dish detergent is cheap and works well.

- As a spot remover add Quic Silver shampoo to rubbing alcohol and spray it on spots to remove stains and then wipe off with a towel. For stubborn stains, let it soak for a bit.

- Baby powder, rubbed in to *slightly* damp legs–when the legs are very wet it will clump–can be used to whiten socks. Do this *before* you apply hoof polish (figs. 15.6 B–D) so you don't make a sticky mess on the feet.

Physical Health: Skin/Feet Problems

Tricks of the Trade

- Witch hazel is a very good astringent and not as irritating and drying to the skin as rubbing alcohol. I use it to treat mild fungal infections like rain rot, and it's very good at lifting dirt from the skin. For a horse that is tricky about having his face brushed and washed, I often spray witch hazel on a towel and use that to gently clean his face and remove any sweat marks.

- I use vitamin E products—oil and creams—on dry elbows, hot spots, or any "rubbed" areas, such as happens with winter blankets on the horse's shoulders.

- For fungus or skin irritation, it might be necessary to bathe the horse with some sort of medicated shampoo. Once the unhealthy skin has been removed, I use a product called Shapley's™ Original M-T-G. For really bad cases on the legs (scratches), I use silver sulfadiazene cream (SSD), available over the counter from pharmacies, which is actually a burn cream that inhibits the growth of bacteria and fungus. Then I wrap the horse's legs overnight. (Any silver products are good at removing fungus and bacteria from the skin: Equifit has a good line, called AgSilver™, which includes a wound spray, talc, and healing balm.)

- It's important to know whether your horse's feet are brittle or soft; if he is turned out in wet conditions frequently you don't want to

15.7 A–C Speed clip (A); trace clip (B); clipping supplies (C).

soften the hooves up too much. To encourage growth of good hoof wall I like Cornucrescine Hoof Ointment (Carr & Day & Martin), rubbed into the coronary band. We use Birdsall's Farrier's Barrier, which you only apply two or three times a week to help balance the moisture level of the foot. For showing, I just use Fiebing's Hoof Dressing, which I paint on and let dry.

Clipping

- On a regular basis, I keep the horses' whiskers, ears, and lower legs tidy with clippers. Body clipping is done October through December. The objective is to remove the heavy winter coat so that horses in work can cool out easier and dry quicker, which prevents them catching a chill. Coats are also much easier to take care of when they're clipped during the winter months. The type of clip depends on the level of work the horse is involved in, as well as the climate and his turnout schedule. When he is turned out all the time, he needs more coat to protect him from the elements; however, if he's mostly indoors, or the climate is mild, you can take more hair off.

- With young horses, three- and four-year-olds that are just in for basic training, I tend to do a *speed clip* or a *trace clip*, both of which take the hair off the belly and neck of the horse. These clips only require light blanketing (figs. 15.7 A–C).

- For horses that are in medium work—Novice or Training Level—and likely to stay in Pennsylvania during the winter, I do a *blanket clip* (fig. 15.8 A). This takes the hair off all of the neck, chest, and shoulders, and under the belly. Basically, the hair that is left resembles an exercise blanket (quarter sheet).

- All our horses that compete in October or head to the popular winter eventing training and competition destination of Aiken, South Carolina, which generally has a more temperate climate than Pennsylvania, get body clipped: The horses at Preliminary Level and below just get a *hunter clip* (the legs are left hairy) as they tend to live outdoors more (fig. 15.8 B), while the Intermediate and Advanced horses have their legs clipped as well—basically, all the hair comes off!

Clipping the Face

There are special clipping considerations for dealing with the horse's face:

Trace clip—only do under the chin.

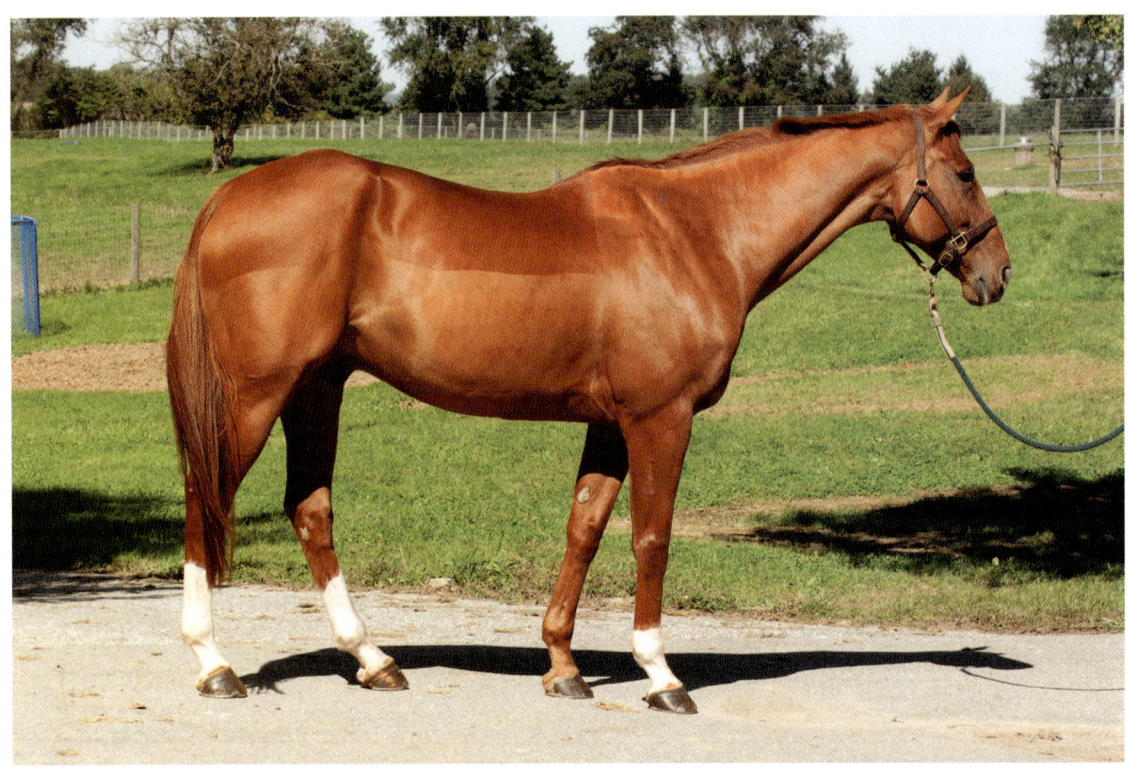

15.8 A & B Blanket clip (A); hunter clip (B).

Blanket clip—I go up to the cheek bones.

Hunter clip—I do the face when the horse doesn't mind; however, if he gets stressed, I only remove the longer hair up to the cheek bones.

Pulling the Mane

To keep the horse looking tidy and the mane easier to braid for competition, it must be kept about 5 inches long and slightly thinned out. This is accomplished by pulling out the longer hairs.

1 A dirty mane is easier to grip, but the hair should be brushed out before you begin. Start by pulling the longest hairs that stick out at the bottom: Pick up a few strands of hair between the thumb and the index finger of your dominant hand and with the other hand push the excess hair back with a pulling comb.

Useful Clipping Tips

- I always completely wash my horse before clipping, spray him with some coat polish like ShowSheen® Hair Polish and Detangler (Absorbine), then dry him off with a towel. The cleaner the coat, the easier it is to clip, and the better it is for the blades. The coat must be completely dry before you clip.

- During clipping it is very important to clean and oil your blades every 10 minutes or so and always be aware of how hot the blades are getting so you don't burn the horse.

- For first-timers I recommend drawing your lines on the horse with chalk before you start clipping the hair off. Always remember that it's better to start low and clip upward, so you have a little room for error. Don't get carried away or before you know it you'll have clipped the whole horse trying to get the lines even. Remember though, if the lines aren't even, no one can see both sides of the horse at the same time so don't panic if it's not completely symmetrical.

- Basically, you start clipping against the hair growth. To remove any track marks left by blades, clip at an angle to the hair growth to clean up any missed patches. You don't want to make really long or short strokes with the clippers—too long and the clippers get clogged with hair, too short and it ends up looking "choppy."

- For aesthetic reasons with the *hunter* and *full body clip*, you usually leave a little triangle of hair over the tail: draw a 45-degree angle from the dock of the tail to the dorsal line and you'll get it right. This leaves a tidy appearance and makes the base of the tail look more appealing.

- For general show trimming, I trim the ears, muzzle, bridle path, and "granddaddy hairs" under the chin, as well as clean up the fetlocks, back of the pastern, and coronary band. When the horse is fussy about the clippers, most of this can be done with scissors. You can also use a razor blade or "shaver" for the muzzle and hair under the chin.

- I always like to bathe my horses after clipping to remove any clipper oil residue, which lessens any risk of a skin outbreak.

- When you think you are finished, brush the horse off and get a hot towel to towel him over. This lifts up the longer hairs, so that any areas you missed show up and you can go back over them.

2 Twist the hair that you are holding around your index finger and the comb, hold the crest steady with your other hand at the base of the hair, and pull out the long hairs with one swift motion.

3 Move along the mane always selecting the longest hair. Keep pulling the hair out until you achieve the desired length and thickness. Be careful not to overdo it–you can always pull it out but you can't put it back!

4 Give your horse a break now and then while you brush him or give him a carrot. When his mane is very thick, spread it over several sessions instead of trying to do it all at once and irritating the horse.

Pulling the Tail

Use latex gloves for better grip. I use Sporty Stick Spray™ made by European Saddlery (normally used by riders to help them have a better grip between them and the saddle) on my fingertips because it's really good for grabbing hold of the hairs. (I like a spray product rather than a paste because it is easier to use.)

1 Always pull the tail from the underside first. When the horse moves, he lifts his tail and it looks clean and elegant if the hair is removed from the sides and underneath.

2 Pull the hair on the sides of the dock, from the base of the tail to about halfway down the bone. The center of the tail should rarely be pulled other than to thin it out when the hair is very thick.

3 After the tail is pulled, it should fall in naturally with the muscle line of the hindquarters.

4 Less is more–as with the mane, you can always pull more hair out later, but you can't get it back.

You also want to "bang" the tail–trim the end–so that it hangs level with the ground when the horse is moving. I am pretty particular about the overall length of the tail hair.

1 First, the tail needs to be thoroughly washed, detangled, and combed through so that all the hair falls evenly.

2 I place my hand under the dock to simulate how the horse carries his tail when he is being ridden.

3 I like the length to fall 7 inches below the point of the hock. I use scissors to cut it straight, making sure that it is level when the tail is up.

COMPETITION GROOMING

Phillip is usually riding many horses, so I have to get all of them looking their best as quickly and efficiently as possible.

Braiding

Mane

1 I use yarn for braiding; you can also use rubber bands, or a needle and thread. It comes down to individual preference (figs. 15. 9 A & B).

2 Fewer braids make a longer neck appear shorter, while lots of tiny braids can lengthen the appearance of a short, thick neck. I personally aim to do 12 to 15 braids on most of Phillip's event horses. For special events, due to fewer horses and more time on my hands, I put anywhere from 15 to 20 braids in. When I am really pressed for time I do 8 to 10 or so (figs. 15.10 A–E).

3 Wet the mane before you start. This prevents little flyaway hairs and makes it easier to manage. I have two ways to separate the hair: either with a hair clip, or I band off the individual hair sections prior to braiding. A good way of keeping them even is to use a proper braiding comb (see fig. 15. 9 A), otherwise you can cut a human comb into the length of the section you want.

4 In general, you want the actual braid to start close to the crest of the neck. This keeps the braids tighter and neater when you pull them up later.

5 When braiding with yarn, halfway to the end of the braid add a length of yarn, say 2 feet or so in length, so that the extra yarn hangs down when you finish. As you reach the end, tie it off by looping the yarn around and back through itself, then pulling it tight (figs. 15.11 A–D).

6 Slide a crochet hook or similar tool through the top of the braid, grabbing the yarn and pulling the braid up from underneath, then

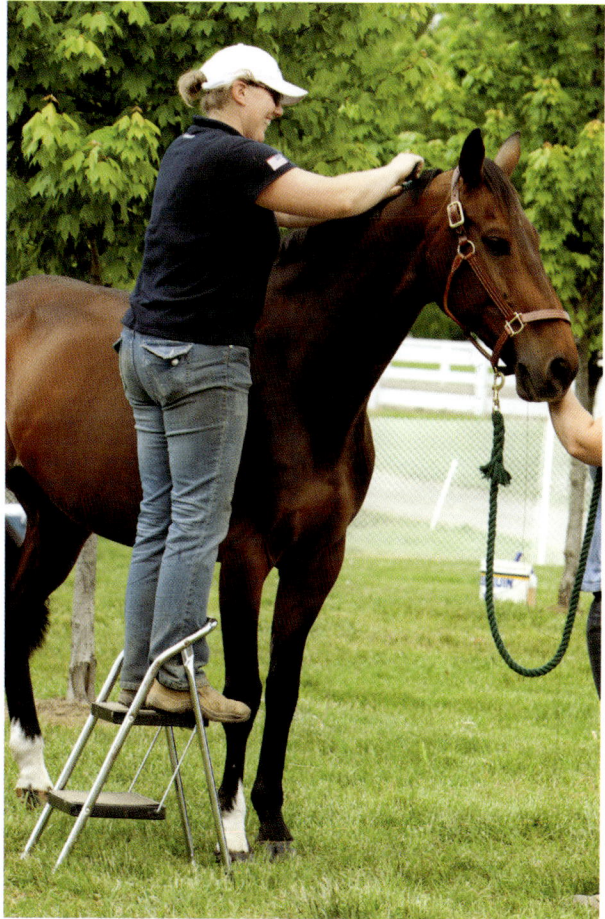

15.9 A & B Braiding supplies (A); Emma on a step stool for braiding (B).

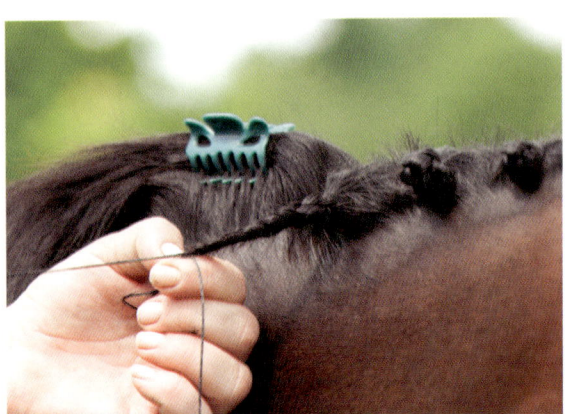 

15.10 A–E Braiding the mane down with thread (A); Quik-Braid™ makes it easier to grip mane hair (B); the end of the braid (C); tying a knot (D); pulling the braid up and making button braids (E).

Grooming 15

wrap the length of yarn around the braid to form a "button" and tie it in a knot. Cut the excess yarn off, leaving about a centimeter of excess so the knot doesn't come undone.

7 For the forelock, you want to do a French braid. Starting at the top, pull the hair tight as you work down. Again, work the thread in halfway down, then using your hook pull the braid up all the way through to the top. Split the two pieces of yarn, and thread each piece through the middle of the braid. Tie it off in the middle, then trim the excess yarn. The key to making this look neat and tidy is to keep the braid tight.

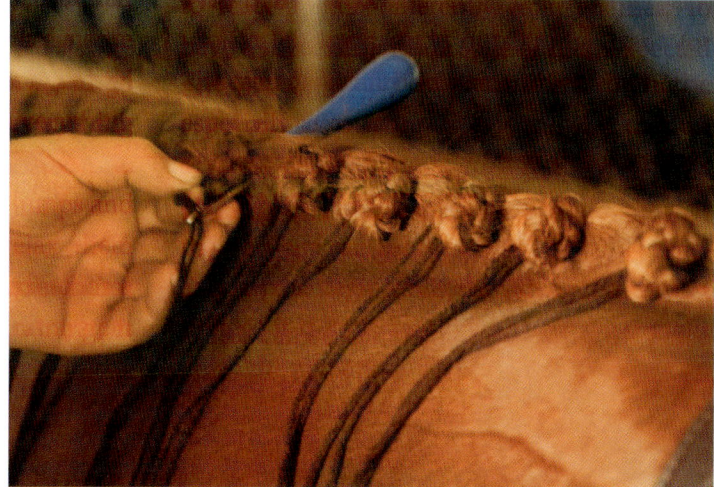

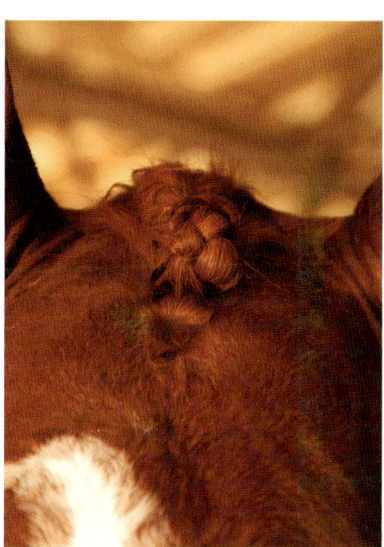

15.11 A–D Braiding down with yarn (A); pulling the braid up with a latch hook (B); a braided forelock (C); a braided mane (D).

Note: Never ever cut off the wispy hairs at the ends of the braids! This just makes it more difficult to braid the next time—if these wisps are unsightly, use a wax-based human hair styling product to make the hair lie flat.

Removing Braids

If you have sewn the braids in, you can use a seam ripper or scissors to cut the yarn and remove the braids. Rubber bands can be easily pulled off by hand.

Tail

My personal belief is that if a tail is long enough and it hasn't been pulled, it should be braided for a show—a very English tradition (fig. 15.12 A)!

After brushing the tail, I apply a tail wrap; when the tail is pulled, it helps to keep the hair smooth and the tail clean (figs. 15.12 B & C).

Final Touches

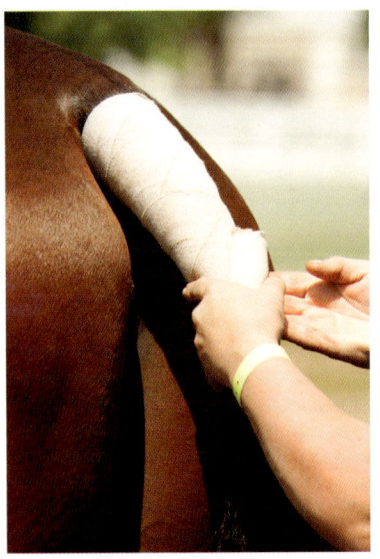
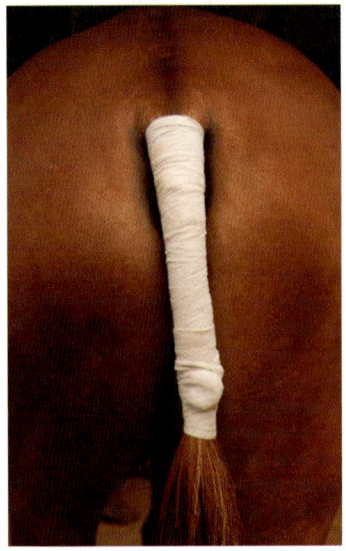

Quarter Marks

Quarter marks are patterns brushed onto the hindquarters of your horse (figs. 15.13 A–D). You can buy a template to create a simple checkerboard or diamond pattern, or you can use material like thin cardboard or a flexible plastic sheet to cut out a stencil and do something more creative (figs. 15.14 A–D).

15.12 A–C A braided tail (A); wrapping a "pulled" tail (B & C).

Grooming 15

1 Whether using a template or creating freehand patterns you need a body brush with short, hard bristles. You can also use a little piece of comb to draw a simple pattern, or something more elaborate.

2 In summer, I use fly spray to wet the hair first, which keeps flies away and helps the pattern keep its shape.

3 To create the pattern I use a small comb or I brush in "racing stripes." For more rounded, muscled hindquarters I tend to use the comb and do a half-diamond with shark's teeth (see fig. 15.3 D). For leaner horses, I tend to brush in stripes to accentuate the horse's hindquarters. I also use the stiff brush for shark's teeth.

Travel

Packing the trailer depends on our destination. If we're going to a local show we stick to the basics: tack for each horse, grooming equipment, hay, and water. For "away shows" you have to think ahead and be prepared for a variety of weather conditions and equipment that your horse needs for overnight: blankets, stable bandages, feed and supplements, and so on (see the packing list on p. 315).

Before we drive to Aiken, all of the horses get bran mashes the night before

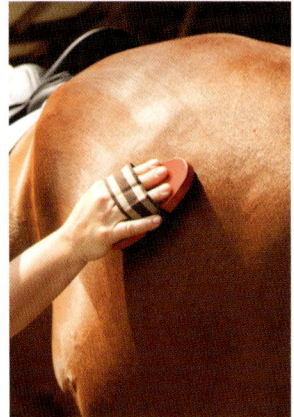
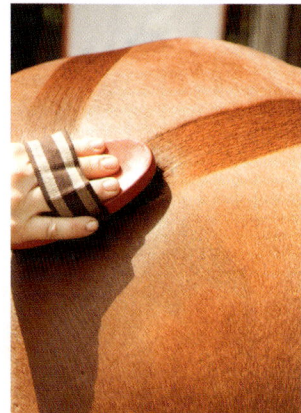
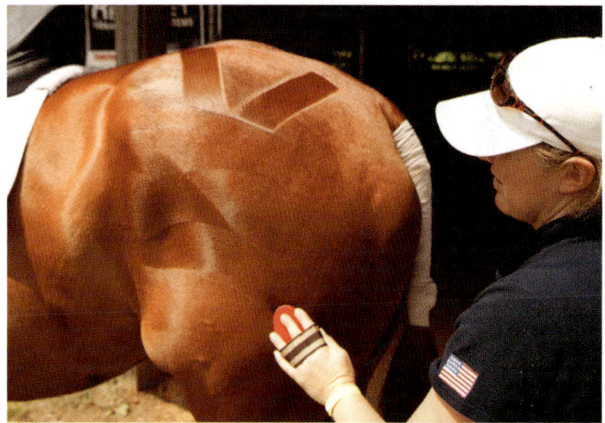

15.13 A–D Applying quarter marks and shark's teeth.

MODERN EVENTING WITH PHILLIP DUTTON 251

15.14 A–D Some very creative quarter marks!

and the vet tubes them with electrolytes and Gastrogard® to keep them hydrated and help prevent ulcers. We also administer a probiotic called Proviable®-EQ (Nutramax) to protect their digestive system from an imbalance before major trips and big events like Rolex in Kentucky. Then they arrive hydrated and as stress-free as possible.

We bring along a few health essentials:

- Something to sedate the horse in the event of an emergency where you need to keep the horse quiet before the vet arrives.

- 3M Vetrap™ Bandaging Tape.

- Antibiotic cream.

- Ice (see p. 257).

How I prepare the horses for travel depends a bit on the individual. When we are going cross-country schooling down the road, I just put their galloping boots and bell boots on for the journey; otherwise, I use shipping boots or bandages.

A lot of people have questions about shipping boots and bandages. I really feel that it's personal choice: There are pros and cons to both. Shipping boots are easier, but some horses won't stand them so you need bandages. In this case, I use thick quilts and flannel wraps, to reduce the risk of a tendon bowing. I use masking tape over the Velcro, and I put bell boots on front and back to reduce the risk of the horse stepping on his coronary bands.

It comes back to knowing your horse. With a couple horses that shipped really badly I even stood in the back of the trailer during travel to see how they like to be shipped! Connaught prefers to stand diagonally so if we put him in a box stall he has no problem. Some horses like to face forward, some backward, so if your horse moves around a lot, try a different position.

Make sure you have a well-ventilated trailer; I think it's better to put on an extra blanket and open the vents—the more air flow the better.

I do not like to give horses a full feed before traveling because I feel that they are less likely to colic without—especially ones that tend to get stressed. When horses have traveled a long distance to a show, on the night of arrival, I give them a bran mash, which is easy to digest and helps to hydrate them.

On long trips horses need to be offered water. Some people do this every time they stop for gas—others, when it's convenient. For horses that are not good about drinking on the road, try wetting every meal as well as soaking their hay. Adding salt to their meal can sometimes increase thirst and encourage fluid intake. Others like the taste of Gatorade®: Try different flavors and find what your horse likes, or try adding apples and carrots to the water bucket.

Flying requires basically the same preparation as driving for a long distance. When the horses arrive at "quarantine" before the flight, they can rest for around four to six hours, so we take off their boots and bandages until just before they are loaded into container stalls and put on the plane; they get hay and water during this break as well as on the flight.

Knowing how your horse travels helps you

decide how to protect his tail; if he stresses and sits on his tail in the trailer or passes a lot of manure, you need to protect his tail (see p. 250). I usually wrap a tail for trips under six hours. Be careful not to put a wrap on too tightly or you can cut off the circulation. For a longer trip, I use a tail guard or nothing at all.

AT THE COMPETITION

Care of the Horse Between the Phases

At a *Three-Day Event* you will have veterinary inspections to prepare for so you will need a friend—or more—to help you in the vet box, but

Preparing for the Jog

At a *Three-Day Event* (One-Star and above at the FEI Levels; also at Training and Preliminary National Three-Day Events), there is a veterinary inspection on the Wednesday afternoon, usually around 2:00 p.m. and again on the Sunday morning around 9:00 a.m. before the show jumping phase. Out of respect for the judges (and because sometimes they offer great prizes for the best turned-out horse and rider), both should be immaculately turned out for the presentation to the ground jury. Below is a step-by-step description of how I (Emma) prepare each horse for the jog.

- For the Wednesday jog Phillip normally rides the horse in the morning and then jogs him by hand to make sure that he is sound.
- I give each horse a full bath including twice cleaning any white socks.
- After the bath I use Cowboy Magic Super Bodyshine™ (CHARMAR ®) and spray it all over the horse and rub it in with a towel. It doesn't make the coat slippery.
- I put some detangler in the tail then put a tail wrap on while the tail is still wet; this remains on until just before Phillip jogs him out.
- I braid the horse, increasing the number of braids from the 12 to 15 that I normally put in for a Horse Trials competition to 14 to 18 for the jog. This lengthens the appearance of the horse's neck—for aesthetic purposes.
- Once the horse is ready I make sure his jog bridle is spotless and use metal polish to bring buckles to a shine.
- Phillip likes to have the horse walking about 20 to 30 minutes prior to his jog time, so 30 minutes before that I bring him out of his stall, brush him off, rub him over with a towel, put Afro-Sheen™ (Johnson Products) in the tail and make sure the tail wrap is still in place.
- I put baby oil on the skin around the eyes and muzzle.
- For chestnuts, bays, and black horses, I rub baby oil into my hands and run it down the crest of their neck and their legs to pick up any dust that might have accumulated.
- I pick out the feet.
- I use hoof oil on the walls and soles.
- I add quarter markers to the hindquarters.
- I like to put boots on prior to the jog to prevent any silly accidents that might prevent the horse from jogging up sound.
- Then, I put the bridle on, and he's ready for Phillip. (If you're riding and by yourself, get the horse ready, then get dressed before you put the bridle on).

generally, unless you are a professional with a string of horses, you have more time on your hands since a Three-Day Event is spread out over several days.

At a *Horse Trials*, the three phases are fitted into two days—sometimes one or three days. With this more condensed schedule, you need to be well prepared to get to each phase ready and on time.

1 When preparing for a Horse Trials or a *One-Day Event* (dressage, show jumping, cross-country—in this order), depending on how early you have to leave in the morning, you

- Be aware of the weather; when it's on the cool side, ensure the horse is warm while you are waiting so his muscles don't tighten up, especially before the Sunday jog.

  Have your horse out of the stall 20 to 30 minutes prior to jog time; don't just pull him out and take him to the jog. Always practice first with someone watching because unexpected lameness can happen. A yellow warning card (issued by the FEI in instances of dangerous riding, inappropriate rider behavior, or poor horsemanship) can be issued for presenting a lame horse at the official veterinary inspection. Receiving two warning cards in a one-year period results in a 60-day suspension from competing in FEI events.

  It is a good idea to practice at home so your horse will jog correctly: going forward without you having to drag him down the jog strip, which can make him look uneven.

  I always take a dressage whip, a hoof pick and a rag to the jog area for last minute touch-ups, and to make sure the horse hasn't picked up any stones in his feet. I also bring spray alcohol to rub anything off: I've had a horse nick himself and I needed to wipe off the blood.

  Preparing for the Sunday Jog
- Typically, I am at the barn at 5:30 a.m. where I feed the horse, immediately take off stable wraps and assess his legs.

- I then take the horse out, wash off any poultice, walk him for 10 minutes, then jog him to make sure there are no surprises. I take him back to the barn and ice his legs while I braid.

- Phillip is at the barn by 6:00 a.m. to assess the horse himself and decide whether he needs riding to loosen up any stiff muscles, or if we should just hand-walk him.

- Depending on the time of year, I tend to use some kind of therapy. When we travel with the US Team I use their magnetic blanket, which increases circulation to the muscles and promotes healing; otherwise, we have an infrared system, consisting of pads with infrared lights in them, which can be strapped onto specific areas to relax muscles, tendons, and ligaments and ease arthritis pain. It operates with a battery pack and I put it on while I'm braiding, usually to keep the back muscles warm.

- When Phillip rides the horse before the jog, I use a spray-bottle with rubbing alcohol to remove sweat marks. A lot of my job on Sunday morning is to make the horse look presentable, with his coat spotless, mane braided, tail brushed and everything shiny.

- I prep the horse in the same manner as for the first jog, absolutely ensuring that the horse is walking for at least half an hour before the jog.

can braid your horse the night before. Give yourself plenty of time to get to the event, go to the secretary, walk both the jumping courses and assess the footing as to whether studs are required (for each phase).

2 For dressage, make sure your horse is clean and tidy (see daily grooming, p. 237, and jog prep, p. 254, for tips on getting your horse looking his best).

3 Ensure your bridle number is affixed to your saddle pad or bridle.

4 If you feel your start times are close between phases, put studs in prior to your dressage test so you don't feel rushed before the jumping.

5 Once dressage is finished, depending on how hot the horse is, either sponge or wash him down and towel him off.

6 While horses at the lower levels can munch on their hay, at Preliminary Level and above, I take the horse's hay away two hours before the start of cross-country so that he is galloping on an empty stomach.

7 Assuming you are show jumping before cross-country, such as you do with your horse at a One-Day Horse Trial, tack up with the appropriate equipment–at a lot of one-day schooling-type competitions you go straight from show jumping to cross-country. Riders generally wear their full cross-country tack and attire, though you may need to quickly change your horse's boots before you head out onto the cross-country course. It can be helpful to have a friend or groom along to assist you.

8 After cross-country remove the saddle and bridle; if the weather is cold, put a light cooler on.

 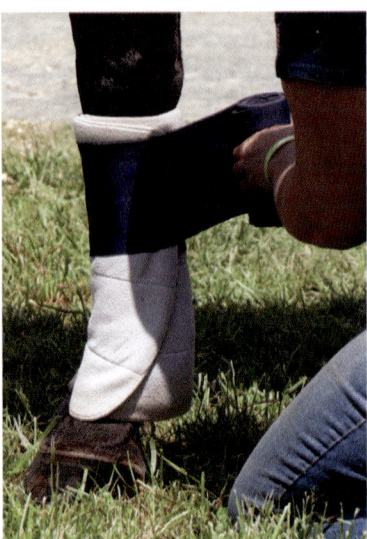 

15.15 A–C Putting on a standing bandage.

9 I like to remove studs before boots to reduce risk of injury from the studs.

10 Give a full shampoo bath, rinse and then walk until the horse is cool.

11 I do not have a problem with a horse drinking as much as he wants when he comes back from cross-country.

12 Once he is fully cooled out, I ice his front legs. (see Number 15 for more on this).

13 When legs are dry, use liniment or poultice, then wrap with stable bandages (figs. 15.15 A–C).

14 If the footing was really hard consider using some type of hoof packing afterward to minimize sole bruising.

15 In very hot or humid weather, purchase ice on the way to the show (or bring with you on shorter trips) to use for cooling out—in buckets of water, for the body, and in ice boots for the legs (fig. 15.16).

16 In cold weather, I like to use knit and wool coolers to wick moisture away as fast as possible.

17 On arriving home it's a good idea to jog the horse that evening to ensure his soundness, and do it again the following morning.

15.16 Dr. Kevin Keane's Fernhill Flutter standing in ice boots after a workout.

For *weekend* Horse Trials, preparation for dressage is the same; for cross-country I might ice the horses twice. I also try to get the horse out of his stall as often as possible and just lead him around to graze and keep him moving so his muscles don't get tight.

Note: See p. 304 in chapter 18 for more information on cooling horses out after cross-country.

CHAPTER 16

Commonsense Nutrition

Horses are grazing animals by nature, with small stomachs and short intestines. The first rule of feeding horses is to feed little and often, which helps prevent colic and keeps them from getting bored. They will naturally not eat large amounts of food at one time; in a natural environment, they graze almost constantly, with breaks for sleep.

The horse's diet is made up of two types of feed: roughage and concentrates. Roughage includes grass or pasture, hay or chaff (a short-chopped blend most commonly of oat, timothy, and alfalfa hays—forage feed that comes in a moisture-sealed bag. Sometimes it is mixed with oil or molasses). Concentrated feed is anything that is palatable to your horse that gives energy in smaller quantities. This includes grain such as oats or a commercial grain mix, vegetable oil, beet pulp, and whole grains.

A horse's stomach is designed for grazing: The total amount that a horse eats in a day isn't that much considering his size, usually around 24 pounds, or 2 percent of his body weight. Of this amount, a horse in heavy work like a Three- or Four-Star event horse eats about 10 to 15 pounds of concentrates with the rest of the diet made up of roughage.

Horses tend to have a sensitive digestive system. To give the delicate intestinal flora a chance to adapt to any dietary changes, be sure to make any adjustments gradually over several days in a row.

With all this in mind, I try to keep the feeding of my horses pretty simple and keep a few basic principles in mind:

- Feed little and often.
- Offer plenty of clean, fresh water.
- Feed according to the amount of work being done.
- When the horse has a day off, reduce his feed by at least half.
- Make feed changes gradually.
- Feed a probiotic like Proviable®-EQ (Nutramax) to protect against any possible imbalances.

Hay

While you may think it's just dried grass, hay quality is extremely important (fig. 16.1). Dusty or moldy hay is very bad for your horse's digestion and respiration. Dust and mold spores can cause inflammation of the alveoli in the lungs, causing coughing and irritation, and mold can cause colic.

- A horse out of work or in light work usually sustains himself quite well on good quality pasture grass or hay.
- Young growing horses need extra calcium and benefit from alfalfa or an alfalfa mix.
- Grass hay is usually sufficient for horses over six years of age in full work.
- Timothy hay is generally regarded as the best grass hay: It has some leaf and is quite nutritious. Other grasses like orchard grass are okay when well grown and of good quality.

16.1 The hay stack at True Prospect Farm.

Commonsense Nutrition 16

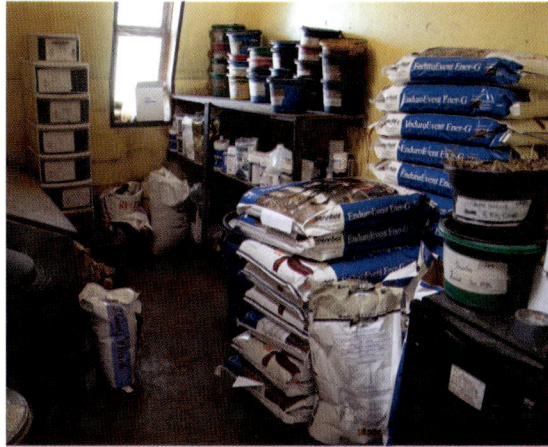

16.2 A–C The feed room and feeding schedule at True Prospect Farm. Emma is measuring feed.

- Alfalfa has higher protein and more leaf. Purchasing hay that mixes alfalfa with grass hay is not a bad idea if the grass in your area is of low nutritional quality (this can be determined by testing through your local agricultural extension office).

Signs of good quality hay:

- Clean and free of dust and mold.
- Sweet and fresh aroma.
- No weeds or "foreign" debris.
- Bright green color.
- Soft, pliable stems.
- Abundant leaves, where appropriate.

Grain/Concentrates

We add concentrates as the work load—thus the need for energy—increases. Try to feed concentrates according to the amount of work the horse is in (figs. 16.2 A–C). When he has a day or two off, it's important to cut the concentrates back, at least in half. Not only will this help to prevent a very fresh horse that's hard to handle when you ride again, but also aids in preventing health problems such as azoturia (tying up).

Protein is essential for growth, resistance to disease, reproduction, lactation, and building muscle. An aged horse (six years or more) does not need protein levels of more than 12 percent in his diet; feeding excess protein can stress the horse's system, especially his liver.

Oats are the most common whole grain fed out, followed by corn, which should not be overfed as it is high in fat and energy. Mixed feeds and pelleted feeds—made palatable through the addition of molasses—contain a reliable nutritional content.

- Grains and mixed feeds should smell fresh and sweet, not moldy or sour.

Complementary Therapies

The Use of Supplements for Joint Health Support

Supplements such as glucosamine, chondroitin sulfate, avocado/soybean unsaponifiables (ASU), and omega-3 fatty acids are being used ever increasingly as another modality to support joint health. They are found in various formulations and are usually given long term. The amounts given may be adjusted based on the level of joint health support needed. This can vary based on your horse's age and discipline, for example.

Glucosamine, chondroitin sulfate, and ASU can improve joint discomfort. They've been shown to support cartilage production and protect cartilage by inhibiting inflammatory mediators and destructive enzymes in the joint tissues.

Omega-3 fatty acids may lower inflammation in the joints and improve lameness from arthritis. It's important to know that there are different forms of omega-3 fatty acids. What are known as long-chain omega-3's—eicosapentaenoic acid (EPA) and docosahexaenoic acid (DHA) found in fish oils—are the preferred omega-3's because they provide more benefits over short-chain omega-3's, which are derived from plant sources. EPA and DHA can help more than just joint health. They also support heart and respiratory health and are useful for breeding stallions and gestating/lactating mares.

These supplements can also be administered to healthy horses for protection. In those horses with arthritis, your veterinarian may recommend using them with NSAIDs, injectables, or other medications.

When considering the use of supplements, you need to realize that, unfortunately, product quality varies. Some products don't contain the ingredients in the amounts that are listed on the label, while others have no research to back their claims. I rely on Cosequin® ASU Plus and the omega-3 supplement Welactin® Equine, both trusted, high quality products from Nutramax Laboratories, Inc., to support joint health and overall wellness in my horses.

- They should be free of bugs, mold, rodent feces, or other debris.

- Make sure to keep feed in closed bins to keep rodents and small animals out (see fig. 16.2 A).

Additives

There are many types and combinations of additives that you can add to your horse's daily diet. Here are a few of the common ones:

- A tablespoon of salt per day, or a licking block in a stall, is useful to maintain the ideal level of hydration and electrolyte balance. While offering salt in the summer, when the horse is sweating a lot is a no-brainer, I particularly like adding salt in the very cold of winter when the horse's drinking water is cold and he needs to be encouraged to drink. Otherwise, he can become dehydrated, an impaction may occur in the gut, and possibly colic.

- Electrolyte replacer is important in the summer months and when the horse is in heavy work. This helps replace the fluids and salts lost through sweating.

- A vitamin supplement in most cases is already added in produced feed concentrates. When mixing your own feed, this supplement is advised. The guidelines usually include an amount for maintenance and for heavy work.

- Joint supplements with ingredients like glucosamine and chondroitin sulfate; avocado/soybean unsaponifiables (ASU)—we use Cosequin® ASU Plus from Nutramax; and methylsulfonylmethane (MSM).

- Respiratory aids including vitamins and minerals, antioxidants and anti-inflammatory agents, and even garlic.

- Digestive aids, such as prebiotics and probiotics (such as Proviable®-EQ).

- Hoof supplements that include ingredients like biotin, amino acids like methionine and lysine, and minerals like zinc and copper (Calxequin® from Nutramax).

Water

Clean, fresh water is crucial to your horse's health (fig. 16.3). Horses require from 5 to 15 gallons of water on an average day. Fifty percent of an adult horse's body is composed of water, and 80 percent of a foal's body. Your horse should have water available *at all times* in his stable and when turned out.

- Automatic waters are convenient but you must keep them clean and free of debris, and make sure that they are functioning properly.

- Buckets should be scrubbed and filled regularly and kept free of debris.

- If your horse drinks from a natural water source, such as a stream, make sure that he has safe access to the water (a slippery, steep or muddy bank can be dangerous) and that the water is flowing so that it stays fresh. Also

16.3 Horses need plenty of fresh water to drink.

be sure that the water is potable—not from a contaminated source upstream.

Turnout

Most stall-kept horses are better off when they are able to spend time outside in a safe pasture, generally for at least two hours a day (figs. 16.4 A & B). Some horses are happier when turned out for longer periods, for example, all day or all night. I find that constantly stabled horses can become irritable, nervous and cranky. They can also develop vices such as cribbing, weaving, and stall-walking.

It is important to get to know your horse's turnout habits. When you get a new horse find out how his turnout has been managed. Here are a few things to consider:

- Is your horse better turned out by himself, or does he get nervous and gallop around without company?

Commonsense Nutrition 16

16.4 A & B
Regular turnout in paddocks with a shelter keeps horses happy and healthy.

- They can be gradually taught to stay out for as long as you like by establishing a predictable turnout and feeding schedule.

- In winter weather, your horse needs adequate shelter from the elements, like a run-in shed. Icy footing can cause slipping and falling for the ill-prepared horse.

- During the summer, take advantage of the cool and quiet nights for turnout, or turn your horse out early in the morning. A run-in shelter can also provide shade and a refuge from biting insects.

Special Concerns

Stomach Ulcers

A stabled life can exacerbate stomach ulcers; the importance of this has only been addressed in recent years (fig. 16.5). When ulcers are present, it can have a negative effect on your horse's behavior. I have seen remarkable changes in the way a couple of horses performed after being treated for ulcers. GastroGard® (omeprazole—produced by the AstraZeneca group of companies) is the only FDA-approved ulcer treatment on the market; it works really well: however, it is not meant to be given every day for long periods. Furthermore, it is priced as a treatment, not a maintenance medicine, so it is best to prevent ulcers in the first place.

I try to feed to help prevent the ulcers from forming in the stomach. It seems that ulcers are caused by grain being digested in the gut. The stomach acid created to digest the feed causes ulcers to form on the lining of the stomach.

16.5 Life solely indoors can exacerbate ulcers.

- How long is an ideal time for him to spend outside before he wants to come in?

- Some horses fight or play with other horses, which can often causes a mild injury—but occasionally, something more major.

- Horses that have not been turned out much can be gradually exposed to more and more time outside.

Adding a leafy type of roughage can help prevent this, but it is often not practical or possible to find the perfect hay for this. I feed the chopped chaff (forage feed) that I mentioned earlier. Adding a pound or so of this with the concentrates at every meal really helps prevent ulcers. During travel or at competitions, I add the GastroGard and Proviable-EQ.

"Hot" or Nervous Horses
Many such horses, particularly Thoroughbreds, react strongly to grain-based concentrated feed by having "too much" energy, sometimes the nervous kind, which is usually not desirable. Experimenting with different concentrates can help you find the right balance for your horse (fig. 16.6).

Adding vegetable oil to your horse's feed allows you to cut back the amount of grain you are feeding. A quart of vegetable oil per day helps to give enough calories or energy for the work, but in most cases, does not make the horse hotter.

Like people, horses' metabolisms vary: Some are "easy keepers" who put on weight easily, while others seem to eat constantly and never gain a pound. The Foreman, for example, could spend six months in a field and his weight would go up only 50 pounds or so, while a horse like Hannigan was nearly always on a diet!

Overweight Horses
Reducing a heavy horse's weight needs to be approached in a healthy way. Just as with humans, cutting back calories and exercising more helps to get rid of excess body fat.

- I usually feed small amounts of concentrate, about 2 to 4 pounds a day, and add a "replacer pellet." This is a feed made by most companies that includes the required daily vitamins and minerals needed for healthy bones and tissue development, without the calories of a normal concentrate. You can then help the horse satisfy his appetite with low-calorie forage (hay).

- Make sure the horse has enough to eat to prevent boredom, otherwise he may eat his bedding, risking colic and other health problems.

- When your horse lives outdoors, he needs to be kept from eating grass by wearing a muzzle at times; spending more time indoors without extra feed; or being moved to a paddock with little or no forage.

Underweight Horses
When underweight, it is essential to make sure the horse is completely healthy, parasite-free, and does not have ulcers before you start pouring feed into him. Also be sure to have an equine dentist check his teeth, particularly if he is "quidding" (dropping balls of half-chewed feed while he eats). Any of these conditions prevent him from putting on weight no matter what or how much you are feeding him.

- Once these are ruled out, give him feed that adds a lot of calories, which you hope will not adversely affect his behavior!

- Fattening feeds that can put weight on are vegetable oil, beet pulp, and rice bran. Most feed companies also make high-fat concentrated feeds to help add weight without adding excess energy.

- Alfalfa hay often adds weight.

Poor Eaters

A poor eater can be caused by being very fit. Check for stomach ulcers first; otherwise try to vary the feed. Try a different kind of feed or experiment to find something he likes. Connaught was notorious for this: He would go on binges where he would only eat a certain type of food and wouldn't touch anything else. Although not ideal, any food in this case is better than not eating. Adding treats to the food like carrots, apples, honey, or molasses can help get a horse started.

Laid-Up and Injured Horses

When horses are rested with an injury or their activity is restricted for any other reason, you need to feed them according to their reduced workload. This means reducing high-energy concentrated feed and offering more roughage to prevent boredom and help prevent colic and ulcers. It also matters that a horse you are trying to rehabilitate be kept quiet so that he doesn't play up and injure himself again.

Anhidrosis

Some horses suffer from a condition called *anhidrosis*, which means they are not able to sweat. This can be a serious problem, especially in hot summer months, since a horse needs to sweat

16.6 Three-star event horse Mighty Nice, owned by Bruce Duchossois, enjoying his feed at an event.

to stay cool. Ironically, this tends to most often affect horses in hot and humid climates.

Getting a proper diagnosis from your veterinarian is essential. Then your vet will most likely recommend a feed additive. I have had great success by adding a pint of Guinness stout beer to the evening meal.

Preventing Azoturia (Tying Up)

I've never seen a horse that is not on grain tie up. So first, I cut out the grain. It is so important with these horses when they have a day off—or are not in work—that you cut out the grain. Horses that tend to tie up need to be very closely managed so that the grain-to-work ratio is always in balance. There are some companies that make a concentrate specifically for these horses. I have had success feeding a low-starch, high-fat, high-fiber feed called Re-Leve®, which is produced by Kentucky Equine Research (KER).

CHAPTER 17

Hoof Care and Shoeing

By Stephen Teichman
Farrier for True Prospect Farm

Introduction to Stephen

With more than 25 years of experience in all facets of the farriery business, Stephen Teichman is a partner at Chester County Farrier Associates in Pennsylvania. In addition to shoeing Phillip's horses he counts among his clients the United States Equestrian Team. As farrier, Stephen has traveled with the USET to the World Championships and Olympic Games in Sydney, Australia, and Hong Kong, for the eventing, dressage and show jumping teams. His creative problem-solving ability and breadth of professional experience make him not only a master craftsman, but also a sought-after consultant nationwide.

    He is an American Farrier Association Clinician, Journeyman Certified Farrier and Certified Tester, and a member of the Pennsylvania Professional Farrier Association. In this chapter, Stephen provides guidelines for properly caring for the event horse's feet.

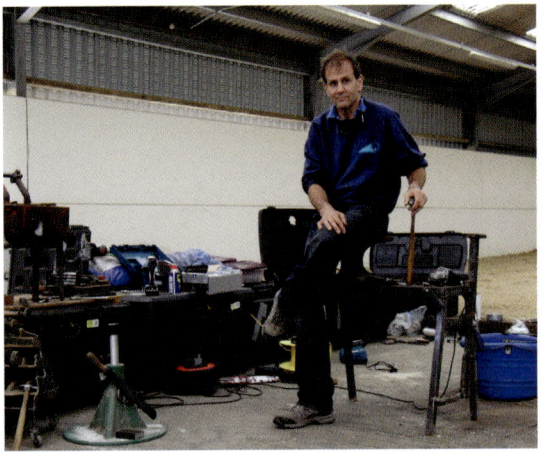

17.1 Stephen Teichman.

Introduction to Hoof Care

I shoe horses in a variety of disciplines and, without a doubt, feel that feet are most critical in the event horse, from the grassroots level up to the professionals like Phillip and Bruce Davidson. For a horse to have a successful career, the farrier is going to be an extremely necessary part of the team—even more so than for a hunter or dressage horse. Regular maintenance is critical. You have to have a relationship with a good, quality farrier—someone above and beyond the average guy—who can work through difficulties whether they are seasonal changes to the hoof, a pulled shoe, or general wear and tear to the feet resulting from the training for eventing.

Communication

I get most of my information about a professional rider's horse's feet from his groom: The rider might tell you how he is *going*, but when I really want to know about how he is *doing*, I talk to the groom who notices things like whether shavings are packing up under the heels, or whether the horse is standing in the corner of his stall all the time.

It is worth asking your farrier to watch your horse move before shoeing since he will

17.2 A & B Most farriers have a mobile shoeing unit. Pictured is farrier Doug Neilson's truck in front of one of the barns at True Prospect Farm and a close up of the tools and equipment inside the truck.

look quite different than he does when standing. This can make a huge difference to your horse's overall soundness and way of going.

Maintenance

The best way to prevent lameness in the event horse's foot is to have good hoof maintenance (figs. 17.2 A & B). Having an adequate length of foot to start with is the best way to avoid any problem because most of the foot problems farriers see in the event horse stem from the feet having been trimmed too short. Event horses can't get away with a shorter foot the way some other show horses can.

Most horses are shod every four to six weeks. A shoeing schedule is paramount: It often revolves around competitions, and horse owners need to be really organized about this schedule (fig. 17.3). At Phillip's barn, Emma and I had the shoeing schedule for each horse planned out at the first of the year, all the way through the Rolex Kentucky Three-Day Event

17.3 The shoeing schedule is posted on a blackboard at True Prospect Farm and updated regularly.

Keeping Your Farrier — TIPS

A good farrier is hard to find. When you find one, you want to keep him, so here are a few suggestions for you to make his job easier:

- Keep your horse(s) on a schedule.
- Let your farrier know how many horses need shoeing/trimming and any special needs or supplies required when you schedule an appointment.
- Have your horse waiting in the barn or a paddock. Don't expect the farrier to chase your horse around a field to bring him in.
- If the horse is muddy, towel off his feet and legs and brush the mud off before the farrier gets to work.
- Provide an uncluttered, level, and well-lit working area out of the sun, rain, snow, and wind.
- Have running water or a bucket of water available.
- Teach your horse to stand quietly without jerking his hoof away.
- Apply fly spray *before* shoeing (not while the farrier is bent over under the horse—you can spook the horse or cover the farrier with fly repellant).
- Hold the horse, if necessary.
- Offer a glass of water or cup of coffee.
- Provide a place for hand washing after work.
- Have your payment ready in full.

in April. With Phillip's Advanced horses I check the feet 10 to 14 days before a big event to make sure the balance is correct and the nails are tight.

Trimming

There are some things we see that are universal problems, including the amount of sole a farrier leaves (or doesn't leave) on the feet, and another is how he trims the frog. A good sole callus and a shaggy, ugly frog are worth their weight in gold. Some farriers trim all the frog material out, then add a product like Equilox™ (hoof repair adhesive) and put a pad on. I say it's much better—and easier—to leave things as nature intended: Trim the wall and take the minimal amount of frog out, leaving it at that. Event horses need to have a solid foot so I leave the exterior of the hoof wall alone and a lot of dead sole on the bottom of the foot. Event horses do much better when you leave the frog and sole alone. It may not look as neat but it's critical to a good healthy foot.

As far as the heels are concerned, many of the older, competitive horses have a lot of pathology in the foot—and sore ankles—and I think farriers are pretty aware they should not arbitrarily take too much heel off. OTTBs tend to have under-run heels and it's going to take about 18 months before you can get a "good hoof." With any career change, it's going to require time and work to develop a good healthy hoof capsule (fig. 17.4).

Returning to leaving enough sole and frog, there's a correlation here to the hoof angle: A lot of off the track Thoroughbreds have a long toe and low heel. Just by leaving the sole and frog you can develop a little more vertical depth in the foot. Usually this takes a little while as the hoof grows out. It's the same with horses that are shipped here from overseas; they experience a change in footing, climate, and shoeing style, resulting in an adaption period of about a year.

Seasonal Impact on Feet

As we get into the competition season and horses are in better shape and moving up the ranks, the weather changes and they're pounding their feet. Their feet are key to your success and when a farrier is not tied into that equation you're not going to get very far—especially if you want to move up the levels and play with the big guys!

Farriers don't like working on feet when they're soaking wet because it makes our job harder. It's common sense to be aware of the

17.4 A barefoot hoof.

Hoof Care and Shoeing 17

17.5 Wet, muddy conditions can be detrimental to the hoof.

environment's impact on the quality of the foot. When you're shipping south to compete in a dry climate with hard footing, don't let your horse stand in the mud for five days prior (fig. 17.5). Changeable footing is a problem all round the world. Before the Athens Olympics, the American team horses first adjusted to the soft footing in England, when training there for a month. Then they were shipped to Greece where the environment was entirely different. This wasn't an ideal scenario for their feet; it takes several weeks for the horse's feet to adapt to a new climate. Keeping this sort of thing in mind helps to prevent feet from becoming a "wreck," and bruised soles.

Types of Shoes

Good shoeing starts with the basics. You should have good coverage from toe to heel—the length of the shoe as well as the width between the heels. This is the basic shoeing concept good for any discipline. Some guys will fit the shoe shorter and tighter, but good length and width is particularly important for eventers. They are tough on their feet and quite often their shoeing schedule revolves around their event schedule, so this is no place to have improper shoe size.

I use a 5/16 ¾ inch shoe—the brand I prefer is Kerckhaert, from Holland, an excellent sport-horse shoe. It's extremely suitable across the board for event horses. It's got a great nail pattern that is very practical: It uses an American-style nail, or "city head" rather than "e-head." It fits better in the shoe and does a little less damage to the feet. It's also got good heel coverage (sore heels are a pretty common occurrence in event horses). Every farrier in this country probably has this shoe in his truck, so it has a universal appeal—whether you compete in Montana or Germany, the farrier probably has a box of Kerckhaert shoes handy.

How we "mark" our shoes is another consideration. Typically farriers mark the outside branch—front shoes are marked between the second and third nail hole; hind shoes between the third and the fourth on the outside. This helps on Sunday morning at the event when people are in a panic: They can bring a horse's extra set of shoes to me and I know right away which shoe goes on which foot.

We see a lot of the European horses using "concave" shoes; they're not as popular here, because they pretty much require an "e-head" nail system. We find that using the smallest nail size to do the job works better for us.

What if Your Horse Loses a Shoe?

Typically, when shoeing a horse, the farrier removes some of the sole; in the event horse though, extra sole is needed to help with some of the punishment that takes place during cross-country. This will be made obvious to you when your horse loses a shoe on cross-country and you are forced to make a repair. Having excess sole callus on the bottom of the foot in this situation is critical.

When your horse loses a shoe on cross-country, have the farrier pack the foot with something like an Epsom salts product, poultice it, and let the foot "quiet down" for a few hours before applying the new shoe. When the farrier is too quick to throw the shoe on after a cross-country run, it can be difficult to determine just how uncomfortable the foot is.

17.6 A farrier's supply of premade or "keg" shoes.

For general shoe loss around the farm, the simplest thing to do is to wrap the foot and try to preserve the hoof wall as best you can until your farrier arrives. Cotton sheeting followed by Vetrap™ or its equivalent, then an outer layer of duct tape, works well to protect the foot.

Shoe Fit

I usually don't make much alteration to *keg* shoes (fig. 17.6). I keep a good normal fit on front feet and hind feet so I don't have to be as worried about the shoes getting stepped on or ripped off (fig. 17.7). I almost never have an issue with the hind feet when it comes to losing a shoe or getting a crack—it's most always the front feet.

- There are some new products on the market like titanium shoes that are extremely lightweight and durable that I think are really going to change the future of shoeing. I think they'll be advantageous because they have good support and good heel cover and some of the horses will be happier wearing them; for the owner a big advantage is that they last two or three times longer than steel shoes. They would also mean horses could wear the same pair of shoes through an entire event.

- Another popular technique is gluing heels, or heel augmentation, which is adding a little acrylic resin to the heel area of the shoe to prevent the horse pulling the shoes off; this way, if the horse gets an overreach on cross-country he hits the synthetic material rather than his hoof. In general, with a reasonably healthy foot, and in deep footing, it's a good way to keep the shoes on (but it is not good for long-toed, low-heeled horses).

17.7 Clinching the nails to finish the shoeing.

Addressing Hoof Lameness

Maintaining perfect feet is all very easy to talk about, but sooner or later you run into problems. Over the years I've found a few specific types of shoes that seem to work best for keeping the hoof capsule in good shape and allowing the horse to move comfortably. Most of these are in the form of a bar shoe, typically a *straight bar* or a *heart bar*.

- A *straight bar* shoe is a quick and easy way to give stability to the hoof capsule—it's as simple as that.

- The *heart bar* shoe, which works on the principle of transferring weight to the frog, is ideal when you need to offload the posterior (rear) portion of the horse's hoof. This nicely takes care of a number of problems, from quarter cracks or corns, to sore heels or under-run heels. The fact that this works well for addressing a variety of problems in the posterior part of the horse's foot makes this a good shoe of choice, since it can save you from reapplying multiple different shoes to solve a problem.

I often go straight to a heart bar shoe for most problems. It's a multi-function shoe: By the way I place it I can put weight on different parts of the foot, and apply varying amounts of pressure.

In addition, there are some good sole preparations that can be applied to the bottom of the feet to help reduce pain, and keep the bottom of the foot tough and durable. Magna Paste and other Epsom salts products are great applications to apply to the soles (see below).

Pads

I use a lot of pads but almost never plastic pads. I use a thick, natural leather pad that can make up for a multitude of sins on horses that come to me with a problem at a competition. The leather pad is a very forgiving product and works fantastically well—it's a blessing! It's the right material for the job.

One of the ways I make up for inadequate hoof length is with the use of a leather pad either as a rim pad (just under the shoe), or as a complete pad that covers the entire sole.

Sole-Support Material

Sole-support material, for example, Equithane™, one of numerous such products, became available around 2000; before that, we used silicone, but this new product hardens in a minute. I started using it without a pad and realized that because it's so sticky, it has the effect of transferring weight to the sole and the frog: I can "shoot" it to the side of the foot or the heel and transfer weight loading on the horse's feet. I can rebuild heels with it. A farrier that doesn't have the best mechanical skills can use sole-support material instead of a heart-bar shoe. A rider can keep it in the tack box, and do a quick repair when there is no farrier on the grounds.

Clips

Both toe clips and side (quarter) clips are used to help keep the shoe in place. With the varied terrain that event horses encounter, the big studs that riders use, and the different footing conditions, side clips seem to be the most practical for event horses because they tend to keep the shoe on tighter. I use a lot of toe clips on driving horses and hunters, and no clips on dressage horses.

Drilling and Tapping/Studs

Drilling and tapping gives riders the option to put studs in the shoes, which give the horse extra traction (figs. 17.8 A & B). Across the board, I pretty much drill and tap everybody. Ten years ago riders didn't bother—except the eventers—but today they realize that it gives them more options for traction (17.9 A & B). There are literally thousands of studs out there to choose from.

1 We put a stud hole in each heel. Since event horses are not wearing studs all the time—the groom or rider puts them in before riding and removes them afterward—it makes it less likely that the horse will injure his leg with a stud when we place stud holes right at the end of the crease (nail line).

2 The top of the stud hole is countersunk, which creates a conical opening near the top of the stud hole, helping the studs to fit better. The hole itself is threaded like a screw with a tool called a "tap," so that the studs can be screwed in. I prefer a 120-degree countersink to the more typical 90-degree countersink because it removes less of the thread, which keeps the studs more securely in place. The strength is in the first three threads so you are less likely to rip a stud out with the 120-degree countersink.

17.8 A & B Drilling holes for studs (A); tapping (threading) the stud holes (B).

3 Pack stud holes to keep them clean. You can use cotton or commercially made stud plugs, which helps with maintenance.

4 Having the smallest stud possible for the job, particularly on the front feet, is better for soundness. In other countries like England, they use very large studs placed near the second nail hole. I tend not to even give

17.9 A & B A groom removes a horse's studs after cross-country (A). Phillip's horse is wearing studs for better traction during a show jumping phase (B).

riders this option. I drill a stud hole in each side of the heel and let the rider decide which studs to use. It's much easier on the horse's legs to have symmetrical stud placement.

Topical Applications

There are a couple of products I recommend:

1 As mentioned, I like an Epsom salt gel called Magna Paste, which is basically magnesium sulfate distilled into a paste. It is sticky and draws well and more importantly, doesn't make the feet soft, so it's ideal to pack the feet with on Saturday night or Sunday morning at the event. You can't go wrong with it: You won't get in trouble with "drug rules" and you don't need a lot of wraps to keep it on. Many other poultices create a soggy foot, which is impossible to work with. With Magna Paste, the foot will be as hard as a diamond, which makes working with the hoof so much easier.

2 During the wet season, I buy Johnson & Johnson® clear floor wax; it's non-toxic, I spray it on the horse's feet, and it dries in about a minute. It seals out moisture and is a simple, safe barrier. I keep it in the truck in

spray bottles and spray it on when I finish shoeing. I stay away from products like hoof sealants and hoof oils that make feet too brittle or too soft.

3 Most of the pine-tar-based hoof packing, commonly used in combination with a fibrous material called oakum and packed into the sole area to moisturize feet is toxic to the hoof wall, so I don't recommend it.

The most important thing is that the bottom of the foot does not get soft like it can when any type of clay poultice or poultice pad is used for packing hooves. These may make the horse feel comfortable, but they can leave the farrier with a soft mess! If the horse has to get back out on cross-country or trot up for soundness, soft soles are too sensitive—plus nailing into a soft hoof becomes a real problem.

Emma Ford on Using and Maintaining Studs — TIPS

Putting the studs in is one of the first things I do after grooming and before tacking up, though when I'm using pull-on bell boots, I put them on first.

I like to organize my studs in a tackle box: At the beginning of the season I line each section with paper towels sprayed with oil like WD-40. Each size and type of stud has its own individual compartment to make it easier for me to find what I need (figs. 17.10 A & B). Also in the kit I have:

- A "tap," a tool used to clean the threads that hold the stud in place when you screw them into the shoe.
- A wrench to grip and tighten the stud.
- WD-40 to lubricate the stud.

Although I do not use stud-hole "stoppers," due to the number of horses I'm dealing with, you can use rubber stoppers, or plug the holes with cotton balls soaked in WD-40 or petroleum jelly to keep the holes clean and free of debris. I prefer to use a horseshoe nail to clean out the holes; however, there are many products available for this purpose—what you use is individual preference. There are various taps available: a round, flat one, which I prefer for safety, in case the horse stomps his foot down, or the more traditional "T" tap.

17.10 A & B A well-organized and well-stocked stud kit ready for any type of footing: A magnetic dish helps a groom keep small studs organized (and from falling into stable bedding during application); a round tap; various studs; and a wrench for applying studs.

CHAPTER 18

Horse Health and Veterinary Care

By Kevin Keane, DVM

Introduction to Dr. Keane

Dr. Kevin Keane spent his youth on a farm outside Chicago and earned his doctorate from the University of Illinois. He has a special interest in Sports Medicine and musculoskeletal disease in horses. His practice at Sports Medicine Associates in Kennett Square, Pennsylvania, is unique in that they treat both racehorses and sport horses. He has traveled extensively as a veterinarian for the United States and Australian Equestrian Teams, and contributed to the textbook by Ross and Dyson, *Diagnosis and Management of Lameness in the Horse.* An active eventing competitor, at the time of publication, he and his horse Fernhill Flutter have competed to the Advanced Horse Trials and CCI Two-Star Level. He was the 2011 USEA Advanced Amateur Rider of the Year and Adult Amateur Rider of the Year.

Note: Certain layman's terms are different around the world. We are using the ones commonly known in the United States.

Dr. Keane says that working with racehorses has helped him apply his knowledge to other galloping sports, which include polo, foxhunting, and eventing. He explains the role of the veterinarian: "Everyone who is successful in this sport needs the veterinarian in several roles. If you choose to have a veterinarian to perform the initial exam and assess the risks of your purchase, that is the beginning of the relationship; going forward the vet is someone to help maintain the health and soundness of your horse and to diagnose and treat injury and unsoundness as they may occur throughout the horse's career."

In this chapter, Dr. Keane provides guidelines for properly caring for the event horse.

18.1 Dr. Kevin Keane and his horse Fernhill Flutter.

THE IDEAL ROLE OF THE VETERINARIAN

Not everybody has the privilege of being at a large stable geared to international competition, and it is up to each individual to work out for themselves the role of the veterinarian. At the lower eventing levels you might monitor your horse's soundness and comfort on your own, especially when you live in an area where you don't have access to regular veterinary care, and just call the vet for emergencies. At some big stables like Phillip's, the vet is often there every day.

One of my favorite methods for management—because this is where I think your vet should be playing a role—is *frequent evaluation*. I think the beauty of this is it allows detection of problems when they are smaller or more minor. The hallmark of my management system is monitoring the problems and monitoring the comfort of the horse regularly—that is, jogging the animals up in an appropriate venue on a regular basis related to a recent competition (for example, the Monday following a weekend of competition).

Frequently evaluating the horse, which is not terribly time-consuming, has the potential to discover a problem that might be very small, such as a tendon that feels slightly tender under palpation, a back that that has become sore, or a small boot rub that looked fine at the competition but is now inflamed and might necessitate the use of antibiotics. This will benefit everybody because the horse will be treated appropriately, quickly, and will miss fewer days of training, helping you achieve your goal of a Three-Day Event or a Championship Horse Trials, typically in the late spring or fall.

Another thing I think is of the utmost value is to have multiple sets of eyes trying to figure out a very difficult problem, such as a group of vets at a large clinic, or as consultants. I think the most ideal situation is when the vet is very familiar with the horse's legs and condition so that small changes in comfort or the condition of a joint or supporting soft tissue can be closely monitored for changes.

A great example is a horse that always had an enlarged tendon, perhaps an OTTB that you purchased with an old injury; knowing the horse's baseline and having a record of what your horse is usually like is very helpful to go on. We begin every evaluation with the history, asking, "What is normal for this horse?"

Drug Rules

Rules under which horses compete vary, depending on which country you are competing in. For example, the BHS (British Horse Society) and the USEF (US Equestrian Federation) both have different drug rules governing events. And when a horse competes at an FEI competition, there is yet a different set of rules.

Your vet should always be aware of the drug rules of any competition you enter and be sure that any medications given are okay. And the "withdrawal" time (for medication to leave a horse's system) is also important: The administration of a medication given simply for maintenance of your horse's health should be given in a timely way so doesn't create an issue with drug testing.

In the United States our rules fall under USEF guidelines, which are mandatory to adhere to during competition so that the horse can compete on a level playing field with the other horses. It is easy enough for someone to fail to understand the rules, which can then create problems and potential action by a governing body against the horse and trainer and/or rider.

As of December 1, 2011, the USEF Drugs and Medication Rules have been revised. Although they allow horses to compete on certain amounts of medication, the rules are very specific and it is necessary that riders and trainers understand these rules. I am unaware of any other country in the world that allows medication to be used in the horse in an identical way to the USEF. It is very important to understand the rules under which you are competing and I think it is relatively safe to say that outside of the US most eventing communities align their medication rules to the FEI's rules. The drug rules in the US appear somewhat liberal in comparison, but it should be pointed out that these rules have been written with great forethought to protect the welfare of the horse.

The beauty of the rules in the USEF are, for example, that a horse injured in transit on the way to a competition, given correct adherence to the rules, may receive medication and still be allowed to compete. What is done for the diagnosis or therapy of an illness or injury is considered for the better welfare of the horse. Although there is too much detail to be written here, given appropriate adherence to drug rules, the horse would likely be able to compete if the injury or illness has been corrected.

Maintenance of Your Horse's Health

Need for vaccination and parasite control (deworming) varies tremendously, even throughout the same country. For example, in the United States, with different climates on the coasts, and horses in the UK and Australia, there are variations on what animals require to maintain healthy.

Through my years of international travel it appears horses in the US require the greatest number of vaccines, in sharp contrast to Australia where, being an island, there is little need for the full array of vaccinations that would commonly be given to horses here. Australia did undergo an outbreak of equine influenza in the first decade of the twenty-first century; however this is uncommon.

Your vet needs to tailor your horse's vaccination schedule based on your geographic requirements. For example, there are two counties in eastern Pennsylvania where botulism can be found—a devastating disease; in many other parts of the US people choose not to vaccinate because the risk is so low that it is almost unheard of for horses to contract this disease.

It is worthwhile to mention at this point that the FEI has its own regulations for equine influenza prevention, which need to be adhered to and recorded in the animal's passport to allow for international competition under FEI rules. This essentially is a primary series of influenza shots followed by a twice-annual booster to keep the passport current and updated.

Parasite Control

Once a very big deal because of the lack of availability of effective and easy-to-administer medications, parasite control has been made much simpler with paste dewormers.

Because many people have more than one horse or keep their horses in a group situation, parasite control is essentially a herd issue. It is often best, under your veterinarian's guidance, to monitor the need for the use of anthelmintics (dewormers) by checking for parasite ova with a periodic fecal exam. This really is the best way to determine the need for deworming.

Over the past 40 years the changes for what is recommended has progressed greatly; at one time it was thought that the horse should

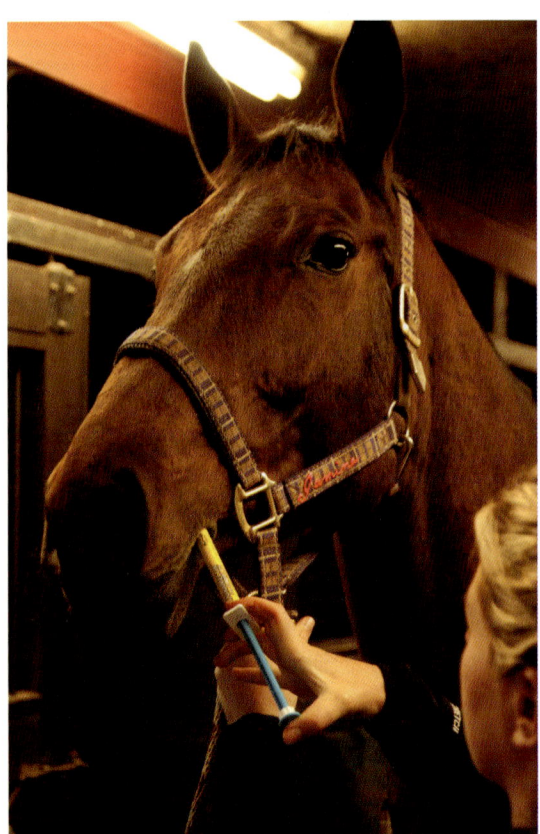

18.2 Deworming with paste.

be dewormed every six weeks with rotating anthelmintics, but now checking for parasite ova and deworming based on need is recommended as opposed to using medication when the parasite burden is so low as to not require its use (fig. 18.2).

COMMON PROBLEMS

Common Unsoundness in Event Horses

Many horses in the eventing countries are bred for the sport. Consequently, they are generally mature in their skeleton by the time they start work, unlike racehorses. If a horse is not purpose-bred, he generally has had a previous career, often as a racehorse, which is still very common in eventing, and some of these OTTBs come with a previous injury.

When a horse is purpose-bred—for example, both Bruce Davidson and Boyd Martin keep their own horses and breed them for the sport—it can positively influence soundness.

However, provided a horse has retired from racing without significant joint disease, racing is looked at as being beneficial because a horse has had his bone density increased; has learned how to gallop—favorable for eventing; his body has been tested; and he has significant core fitness (see chapter 5).

To get a horse to the Four-Star Level or the pinnacle of the sport it might take five to six years of training; this is significant in that much like a human marathon runner takes years to develop, an event horse needs to stay in training for half a decade, and many things can affect his soundness as he rises through the levels.

There are four- and five-year-old Young Event Horse classes at some competitions, an age that is quite mature compared to racehorses. This influences the type of injuries that event horses typically have. Horses with mature skeletons are less likely to get the severe orthopedic injuries that racehorses tend to have simply because of their bone mass.

Event horses have what we call "cyclic loading of the leg": basically repetitive concussion of the leg, which probably predisposes them to DJD (degenerative joint disease, or arthritis). In general, the young horse competing at a lower level is going slower, which influences against significant orthopedic injury in the long bones, such as fracturing cannon bones, and so forth. As he goes up the levels and the intensity of training increases, there is increased cyclic loading.

Again (generally not until the higher levels of eventing, when horses occasionally have falls on cross-country), event horses may sustain an unpredictable type of injury, such as a shoulder injury or bruised stifle from hitting a jump.

The most common injuries include:

1 Osteoarthritis from concussion.

2 Traumatic injury from falls.

3 Soft tissue injuries on supporting structures such as tendon and ligaments (occurs with increased speed, thus unusual in Novice and Training Levels, but more common in Advanced horses).

Common Lameness Conditions

- Pain in the foot. A significant amount of lameness comes from bruising and concussion in the feet, for example, having run on hard ground.

- Traumatic osteoarthritis (degenerative joint disease)—both in front and hind legs.

- Supporting limb injury (tendons and ligaments/suspensory apparatus).

- Muscle and bone pain in the back, under the saddle area and in the sacroiliac region, basically along the topline of the horse.

Hoof Pain

It is essential to select a horse with good feet and a thick sole, which influences against foot problems. Also, you need to have an excellent relationship with your farrier. There are extremely talented farriers all over the world and you should find someone that fits your needs (see chapter 17).

- We like to start by assessing the foot balance, since foot imbalance can cause problems throughout the horse's body. Horses that don't have ideal foot conformation are more likely to be prone to bruising, especially when competition conditions are less than ideal. In Australia and the US it is common for horses to compete on hard, uneven ground, so thicker soles and well-balanced feet are built-in protection against concussion.

- One of the worst things to have in horses in any discipline is under-run, rolled-in, and collapsing heels. These horses are prone to development of chronic heel pain and corns. This is common in horses off the racetrack that are selected for speed but not always conformation, so if you are looking at an ex-racehorse be mindful of the conformation of his feet.

- Although abscesses can occur in any horse, I find that hoof abscesses in eventers are relatively infrequent because event horses tend to have high-quality farriers shoeing them and management is good: The feet are picked daily, stabling conditions tend to be clean and dry, and they are on a regular shoeing schedule at fairly short intervals. Foot lameness tends to occur more often as the result of galloping on hard ground.

- Arthritis of the coffin joint and problems with the navicular bone, which both occur in the hoof capsule, are common, but this falls under the category of osteoarthritis (see below).

Musculoskeletal

The main conditions we treat are:

1 *Degenerative joint disease (arthritis).* This is likely to affect most animals at some point in their competitive careers. Fortunately, in the early twenty-first century, we have an enormous number of avenues with medication to alleviate symptoms of arthritis and also to manage it in not particularly invasive ways that help reduce advancement of the disease. The beauty of this is that the horse is able to perform for a longer period of time, with comfort, just as an elite human athlete would see their doctor on a regular basis to manage joint injuries.

2 *Soft tissue injuries of the supporting structures.* This means that there is either a strain to a tendon or ligament, which comes in all magnitude of seriousness. Frequently, injuries such as a suspensory ligament strain or tendonitis make it mandatory that the horse have time away from competition. As with degenerative joint disease, there are many ways of helping to heal the injury in fairly predictable periods of time, so that one might be able to plan what to do with the horse. There is usually good quality of healing, which is important for future performance. The days of turning a horse with a tendon injury out in a green field to wait for it to heal are gone. Today, treatment may include controlled exercise in a buoyant medium, such as treadmills in water, to salt-water spas, to stem-cell therapy for helping to provide quality of healing.

3 *Performance-limiting musculoskeletal issues.* Probably the most challenging thing for veterinarians to diagnose is "clandestine" pain, which creates resistance and, consequently, performance issues in the horse. This is one of the more vague and challenging areas for the rider, trainer, and vet to succeed in. Although I'll go more into it later, an example is a horse at the Advanced Level that changes his leads cleanly in one direction and is late behind in the other. The vet must determine whether this lack of ability is based on the way the horse is being ridden, or if it is based on a physical problem because no overt lameness is in existence. These issues often turn out to be interesting areas for the rider and vet to work on and correct. This is one of the biggest things we do—if the client is riding at Training Level, say, the dressage is less difficult, but as the horse moves up the levels these small problems become more apparent.

Legs

When it comes to the limbs our categories of injury are degenerative joint disease and supporting limb injuries.

- In the front legs especially, the joints that are most affected are the coffin joint, pastern joint, and fetlock joint. These are most commonly afflicted with arthritic conditions.

- In the hind leg, the two lowest joints of the hock and the hind fetlock are also commonly afflicted with arthritic changes. A moderate amount of stifle lameness does exist, more commonly in the inside or medial joint. Frequently there is little change radiographically (on X-rays) and even the highest quality imaging does not always yield a definitive X-ray lesion; however, a large number of horses tend to benefit from treatment of stifle soreness.

Note that horses develop stifle soreness without having dramatic lesions evident in imaging, but when we can rule out certain types of concerns such as meniscal tears or cruciate ligament problems, which are associated with high degrees of lameness, it is generally observed that they respond well to treatment of the stifle the same as they would with other joints.

Treatment of the Joints
There was a period of about 10 to 15 years during which veterinarians treated high-performance horses with an aggressive (frequent intra-articular medication or joint injections) treatment and management system. In recent times, the pendulum has swung the other way, and now people are getting more conservative. They are finding a middle-of-the-road way to manage horses successfully, without the frequency of invasive treatment.

Fortunately, in this day and age there are many anti-arthritic treatments for horses, generally available worldwide. In the United States, horses commonly get medication called Legend® (hyaluronate) and Adequan® (Polysulfated glycosaminoglycan–PSGAG); in other areas, such as the UK and Australia, it is called Pentosan®.

These are available for systemic use, meaning that they can be administered by intravenous or intramuscular injection by a veterinarian, or dispensed to appropriate personnel for use periodically by owners or stable management. These things help to influence degradation of the joints by blocking inflammatory environments in the cells. Medications like Adequan basically help prevent further cartilage degeneration in the joint.

- It is a widely accepted pain-management technique to directly inject medication into the joint in order to reduce inflammation caused by osteoarthritis. Although a variety of different agents are available, the hallmark of the treatment is the injection of a corticosteroid, of which a number are available with different durations of action, often in combination with hyaluronic acid (HA).

- Different joints are "high-motion" or "low-motion," and the vet may select a certain corticosteroid based on the location of the arthritis as some are more appropriately used for high-motion joints. As previously mentioned, the lower joints of the hock have a different type of stress when the horse is weight-bearing; these are low-motion joints that tend to have different medications used in them.

- In general, cortisone (corticosteroids) is essentially very inexpensive while HA is relatively costly, and your veterinarian will prescribe an appropriate treatment based on the location of the arthritis in your horse (i.e. high- vs. low-motion joint), the age of the horse, and severity of the condition.

A new and exciting area in treatment of joint disease is the whole category of regenerative medicine. As of publication, some of these have been used for less than a decade.

- *Interlucan receptor antagonist protein* (IRAP). This is a technique whereby the antagonist protein is developed after a harvest of the animal's blood and an incubation period, then reinjected at intervals to prevent the occurrence of arthritis. One of the strong benefits is that this is essentially a drug-free treatment, which allows horses to be treated when medication is not possible due to competitive drug rules.

- *Platelet rich plasma* (PRP). Originally used for lesions within soft-tissue tears of supporting limb injuries and now used in joints, PRP is blood plasma that has been enriched with platelets. It contains different growth factors and other cytokines that stimulate healing of bone and soft tissue. Much ongoing research is being conducted at this time.

- *Extracorporeal shock wave therapy* (ESWT). This is typically used to treat bone/ligament union inflammation, such as back pain. In racing, a horse is not allowed to be "shock waved" within 10 days of a race because of its analgesic effect, which could mask pain and cause serious injury when the horse is put in work too soon.

Supporting Leg Injuries

Bowed Tendons and Suspensory Injuries

Essentially, injuries from mild strains to significant tearing of structures that necessitate lengthy convalescence and rehabilitation, mean

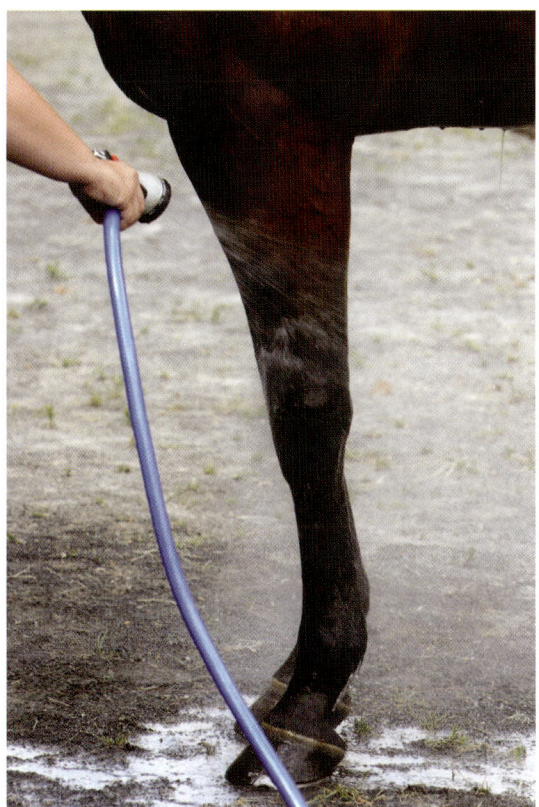
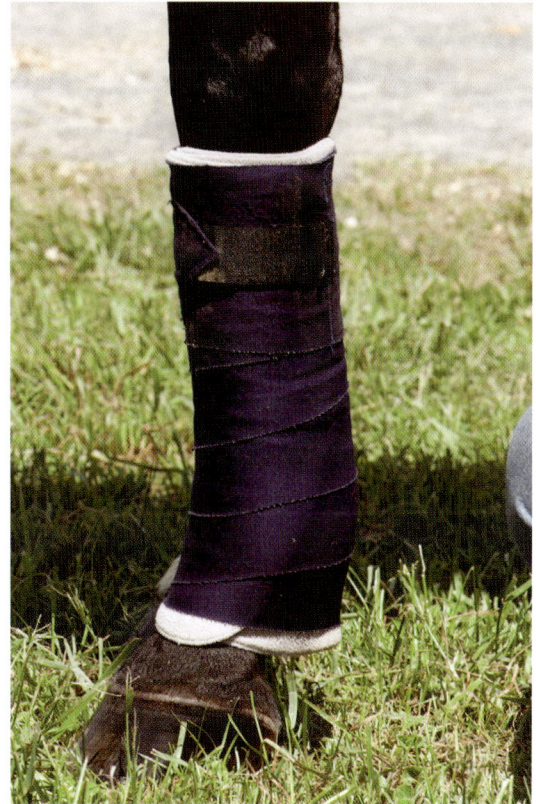

18.3 A & B Cold hosing and bandaging can help reduce heat and inflammation.

time away from competition (figs. 18.3 A & B). These occur at all levels of training and may involve:

- Superficial flexor tendon.

- Suspensory ligaments.

- A number of important ligaments on the palmar (back side of) the pastern, which can become injured—especially in the front limb.

As previously mentioned, the speed at which the horse must gallop over a sustained period of time (up to 12 minutes or greater), and the fact that he sometimes lands on one leg over a jump—with varied footing—can affect whether or not supporting injuries develop.

Subclinical Injury

It has been observed that certain *subclinical* injuries—specifically *superficial flexor tendinitis*—may not be noticed for some time after the horse has competed in a Three-Day Event. Consequently, riders have taken to monitoring for tendon injury either by periodic evaluation or by ultrasound to prevent worse injuries from occurring. It is well documented that horses may not demonstrate this type of injury until they return to exercise after taking their routine rest period following a Three-Day Event. This can happen a couple of months after a competition: for example, a horse runs at Fair Hill, Maryland, in the fall, then during a little Horse Trials a few months later, he gets a bowed tendon.

The occurrence of a *bowed tendon* or a *tear of a superficial flexor tendon* generally means a long rest period, which can significantly interrupt the horse's competition schedule. Some riders at the higher levels of the sport whose horse has experienced a significant injury choose to aim at a lower level of competition going forward. Trying to attain too high of a level again may put the horse at risk of serious re-injury.

- A significant tear, which is seen as a dark hole on an ultrasound, is known as a "*core lesion.*"

- Probably due to speed, the kind of catastrophic tendon injuries that you can see in a racehorse do not typically occur with event horses.

- We tend to see a lot of proximal suspensory desmitis (injury of the most upper portion of the suspensory), a condition that has been recognized for the last 35 years as a "*high suspensory.*" This occurs at the origin of the suspensory, basically at the base of the knee in the front limb. It also occurs at the hock in the hind limb.

- Injury at the lower aspect of the suspensory, in the branches that occur at the fetlock, is also common.

- There are a group of ligaments that are essentially referred to as the "XYZs." Medically known as the *distal sesamoidian ligaments*, these can also develop strains and tears, although this is significantly less common than a tendon or suspensory injury.

Muscle Conditions

Myositis (also known as *tying up* and *azoturia*) is not that commonly seen at Three-Day Events simply because it would have already occurred in training prior to a horse arriving at an event. Sometimes requiring careful dietary management, this type of problem generally would have been observed and treated as the horse was developing and moving up the levels, although the odd case does periodically show up once the horse has reached the higher levels.

- Horses have to travel to competitions and a number of issues are related to dehydration during travel–a known stressor for horses. Changes in the horse's eating regimen surrounding travel and competition can all have an influence on tying up.

- Some horses are more prone to tying up based on their metabolic makeup; provided the horse does not have a genetic predisposition for it, such as *Equine Polysaccharide Storage Myopathy* (EPSM), which is common in certain heavy breeds of horses, tying up basically shows significant muscle stiffness, often notable at the walk.

- Certain episodes can cause the horse a great deal of discomfort, including reluctance to move. Most often the muscles of the hindquarters are affected; signs include muscle cramping and passing reddish-brown urine. Detection via laboratory work to detect elevated levels of certain muscle enzymes is quite easily done and is reliable.

- While proper conditioning may prevent tying up, the hallmark of treatment is through dietary management: The current recommendation is a reduction of grains and concentrates, especially important when the horse is not in work. For example, there should be a significant reduction in the daily feed on a day off. Also, a whole host of commercially available feeds that are high in fat and low in starch are available to help manage such a condition. Some horses need more rigid management than others: Simply altering the type of grain intake works for one while another needs careful monitoring of soluble carbohydrates.

Back Pain

Back pain typically occurs along the thoracic and lumbar region of the back, underneath the saddle. In recent years, veterinarians' diagnostic ability has improved for evaluating conditions of the back and pelvis. There are two broad categories:

1 Low-grade, ongoing muscle soreness of the back from the withers to the lumbar area behind the saddle–a kind of soreness that can be diagnosed by the vet simply through palpation of the area.

2 Some horses with more severe manifestations may even have loss of musculature in the area, as evidenced by lack of development of the long muscles of the back. Causes range from improperly fitting tack to dorsal spinal processes being too close

together (known colloquially as "kissing spines"). Such horses are prone to periodic, or chronic, lingering back discomfort.

There are a whole host of management and treatment options, although the very worst cases can be difficult to get under control. Treatment ranges from regional injections of *cortisone* to commonly employed alternative therapies, such as *acupuncture, chiropractic*, and *massage*. Additional techniques include Mesotherapy and *extracorporeal shockwave therapy* (ESWT), both performed by your veterinarian, who will select the treatments that would be most appropriate for your horse.

Probably underestimated, one of the best ways to improve back pain–similar to humans–is through stretching and exercise. Some people are experts at this, getting the horse to jog in a "long-and-low" outline, so that he is stretching in a relaxed, long frame and strengthening the back over time. This helps to reduce discomfort through the development of appropriate muscle groups and is highly effective, unless the horse has the most significant bony changes, which may not respond much to treatment.

People often want a "cure in a syringe," but riding the horse like this for a few months, jogging and stretching in a relaxed manner, and in a correct, round frame, can be highly effective. Once they learn how to stretch, horses become so comfortable that they actually enjoy this. It's surprising how quickly the horse can change for the better–you can start to see a difference after just a couple of weeks.

Sacroiliac Pain

The sacrum is the end portion of the horse's spine, and the ilium is one of three bones that make up the pelvis. The sacroiliac joint anchors the pelvis to the spine. In event horses, sacroiliac pain tends to be a low-grade soreness, which causes a lack of impulsion (pushing strength), usually due to sore ligaments in the area. Generally, when the horse is fitter, this is less likely to be a problem because better muscle tone will help to stabilize the area

An assessment is done through a physical examination, which can indicate peri-sacral pain (pain around the sacrum). It can be diagnosed with a clinical assessment; or an ultrasound can detect injury to the ligaments that help to stabilize the pelvis. Again, I think this is an area where chiropractic treatment (see below) can help improve the horse's soundness, and regional injection of corticosteroids can help reduce inflammation.

This is a very common area of treatment in our practice. In some cases the judicious use of medication or treatment, along with improved fitness, can yield a positive result.

Alternative Therapies

The main goal of alternative therapies is to reduce the animal's discomfort. One of the reasons they are popular is that with FEI rules being what they are, people are getting away from wanting to use drugs of any sort. These therapies allow animals to be treated by techniques that are longstanding, accepted methods (over centuries) and highly compatible with FEI drug rules.

Some of these techniques are unproven and kind of anecdotal, though if an appropriately trained professional who is skilled in an alternative therapy such as chiropractic and acupuncture is available, he or she can be part of the management team to aid in reducing discomfort for a variety of issues related to the skeletal system. In the UK there are people who work as physiotherapists rehabilitating horses. Some of them are extremely well-trained and highly effective.

It appears most people use alternative therapy modalities for problems involving the trunk, neck, and croup rather than the limbs. Usually, conditions of the limbs are well studied and well treated by a conventional vet. In any barn, there are cases that are more nebulous: muscle pain, lack of flexibility, stiffness, and an inability to flex or bend in one direction more so than the other. Consequently, a number of well-trained professionals are frequently available, especially at the larger competitions, to evaluate horses and use safe procedures to improve performance. The FEI does allow for use of alternative therapies at events, under conditions for which there are forms requiring authorization.

Improvement with alternative therapies is often an adjunct to improvement by conventional therapies being administered to the horse. Some of the benefits noted are anecdotal and difficult to measure, and are often concurrent with therapies like Adequan®.

A number of alternative therapies are available and are approved by the FEI, including:

- Chiropractic.
- Massage.
- Dry acupuncture (using needles without injections).
- Radiotherapy.
- Electrostimulation.
- Infrared.

Rehabilitation

Event horses are especially prone to soft-tissue injury. During rehabilitation a key component is monitoring recovery in a precise fashion so as to get the highest quality healing in the shortest, most reasonable period of time. About 25 years ago, a horse with a bowed tendon was frequently turned out to pasture; now it is more common to rest the horse with controlled exercise, at least for the initial period of recovery.

Orthopedic

Needless to say with orthopedic injuries (a broken bone), immobility is crucial. Although not terribly common in event horses, the rehab for any fracture would likely necessitate a period of stall rest based on the severity of the fracture, under the veterinary surgeon's express recommendation based on the magnitude and severity of the injury.

Soft-Tissue

The majority of rehab is used on soft-tissue injuries such as tendinitis or suspensory ligament inflammation (front and hind leg). Due to the number of regenerative procedures now commonly being employed, such as PRP (see p. 291), bone-marrow treatment, and cultured stem cells, a structured, slow progressive exercise schedule is generally recommended.

Each vet may establish a rehab program for the specific patient. In our practice, we have a number of pre-written exercises that we can recommend, or we can tailor something to the individual. The hallmark is:

1 An initial period of hand-walking, which is successful when the horse cooperates; when too difficult to handle, judicious and safe use of tranquilizers can be helpful.

2 A period of "tack walking." Under saddle, this is sometimes safer than hand walking, depending on the horse's temperament and the weight of the rider.

3 A period of slow, incremental increases in timed jogging exercises over 18 weeks or longer.

A periodic examination, along with ultrasonographic monitoring of the quality of healing, is performed, which may allow the veterinarian to grade up or grade down the level of exercise the horse is currently doing. For example, when a horse is 12 weeks into tack-walking exercise after sustaining a core lesion in a tendon, and there is a sudden increase in the size of the tendon, the scale of walking may be reduced for several weeks until the swelling has subsided, as this may indicate a too-rapid progression in exercise for that particular animal.

Keep in mind there is no single, set program that is successful for every case so this is by no means an all-encompassing recommendation for all horses. Basically, a large number of skilled horsemen participate in the sport of eventing and they may have successful methods and programs that work for them. Recommendations change every decade or so: As I said earlier, at one time, it was commonplace to simply turn out a horse with a badly bowed tendon. But as greater medical knowledge is

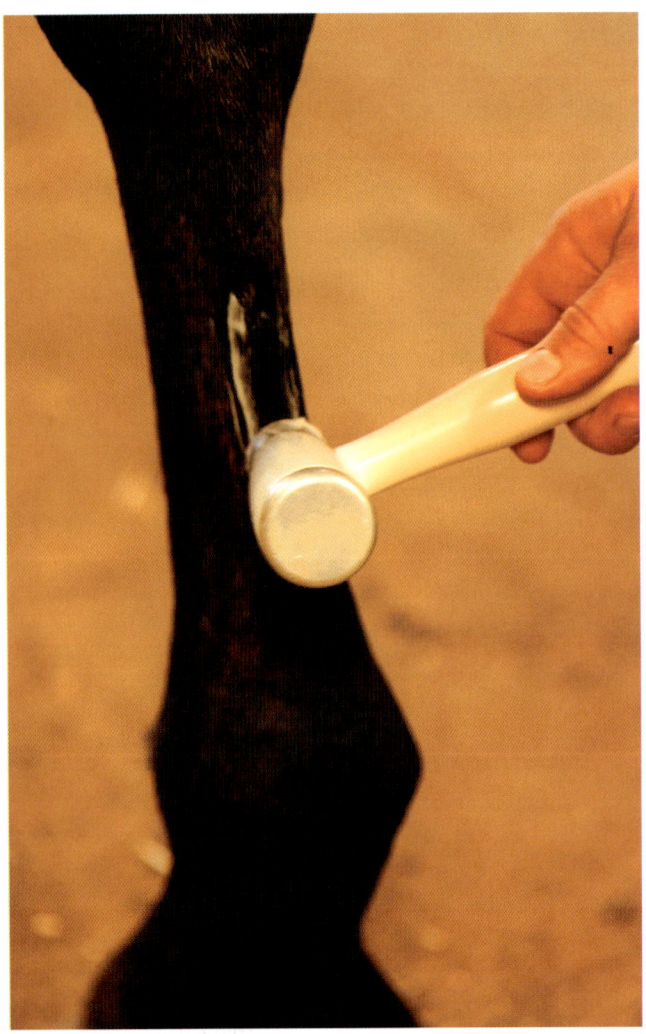

18.4 Therapeutic ultrasound.

gained, the current trend is to control exercise, at least in the early healing stages, after which time the movement of the horse in small turn-out makes it less likely for the animal to reinjure the affected limb.

Therapeutic ultrasound (as opposed to diagnostic) has been shown, when used correctly, to be useful during the rehabilitative process. It is relatively easy to use and safe, and the stimulation provided by topical ultrasound can assist in quality of healing (fig. 18.4).

Many of the traditional techniques for treatment of tendinitis, such as pin-firing, are seen to largely have fallen out of common use based on more contemporary techniques that are now available. However, this can still be seen mainly in racehorses.

Cardiovascular

The heart is the most important muscle in the horse's body. Given the endurance aspect of eventing, heart health is an important part of the pre-purchase exam (see p. 31). Evaluation of the horse's heart during a pre-purchase exam gives one a baseline for heart health.

- *Heart murmurs.* In our practice it is not uncommon to hear a heart murmur, in which case, we pursue the evaluation further with an echocardiogram to evaluate blood flow and assess risk. Murmurs in horses are noticed frequently and as the majority of them are benign, many horses are competing at the high levels with a murmur.

- *Patency of the jugular vein.* The jugular vein, which runs along the groove in the horse's neck, is a good estimation of hydration status. Any distention or pulsation of the jugular vein may indicate a pleural effusion or cranial thoracic mass obstructing the return of blood flow to the heart.

Anhidrosis

Anhidrosis is the inability of the horse to sweat properly. This puts him at risk because his core temperature can rise to dangerous levels, depending on the amount and type of exercise and the ambient temperature. The ability to sweat is an important cooling mechanism; an inability to do so can occur in different magnitudes, from reduced sweating to not sweating at all.

You can find a common "history" in some anhidrosis cases when they experience sudden climate change—for example, the horse that is moved from the temperate climate of Northern Europe to the heat and humidity of the Eastern United States in the summer time.

There are oral medications, essentially containing amino acids, which have some success in managing anhidrosis. A common, old-horseman's remedy is to feed the horse alcohol in the form of beer, which horses actually like very much top-dressed on their feed. A pint of Guinness is popular; although Guinness contains a lot of minerals, it is likely the alcohol content of the beer that is effective. Peripheral vasodilation (widening of the blood vessels)—the same thing that causes the ruddy face of an alcoholic—is probably helpful in stimulating sweating. Diagnosis and treatment under a vet's guidance is preferable to an owner managing her horse's anhidrosis on her own.

Respiratory

The health of an event horse's respiratory system is essential to peak performance, and there are a number of horse-management areas to address for keeping your horse's lungs and airway healthy. The basic things that we look at, diagnose, and manage when it comes to the lungs are *infection* and *allergy*.

1 Starting from the beginning, management of mold and dust in the stable, as well as quality of feed, is key to keeping your horse's lungs healthy. Because a horse is a nose breather (not a mouth breather), the importance of the air quality in his stable and during shipping is very important. Large amounts of dust and other pollutants are filtered out as air is drawn into the nose.

2 *Inflammatory airway disease* (IAD). This is a diagnosed category of disease that requires management. We used to say a horse has "heaves" but now we would call it IAD or *recurrent airway obstruction*, using terms that are more specific.

3 *Exercise-induced pulmonary hemorrhage* (EIPH). Horses that are "bleeders" need to be managed in a specific way, which is made more challenging because FEI horses can't compete on medication.

4 Upper (lungs) versus lower airway (larynx and pharynx). Given that eventing is a galloping discipline, the horse needs to be able to breathe well so that he can perform at his best. At the high levels of the sport, horses need to be at a full gallop for about 10½ minutes, so this is vital. Many horses can have an impairment called *laryngeal hemiplegia* (roaring)—a condition of the upper respiratory tract involving paralysis of one side of the larynx, which causes decreased performance and respiratory noise in the horse—and compete up to a limited level.

Dermatologic (Skin Problems)

We can classify skin issues in event horses just like any other horse. Horses being horses, and given turnout conditions and varying weather

> # Fatality
>
> Eventing is a high-risk sport and, as with any sport, there are risks associated for both horse and rider. No one willingly takes her horse out and starts an event knowing her horse is at risk; but it is beyond reason to know every risk that might occur to your horse. Sadly, the rare event of a horse collapsing on course does occur, just as with people.
>
> While it is beyond the scope of this book to delve into many cases, one example is the show-jumping stallion Hickstead, enormously popular and whose death was widely publicized. It was determined that he had had an acute aortic rupture while leaving the ring at a major horse show in 2011. Horses ridden to the highest level of the sport, even under the best possible veterinary care, may have a hidden health issue that only reveals itself under acutely stressful situations.

conditions that they have to live in—from a dry climate in Australia or a very wet climate in New Zealand or England, to everything in between across the US—there are many factors that can contribute to dermatologic issues in horses, including but not limited to:

- Wearing blankets.

- Dry conditions.

- Mud.

- Bacterial infection.

- Fungal infection.

- Body clipping is necessary in certain times of the year, necessitating that the horse wear a blanket. Dirty blankets can cause rubs, pressure points and skin infections, so it is imperative to keep them clean and make sure that they fit the horse well.

- Because of the long time event horses are ridden—say you have to ride a good distance to a galloping site—the saddle pad can contribute to changes in the horse's skin health.

- Fungal problems like ringworm are more common in young horses. It is not seen so often in older horses and ones that spend time outdoors in the sun. It is more commonly noted in winter months. Although it sounds bad, this fungus is easily treated.

Common Skin Issues

- *Direct trauma*. This is the sort of trauma caused by contact with an obstacle—in competition or in schooling. What's important is its location—proximity to vital joints and tendons—and its depth: you need to ascertain whether it requires stitches or other veterinary attention. Using small clippers to shave around the wound is helpful for evaluating the extent of the injury—and keeping it clean.

- *Puncture*. It is always a matter of urgency to assess the damage. One of the direst situations we evaluate begins as an innocuous-looking wound that later turns out to be a serious puncture requiring extensive (and expensive) veterinary treatment.

- *Bacterial infection*. "Scratches," a horseman's all-encompassing term for an infection generally of the lower limbs and, specifically, the back of the pasterns in the front and/or hind legs that often creates swelling, significant pain and lameness generally requiring medical treatment. It's basically a severe inflammation and infection. Fortunately, under FEI rules written as they are, horses may be given antibiotics and are allowed to compete when, in fact, an infection occurs in the lead-up to, or during a competition.

- *Boot rub*. It is important to realize that unlike in show jumping where the round is relatively short in duration, event horses may be wearing their protective leg gear for more than 40 minutes when you include warm-up. Consequently, they can sustain trauma to the legs from rubberized products in the boots. Check legs for heat, rubs, or other irregularities after every ride.

A condition that presents like scratches is an irritation from a galloping boot. This type of injury has created enormous disappointment for riders when the horse is not able to be presented at a Three-Day final veterinary inspection because of lameness. This is why you have to be quick to evaluate and treat even minor-looking skin problems.

- *Fungal problems.* The term "fungal infection" is used very generically among horse people. Unless the diagnosis can be reasonably certain from the presenting signs, our preference is to scrape the lesion for culturing purposes so that a definitive diagnosis can be made before we prescribe treatment.

- *Dermatophilosis.* Commonly known as "rain rot" or "rain scald," this is not truly a fungus but an organism with both fungal and bacterial properties. It's actually the only organism in the world that fits in this phylum (a group of organisms with a relative degree of similarity or relatedness). You actually treat this with antibiotics. Although often unsightly, appearing as circular raised crusts with *exudae* below, rain rot is relatively easily treated, both locally with iodine-based shampoos, and with antibiotics prescribed by your veterinarian. In mild cases, frequently patch-washing the area of the affected site can be effective, and for cases of greater severity, antibiotics are successful.

Classic-presenting rain rot, over the back and loins of the horse, is from the organism that presents the same type of lesions on the front of the hind cannon bones, commonly known as "stud crud." Bath water running off the gaskin and down the legs can cause this problem, so dry the legs and belly well with a towel after bathing your horse.

Gastrointestinal

Horses have a very primitive gastrointestinal system. Essentially, their gut is unchanged since Biblical times; what we do know is that gastrointestinal health has been affected by modernization. In nature, horses are constant grazers that have food in their stomachs at all times, but the modern, domesticated horse—especially a competition horse—spends certain hours of the day confined to the stable and in transit, sometimes without feed prior to training or competing.

Due to the rigors of the sport, it is necessary to provide certain amounts of hard feed (grain or concentrates) to supply energy to the horse. These factors are all different from the horse's behavior in nature and, consequently, can affect his gastrointestinal (GI) tract health and comfort. Many stables only feed twice per day, however, feeding small amounts of hard feed more often would help to simulate the natural grazing habits of the horse.

There are many GI issues, such as chronic diarrhea and wasting conditions, that are beyond the scope of this book; however, I will focus on prevention of *colic* and *equine gastric ulcer syndrome* (EGUS).

Colic

Colic means abdominal pain in the horse. The very word "colic" instills fear in every rider and owner. There are many causes: dehydration; the difficulty of ingesta being expelled as manure (impaction); gastric ulceration; infection; and parasitic migration in the bowel, though parasite infestation is not common in event horses since most owners are likely already well-advised by their veterinarians on parasite control.

Veterinarians broadly classify colic as *medical* or *surgical*:

Medical are types of colic that can be treated with anti-inflammatory medications, antispasmodics, or correction of bowel dehydration.

Surgical colic cases are those that through careful evaluation it is determined that either torsion or volvulus of the intestinal tract is present, which, unfortunately, requires surgical intervention to correct. This necessitates extreme urgency at an appropriate location.

Note: Many riders carry flunixin meglumine (Banamine®), a non-steroidal anti-inflammatory drug (NSAID) in their emergency kit. However, we prefer Banamine to be administered under the guidance of a veterinarian: one or more doses of a pain-reducing medication such as this can *mask* vital signs needing to be monitored, delaying a timely referral for surgical correction.

Prevention

Some forms of colic can be prevented—*impaction,* for example, as this relates to an animal's hydration of the GI tract. Probably one of the biggest challenges facing the owner is working out feeding schedules when a horse is traveling to a competition over a long distance. Some stables add an ounce or two of plain white table salt to the top of the feed to encourage the horse to drink water.

Consistency in a feeding program is important. There is a very well-documented study showing that feeding high-quality alfalfa hay to horses reduces colic, although quality and availability of hay varies throughout the world and needs to be determined on an individual basis (see chapter 16).

EGUS (Equine Gastric Ulcer Syndrome)

Dogs (and humans) are monogastric, that is, they have one stomach. Horses have one stomach, but they are also "hindgut fermenters," so we should avoid treating them like dogs. A wild dog can hunt for some prey, gorge himself, and then not eat for two days. A horse is just the opposite and needs to eat little and often. When he ingests a large meal, hydrochloric acid—essential to digestion but can cause ulcers when it is constantly being produced—rushes into the stomach. This is why smaller and more frequent meals are recommended. With today's recognition that *gastric ulcers* are common in sport horses, dividing their feed and administering it many times per day, is, in itself, very helpful in management of your horse's GI tract.

For example, if a horse receives a total of 12 pounds of hard feed a day, it's better to break it up into 3 or 4 pounds, fed three or four times a day, rather than 6 pounds twice a day.

At Phillip's barn the horses are given enough hay to keep them satisfied between hard feeds, and at a Three-Day Event are fed four times a day so that they receive smaller meals more often, since they are without their usual turnout schedule. You also have to plan for the eventuality that the horse may need to perform at his normal dinner time, and plan your feeds accordingly—maybe delaying the evening feed until after the horse has been ridden and thoroughly cooled down.

Detection

The way to definitively diagnose ulcers is with *gastroscopy*. This is a relatively straightforward procedure, performed either at an owner's farm or at our clinic, where we essentially "scope" the stomach, assess the ulcers, and use a grading procedure to determine their severity.

We veterinarians prefer to scope horses for a definitive diagnosis; however, many people, sometimes to avoid the cost of scoping, choose to treat their horse based on his previous health history, response to stress, and his potential likelihood for developing ulcers.

Horses that receive *phenylbutazone*, an NSAID often called "bute," are more prone to hind-gut ulcers (right dorsal colitis), which can be difficult to treat.

Treatment

- Colic from a perforated ulcer is a *medical* colic. For horses needing medical management for EGUS, as of writing, the FEI allows the use of Gastrogard® (omeprazole), which is the only FDA-approved ulcer treatment at this time and Zantac® (ranitidine), which is FDA approved for *humans*, though its use in horses is common and considered accepted practice. Simply said, these medications help reduce the hydrochloric acid in the horse's stomach.

- It is now recognized that ulcers are probably a big cause of GI pain—more than was thought 30 years ago. The downsides of treatment for ulcers are the longevity of treatment and the medication's cost.

- With horses already successfully treated for gastric ulcers, it is common to give them preventive doses during times of stress, that is, during travel and competition. Let's say you have a high-risk horse: You may choose to begin treating two days prior to travel, during travel, and for several days after.

Emergency Kit

Both in your barn and for travel, you should have an emergency kit that is easy to carry around. Items in the kit are to help when, among other situations, you need to:

- Evaluate whether a horse has a fever.

- Be able to control a fractious animal in the case of a shipping accident, for example.

- Deal with an eye emergency until a vet is available.

- Contain bleeding in the event of significant trauma.

Contents
- At least one rectal thermometer. These are available in digital form, though I still prefer the reliable old-fashioned mercury thermometer with some string and a clip on the end that you can fasten to the horse's tail.

When a digital thermometer doesn't work, usually because of a dead battery, the mercury one likely will.

- A sedative, such as acepromazine. Only a small amount would need to be used.

- Types of NSAIDs, such as phenylbutazone, known as "Bute." These are inexpensive, so there's no reason not to carry one. Also a bottle or tube of flunixin meglumine (Banamine), which is most veterinarians' choice for treating colic. As said, it's best when administered under the advice of a veterinarian, but in certain circumstances (late at night) it can be very useful to have it on hand.

    Note: Although Bute is very effective for musculoskeletal pain, it should not be used for colic since it limits the types of medication your veterinarian can administer as treatment.

- Two tubes of eye ointment that do *not* contain corticosteroids for a scrape on the cornea; most vets agree this is safe until the horse can be evaluated.

- Bandaging material, such as Vetrap. There are a wide number of commercially prepared bandages to cover large joints and difficult-to-cover areas. There are multiple reasons for bandaging horses: keeping medication in contact with a wound site for a prolonged period of time, or in an emergency providing compression to control bleeding.

- Sheet cotton, Gamgee® (commercially available padding consisting of cotton between layers of gauze), or self-prepared cotton rolls for application over swollen, bleeding, or abraded areas.

- Topical ointment or antibiotic cream.

- A broad-spectrum antibiotic and a dosing syringe for its administration.

- Battery-operated, hand-held clippers for shaving around a wound site. (Be sure you bring the battery charger! We always keep a

The Importance of a Flashlight

True Blue Girdwood sustained a very serious, career-jeopardizing injury at the Open European Championships in 1995 held in Pratoni del Vivaro in Italy. It was a widely publicized and photographed incident: There were pictures in the following day's Rome newspaper of me prepping and suturing a circumferential degloving injury, with the skin pulled off his entire leg down to the pastern.

It was an incident that led to changes at FEI competitions. He was the last horse on course, and it was autumn with dusk arriving quickly. After he was vanned back from the cross-country course, we had to use flashlights to suture him outside his stable. We were able to successfully treat the wound and he made it to the Olympics the next summer. A flashlight or "adequate light" is now recommended for FEI vets. I use one all the time for tasks like looking underneath the horse's abdomen or the inside of his hind leg.

spare battery charging.) This can do double-duty in your grooming kit as well.

- A flashlight. Sometimes it's difficult to see an injury clearly at competition (see sidebar, p. 303).

CARE OF THE HORSE DURING A COMPETITION

Vital Signs

Pulse

A mature horse's normal resting heart rate is 28 to 40 beats per minute (bpm). A young horse such as a weanling may have a more elevated heart rate. A horse that is excited may be closer to 40 bpm, while one resting in his stall will be closer to 20. A horse that has been suddenly alarmed or one that has just finished being exercised can have a higher than 40 bpm—also quite normal.

How to Check

You can take the pulse right below the large jaw bone from the jugular artery in the groove of the throat, or from the digital arteries on the side of the limb. However, I find it easier for people to invest in an inexpensive stethoscope and learn to take the pulse above and behind the elbow on the left side of the chest. This is much easier, particularly when a horse is moving around, as he might well be doing when he has GI distress, for instance.

Temperature

A normal temperature range is 99 to 100.8 degrees F. Frequently, the horse's temperature is slightly higher in the evening than in the morning. The first sign of fever is 101 degrees F.

How to Check

Use a rectal thermometer. You can lubricate the thermometer with a little petroleum jelly (be sure to tie string to it first, see p. 303).

Respiration

A normal respiration range at rest is 8 to 16 bpm. Again, young horses have higher rates because of their active metabolisms. I think any change in respiration is what you notice immediately: In warm or humid weather it can be much higher. When a horse has a fever, his respiratory rate can be around 32 bpm. There is a lot of variation.

How to Check

Watch the rise and fall of the flank, easily seen when the horse is without tack, to count the breaths.

Cooling Out

The length of a cross-country course, ambient temperature, and the overall effort required by the horse to complete the exercise all have a high influence on the increase in his vital signs once he crosses the finish line. Additional factors need to be considered, such as:

- Has the horse started to grow a winter coat?

- Is the day unseasonably warm or humid?

18.5 The vet box at Fair Hill International.

- Is the horse truly fit for the level of competition?

Conventionally, vital signs are not measured at Horse Trials, so it is up to the rider or trainer to monitor them. However, it is common to have veterinary assistance and guidance at major Three-Day Events where vital signs are monitored until the horse recovers to the point of being discharged by veterinary staff and personnel (fig. 18.5). (Usually, the cross-country course at a Horse Trials is 50 to 60 percent shorter than at a Three-Day Event, so horses are less likely to get so stressed.)

At Three-Day Events, under the discretion of the veterinarians on staff, the pulse, respiration, and rectal temperature will be evaluated along with the horse's general condition before the horse is released to stabling under the direction of his groom.

Although conditions vary from event to event, many organizers are excellent at providing tubs of water, ice chips, and in the case of the Atlanta Olympic Games, tents (for shade) with fans and a misting system.

Essentially, what we're doing with cold water and a fan is cooling the horse by 1) conduction (application of cold water), and 2) convection (cold air blowing over the horse's body—much like sticking your arm out the window of a car immediately makes you feel cooler).

Although it was once believed that putting ice water over the large muscles such as back and croup caused tying up, this is now considered an old wives' tale; instead it is recognized as an effective way of cooling the horse out (figs. 18.6 A & B).

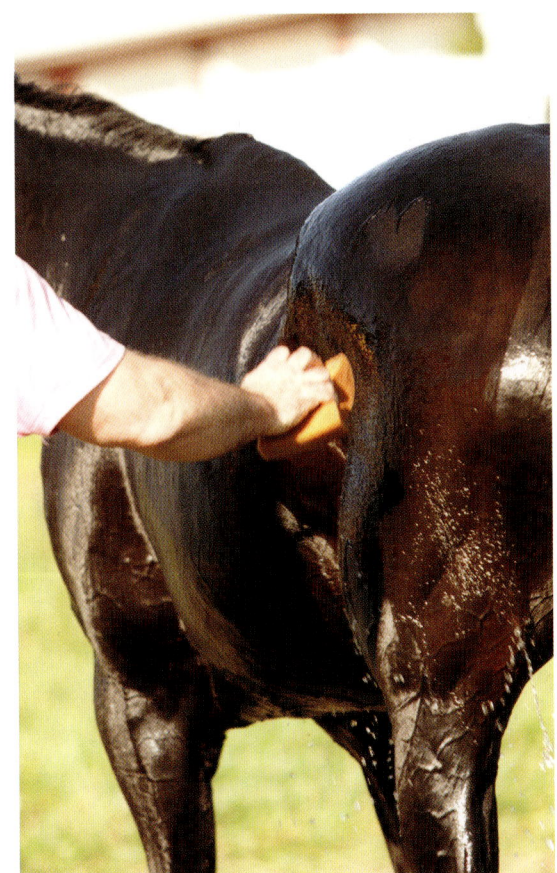

18.6 A & B Ice can help with effective cooling of a hot horse.

Horse Health and Veterinary Care 18

18.7 A–C Lots of cold water on the major muscle mass of the horse will help cool him down quickly after the exertion of cross-country. My group of helpers are cooling down Young Man after completing cross-country at the Fair Hill International CCI**.

TIPS

- Move the horse to a shaded area to help cool him down on a hot day.

- Apply cold water, leave on for maybe 10 seconds to pull heat from the body, then remove with a sweat scraper. When done repeatedly, it is very effective.

- Hold bags of ice over peripheral veins such as the jugular vein.

- Put a cooler made of netting or other light material over the horse to prevent him from getting chilled on the long walk back to the stables. Don't use a heavy wool cooler while you are trying to cool the horse down. This can be counterproductive.

- Walk the horse as you cool him out and to calm him down: With all the excitement in the vet box, a horse is often still fresh and excited after cross-country. I think that having a "station" with a team of people with ice water and sweat scrapers (figs. 18.7 A–C) then periodically walking the horse, is most effective.

- When a horse completes a Three-Day cross-country course (or at any other level, too) he should not be gasping for breath at the end.

Appendix A

Glossary of Eventing Terms

From DiscoverEventing.com and used by permission of the United States Eventing Association (USEA)

Amateur A USEA member may compete as an amateur as long as he/she accepts no money for riding, showing, training, schooling, or conducting clinics or seminars.

American Eventing Championships The USEA American Eventing Championships are the national championships for the sport of eventing, held at a new location every three years.

Area The USEA is divided into 10 Areas. Each Area has its own governing body and organizes activities for its members. The areas must abide by the rules of the USEA.

Arrowhead A type of cross-country fence, also called a chevron, shaped like triangles, with the point facing toward the ground. They tend to be very narrow, usually only a few feet wide.

ASTM/SEI Organizations that certify riding helmets. The ASTM (American Society for Testing and Materials) sets standards for many types of safety equipment. The SEI (Safety Equipment Institute) tests helmets to be sure they meet the ASTM standard.

Bank Jump Cross-country bank jumps are steps up or down from one level to another, and can be single jumps or built as a "staircase" of multiple banks.

Bit Check In the dressage warm-up, riders are required to get their bit, spurs and whip checked to make sure they are acceptable according to USEF rules.

Bounce A bounce is a fence combination sometimes found on the cross-country, of two fences placed close together so the horse cannot take a full stride between them, but not so close that the horse would jump both fences at once.

Brush Jump Brush jumps consist of a solid base with brush placed on top. The horse is supposed to jump through the brush in a flat jump, rather than over the top of it in a more rounded arc.

Bullfinch This fence has a solid base with several feet of brush protruding out of the top of the jump up to 6 feet high. The horse is supposed to jump through the brush, rather than over it.

CCI *Concours Complet International* (CCI) is an international Three-Day Event as opposed to a national competition or a one- or two-day FEI Horse Trials (CIC) (see below). CCI competitions are held under FEI rules for Three-Day Events, including the general rules and veterinary regulations, and offer One- to Four-Star events.

Chef d'Equipe The coach of the national eventing team.

CIC *Concours International Combiné* (CIC) is an FEI Horse Trials. The CIC may be held over one day, and is thus considered an international One-Day Event. However, it must follow FEI rules. The CIC is held only at the One- to Three-Star levels.

Classic Format The traditional long format of the endurance day, which includes roads and tracks (Phases A and C) and steeplechase (Phase B) before the cross-country over fences (Phase D). The Classic Format is currently being held at the Training and Preliminary Levels.

Closing Date The closing date is the Tuesday four weeks after opening date (see p. 311). Organizers may accept post entries after the closing date.

Coffin Also called the ditch and rails, the coffin is a combination fence where the horse jumps a set of rails, continues to a ditch, then to another jump.

Combination Groups of multiple jumping elements. All the jumps are placed within one to three strides of each other, and are meant to be jumped as a series in a specific order. Combinations are named by their number of elements. Double and triple combinations are the most common.

Combined Test A combined test is a competition that includes dressage and show jumping, but leaves out the cross-country phase.

Corner Corner fences are a triangular shape with the horse jumping over one corner of the triangle.

Course Designer The course designer is responsible for the layout, measurement, preparation, and marking of the route for cross-country test, as well as the design of the cross-country fences. He or she may or may not also be the course builder.

Course Map The map received by competitors that shows the route and all of the elements on each cross-country course at a Horse Trials or Three-Day Event.

Cross-Country The second phase of an event, involving the horse and rider galloping over natural terrain and jumping a variety of fixed obstacles along the way.

Dangerous Riding Any competitor who rides in such a way as to constitute a hazard to the safety or well-being of the competitor, horse, other competitors, their horses, spectators, or others. Dangerous riding is penalized by 25 penalties or elimination and/or the issuance of a warning card, at the discretion of the ground jury.

Developing Riders The USEF Eventing Developing Rider Program is available to riders of any age who aspire to compete at the highest levels of the sport. To qualify, each horse/rider combination must have completed a CCI** or above. Precedence is given to riders without prior team experience. Riders can apply or be selected by talent spotters.

Disqualification Disqualification means that a competitor and his horse(s) may not take further part in the event. It is applied at the discretion of the ground jury.

Ditch An element on cross-country courses, ditches can be used individually, or in combinations such as the coffin (ditch and rails).

Dressage The first phase of eventing, demonstrating the horse and rider's ability to perform a series of prescribed classical movements on the flat in an enclosed arena.

Elimination Elimination can be enforced due to many different circumstances. A rider who has been eliminated may not continue on with the competition except with permission of the ground jury.

Endurance The second day of the classic long-format event, the endurance phase consists of roads and tracks, steeplechase, and cross-country.

Error In dressage, the first error is penalized by two points, the second by four, and the third results in elimination.

FEI The FEI (*Fédération Equestre Internationale*) is the sole authority for all international events in dressage, para-equestrian dressage, jumping, eventing, driving, para-equestrian driving, endurance, vaulting, and reining.

Frangible Pins A frangible pin is a breakable pin installed in certain cross-country jumps with the precise failure strength that allows the rail to drop when a horse hits it, thereby stopping the horse from rotating or somersaulting in a fall. This means the horse can hit the rail fairly hard without the fence collapsing and still keep its feet, but if the critical load is reached, the pin would fail with the potential of minimizing risk of injury to both horse and rider.

Future Event Horse The Future Event Horse (FEH) series was introduced in 2007 and focuses on yearlings, two-year-olds, and three-year-olds, and judging the potential they have to become successful event horses. Each age group is judged separately, and genders within the age group are judged separately when the number of entries allows.

Ground Jury The ground jury is responsible for the judging of the event and for settling all problems that may arise during its jurisdiction. If, after consultation with the technical delegate, the ground jury is not satisfied with the arrangements or courses, it is authorized to modify them.

High Performance Divided into A and B squads, the High Performance Squad is made up of riders who receive additional training and grants from the USEF in preparation for major international competitions.

Hog's Back A type of spread fence with three rails, where the highest rail is in the center.

Hors Concours A competitor who enters an event *hors concours* will pay the entry fee, be judged in the normal manner and in accordance with the rules, but will not be counted in the final standings.

Horse Inspection A horse inspection (or jog or trot-up) is required at CCI and CIC competitions. The first one takes place before the dressage test, normally the day before and the second before the show jumping phase. They are conducted by the ground jury and the veterinary delegate acting together as a committee with the president of the ground jury in charge. The horses must be inspected in hand, at rest and in movement, on a firm, level, clean but not slippery surface. The committee has the right and the duty to eliminate from the competition any horse that it judges is unfit, whether on account of lameness, lack of condition or for any other reason.

Horse Registration Horses are required to be registered with the USEA (a one-time fee) in order to compete at the Novice Level and higher.

Horse Trials A Horse Trials is a national competition run under the rules of the USEF. Horse Trials may take place over one to three days. Internationally, the term is CNC ("N" meaning national).

Instructor Certification Program (ICP) The USEA Instructors' Certification Program is a professional education and certification program for instructors of event riding, competing, and horse care. The six levels of ICP certification correspond to the levels of national and international competition from Novice through Advanced and from CIC* through CIC*** and Training Level Three-Day Event through CCI****.

Jump Judge A volunteer at each jump on the cross-country course who is responsible to assess penalties at jumps, respond in case of emergency, and ensure that the area around the jump is clear when each competitor approaches.

Junior A competitor is considered a Junior through the end of the calendar year of his/her eighteenth birthday.

Leaderboard The top riders in the country in various categories are tracked via a point system. The top horses and riders on USEA Leaderboard earn prizes at the end of the year.

Medical Armband A current USEA medical armband, containing valuable information in case of emergency, is required to be worn by the rider in both the cross-country and show jumping phases of USEA recognized competitions.

Normandy Bank A Normandy bank is a combination of obstacles. A ditch precedes the bank, so the horse must jump over the ditch and onto the bank in one leap. There is also a solid fence on the top of the bank, which may produce a drop fence to get off the obstacle, or may allow for a stride off. Because this obstacle incorporates several different types of obstacles into one, it is considered quite difficult, and is usually not seen until the upper levels.

Officials Eventing officials include judges, technical delegates, and course designers, and are licensed by the USEF at the "r", "R", and FEI Levels.

Omnibus The USEA Omnibus provides everything you need to know about all the recognized events throughout the United States. The Omnibus is where you will find a calendar of events so you can choose the best events to compete in. The Omnibus can be accessed on the USEA website or purchased on the USEA online store.

Opening Date Opening date is the first day an event entry can be legally postmarked or time stamped. It occurs on the Tuesday six weeks prior to the first day of competition.

Optimum Time The distance divided by the designated speed gives the optimum time. Completing the course in less than the optimum time results in zero time penalties. A competitor exceeding the optimum time will be penalized.

Oxer An oxer is a type of jump with two rails that may be set even or uneven. The width between the poles may vary. There are several types of oxers including ascending, descending, parallel, square, Swedish, and triple bar.

Palisade A palisade is a fence on a slight 45-degree angle, which leans into the direction you are jumping it. This fence can easily be made more technical by the addition of a ditch in front, so that both the ditch and palisade have to be jumped at the same time.

Preliminary Three-Day A nationally recognized long-format event held at the Preliminary Level (P3D, CCN1*).

Qualifying Results Qualifying results are required to move up to certain levels and qualify for certain competitions. To achieve a qualifying result one must score not more than 50 penalty points in the dressage test (for FEI dressage tests, the score is no more than 75 penalty points); have no jumping penalties at obstacles on the cross-country test, and not more than 90 seconds (36 penalty points) exceeding the optimum time; and not more than 16 penalties at obstacles in the show jumping test.

Red Flag Boundary flags mark obstacles on the jump courses. The red flag must always remain on your right.

Refusal A disobedience in which the horse resists going over the element. At obstacles or elements with height (exceeding 30 cm), a horse is considered to have refused if he stops in front of the obstacle to be jumped. At all other obstacles (30 cm or less in height) a stop followed immediately by a standing jump is not penalized, but if the halt is sustained or in any way prolonged, this constitutes a refusal. The horse may step sideways but if he steps back, even with one foot, this is a refusal.

Rider Fall A competitor is considered to have fallen when he is separated from his horse in such a way as to necessitate remounting or vaulting into the saddle. A fall results in elimination from the competition. *Note 2013 rule change, p. 314.*

Roads and Tracks Phases A and C on endurance day in a long-format event.

Roll Top A roll top has a rounded half-barrel appearance on top.

Runout A disobedience in which a horse avoids the obstacle or element in such a way that he has to be re-presented to the fence.

Senior A division in events that is open to competitors from the beginning of the calendar year of their nineteenth birthday.

Show Jumping/Stadium Jumping The final phase of an event where horse and rider jump a series of fences in an enclosed arena.

Skinny A skinny is any fence with a narrow face, requiring accurate riding and the ability to keep the horse straight.

Small Arena The arena in which lower-level eventing dressage tests are performed. The small arena measures 40 meters long and 20 meters wide.

Speed Fault For the Beginner Novice, Novice, and Training Levels, the distance divided by the speed fault speed gives the speed fault time. Completing the course in less than the optimum time is not penalized up to the speed fault time. Completing the course in less than the speed fault time will be penalized. Speed faults discourage riders from completing cross-county too fast at the lower levels.

Standard Arena Also known as a large arena, the dressage arena is 60 meters long and 20 meters wide. (A small arena is 40 meters long and 20 meters wide.)

Steeplechase Phase B on endurance day in a long-format event. At the end of the steeplechase, the horse and rider go directly into Phase C, the second roads and tracks.

Studs Studs are traction devices screwed into the bottom of the horse's shoe to improve a horse's grip over uneven or slippery terrain. The shoes are "tapped," or drilled, on either heel of the shoe, so that different studs that come in different types and sizes, may be applied as needed and changed according to the footing conditions and the type of work performed by the horse.

Sunken Road A combination jump involving banks and rails. At the lower levels, it may consist of a bank down, with a few strides to a bank up. At the upper levels, the sunken road often is quite complicated, usually beginning with a set of rails, with either one stride or a bounce distance before the bank down, a stride in the "bottom" of the road before jumping the bank up, and another stride or bounce distance before the final set of rails.

Glossary

Table A table is a fence with height and width, with the top of the table being a solid piece of material.

Technical Delegate (TD) The technical delegate will approve the technical and administrative arrangements for the conduct of the event, for the examinations and inspections of horses, for the accommodation of horses and athletes and for the stewarding of the event.

Technical Elimination Abbreviated as "TE" for the score sheets, technical elimination is to define an error strictly related to the actions of the rider, such as, but not limited to: entering the arena with prohibited saddler or prohibited dress; or missing a jump, mandatory flag, or finish line.

Ten-Minute Box The area set aside during a long-format event where the veterinarian performs the mandatory check on horses having completed the steeplechase and roads and tracks before they head on to the final phase of cross-country.

Three-Day Event An equestrian event incorporating the three equestrian disciplines of dressage, cross-country, and jumping in one series of tests for horse and rider. Each phase is held on a distinct day with the entire event lasting three or four days.

Time Limit The time limit is twice the optimum time. A competitor exceeding the time limit will be eliminated.

Training Three-Day A long-format event held at the Training Level (T3D or Half-Star).

Trakehner A Trakehner consists of a rail over a ditch. Trakehners are first seen at Training Level.

United States Combined Training Association (USCTA) United States Combined Training Association was the former name of the USEA. The name was changed in November of 2001.

United States Equestrian Federation (USEF) The United States Equestrian Federation is the National Governing Body for Equestrian Sports in the United States. It was formerly the American Horse Show Association (AHSA). The USEF trains, selects, and funds the United States Equestrian Team. The USEF also licenses equestrian competitions of all levels across the United States each year. The USEF serves as the the National Federation (NF) to the FEI and is a member of the US Olympic Committee.

United States Equestrian Team Foundation The United States Equestrian Team Foundation supports equestrian athletes, promotes international excellence, and builds for the future of equestrian sports. The eight High Performance equestrian disciplines supported by the United States Equestrian Team Foundation are dressage, driving, endurance, eventing, para-equestrian, reining, show jumping, and vaulting.

United States Eventing Association (USEA) The United States Eventing Association is the national organization dedicated to the education and development of horses and riders in the sport of eventing.

White Flag Boundary flags mark obstacles on the jump courses. The white flag must always remain on your left.

Willful Delay A competitor is considered to have willfully delayed his finish if, between the last fence and the finish line, the horse halts, walks, circles, or serpentines. The competitor will be penalized at the discretion of the ground jury.

Young Event Horse An opportunity for owners and breeders to showcase the potential of their four- and five-year-old horses, Young Event Horse classes focus on education and preparation of the event horse in a correct and progressive manner. Youngsters are asked to complete three sections: conformation and type; dressage; jumping test/gallop/general impression. The ultimate goal of the Young Event Horse Series is to choose the youngster that possesses the talent and mindset, and who with proper training, will excel in the uppermost levels of the eventing world.

Young Riders Program The Young Riders Program is offered through the USEA for riders 21 years of age and younger.

Appendix B

Quick Reference: Scoring Cross-Country and Show Jumping

Cross-Country

- Refusal, run-out, or circle
  At the same obstacle: First = 20 penalties; Second = 40 penalties
  In the round: Third (total) = Elimination (E)
- Fall of rider
  *Elimination (*As of 12/01/2013, if you fall off but land on your feet at Beginner Novice or Novice Level, you are NOT eliminated)*
- Fall of horse (shoulder and hip touch the ground)
  Elimination
- Exceeding the time
  Optimum = 0.4 penalties per second
  Limit (twice the optimum) = Elimination
- Coming in under speed fault time
  1 penalty per second (lower national levels in some countries only)
- Competing with improper saddlery
  Elimination
- Jumping without headgear or a properly fastened harness
  Elimination
- Error on course not rectified
  Elimination
- Omission of obstacle
  Elimination
- Jumping an obstacle in the wrong order or direction
  Elimination
- Retaking an obstacle already jumped
  Elimination
- Dangerous riding, at determination of the ground jury
  Elimination (usually with a warning first)
- Failure to wear medical armband
  Elimination (at discretion of ground jury)

Show Jumping

- Knocking down an obstacle
  4 penalties
- Disobedience (refusal, run-out, circling/crossing your tracks, moving backward) over the whole round
  First = 4 penalties; Second = 4 penalties; Third = Elimination
- Fall of rider
  Elimination
- Fall of horse
  Elimination
- Exceeding the time allowed
  1 penalty per second
- Jumping an obstacle in the wrong order
  Elimination
- Error of course not rectified
  Elimination

Appendix C

Event Packing List

Note: Items are listed in alphabetical order.

SHIPPING
- Bandages and Cottons
- Bell Boots
- Chain
- Coggins Test/Vet Papers
- Full Hay Net
- Flashlight
- GPS
- Head Bumper
- Health Certificate
- Lead Shank
- Pins, Tape
- Shipping Boots
- Spare Tire
- Tail Bandages
- Travel Sheet, Rug
- Water Jugs/Fresh Water
- Watering Bucket
- Wheel Chock

FEEDING
- Electrolytes, Salt
- Feed Bucket
- Feed Scoop
- Grain
- Hay and Hay Net
- Supplements
- Treats
- Water Buckets (2)

BANDAGING
- Alcohol
- Bandages
- Liniment
- Paper Bags/Paper
- Plastic Wrap
- Poultice
- Sheet Cotton
- Standing Cottons
- Towels

STUD KIT
- Easy Boot
- Lubricant/ WD-40
- Nail Clincher
- Spare Horseshoes
- Stud Hole Plugs
- Studs
- "T"Tap
- Wrench

STABLE EQUIPMENT
- Apple Picker/Pitchfork
- Broom
- Chairs
- Double-End Snaps
- Duct Tape
- Extension Cord
- Fan
- Hammer and Nails
- Hay String/Rope
- Hose
- Hot Water Heater
- Leather Punch
- Manure Bucket
- Pliers, Wire Cutters
- Rake
- Scissors, Knife
- Screw Eyes
- Screwdrivers
- Scrub Brush
- Shavings, Straw
- Shovel
- Stall Guard
- Tape Measure
- Writing Paper and Pen

HORSE CLOTHING
- Anti-Sweat Sheet
- Dress Sheet
- Fly Mask
- Fly Sheet
- Quarter Sheet
- Rain Sheet
- Rug
- Stable Sheet
- Tail Bandages
- Wool Cooler

TACK CLEANING
- Leather Cleaner
- Leather Conditioner
- Metal Polish
- Rags
- Sponges
- Tooth Brush
- Boots Polish

MEDICAL KIT
- Antibacterial Cream/Ointment
- Banamine
- Bandage Scissors
- Band-Aids
- Betadine
- Clean Towels
- Disinfectant
- DMSO
- Electrolytes
- Epsom Salts
- Eye Wash
- Gauze and Gauze Pads
- Hydrogen Peroxide
- Ice Pack
- Ichthammol Ointment
- Liniment
- Needles
- Paper Towels
- Prescription Medications
- Scrub
- Sheet Cotton
- Stable Bandages
- Syringes
- Tape
- Thermometer
- Twitch
- Vaseline
- Vetrap, Elastoplast
- Witch Hazel

TACK
- Bell Boots
- Breastplate
- Bridles
- Dressage Saddle/Jumping Saddle(s)
- Extra Bits
- Extra Reins
- Galloping Boots
- Girths
- Halters
- Lead Rope
- Longe Line
- Longe Whip
- Martingales
- Overgirth
- Saddle Pads
- Side Reins

BRAIDING
- Hair Clips
- Mane Comb
- Needle and Thread
- Pull-Through
- Quic Braid or Hair Spray
- Rubber Bands
- Scissors
- Seam Ripper
- Spray Bottle
- Sponge
- Step Stool
- Tape
- Yarn

RIDER
- Alarm Clock
- Air Vest
- Barn Boots
- Belt
- Body Protector
- Boot Jack
- Boot Pulls
- Boots
- Breeches
- Dress Clothes
- Dressage Whip
- Equipment Bags
- Gloves
- Helmet
- Helmet Covers
- Insect Repellant
- Jacket
- Jumping Whips
- Medical Armband
- Mirror
- Omnibus
- Rain Gear
- Rule Book
- Running Shoes
- Sewing Kit
- Shirts
- Spurs and Spur Straps
- Stock Tie and Pins
- Sunscreen
- Toiletry Kit
- Work/Barn Clothes

Appendix D

Jumping Exercises

The following are jumping exercises that I use to train and teach my horses and students, working on the same principles that I have covered in this book:

- The horse stays in front of the leg at all times.

- The jump "holds" the horse.

- The horse understands that he should stay straight on the line he is presented on and committed to jumping.

Generally, I set the distances a little shorter than you will find in a competition. This is for two main reasons:

1. In competition your horse tends to be on a more forward-riding stride, whereas in training there is a lot more stopping and starting, so the horse is not naturally covering the ground as well.

2. In most cases, compressing the horse on shorter distances will help his jump, form and rideability. Too much jumping with longer distances will get the horse flatter in the jump. Too much of either long or short distances is not ideal either; it is important to combine the two and with most horses, keeping the emphasis on training a little shorter than in competition.

Also note:

- I like to have fair jumps for horses: nicely placed ground poles, good approaches and good footing. Adding fillers wherever possible is ideal because it gets the horses used to the "real world"—that is, jumps that are similar to what they will encounter in competition. Liverpools, flower boxes and barrels are all good examples of jumps that can be easily made at home and inexpensive.

- I like heavy rails because in my opinion it is important for the horse to understand that the poles are not meant to be rubbed. If this concept can be instilled in your horse at an early age, then your partnership together will have the chance to ultimately be much safer and successful.

In the following exercises, you'll see that some of the distances between fences are not measured. These are "unrelated" distances and can be set to whatever distance works in the space available (see p. 157 for more about "related" distances).

Jumping Exercises

HOW TO: 11 JUMP EXERCISES EXPLAINED

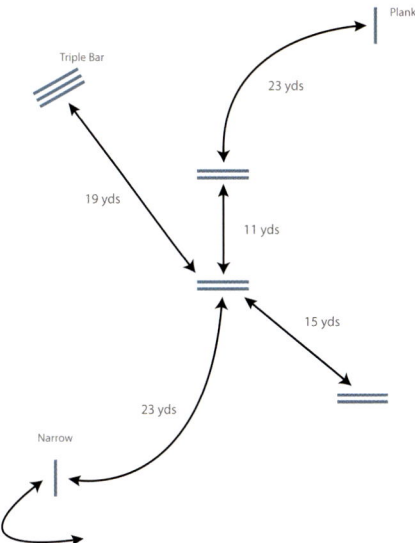

Exercise 1

For the bending line set at 23 yards, the horse should canter through in five easy strides or a "waiting" (shorter) six strides. The plank and narrow fences require balance and control, while the oxer to oxer requires precise, controlled riding through the turn to get the horse straight for the in-and-out.

The triple bar, 19 yards to the angled oxer, then 15 yards to another oxer requires forward riding to the triple bar, a "holding" four strides to the angled oxer, then three strides to the final oxer.

Distances:

11 yards = two strides

15 yards = three strides

19 yards = "holding" four strides

23 yards = five easy or "waiting" six strides

Exercise 2

To practice straightness and holding a line to a narrow-faced jump, I like to use this exercise.

In the line of offset verticals, there should be an overlap, or "eye," of about 2 to 3 feet for the horse to jump through.

To work on being able to ride forward through a turn, the 20-yard bending line can be ridden in a forward four strides. This can also be a "waiting" five or six strides.

Distances:

22 feet = one stride

20 yards bending = forward four or "waiting" five or six strides

MODERN EVENTING WITH PHILLIP DUTTON 317

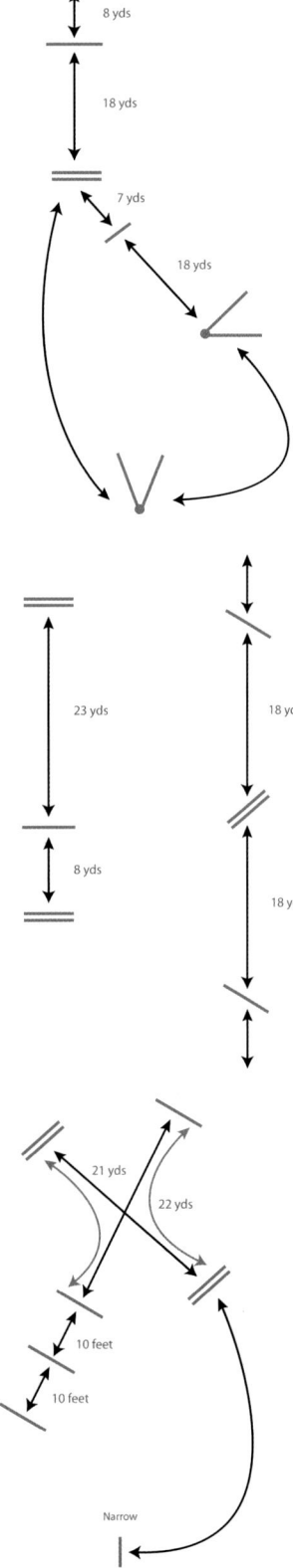

Exercise 3

This exercise is useful when set up in the arena in preparation for cross-country jumping. This is a great exercise for practicing control and straightness, to help the horse and rider understand how to jump apex/angled fences, and to instill honesty in the horse when asked such questions.

Distances:
7 yards angled = short one stride
8 yards = one stride
18 yards = four strides

Exercise 4

For practicing adjustability in the horse's stride, I like to set up the line on the right, which can be jumped straight through or on a bending line to a bending line. The bending line can be four or five strides, while the direct line will be three strides between fences. The 8 yards to 23 yards is a long one stride to a steady five strides. On a forward canter, once you are through the one stride, compress the horse for the short five strides.

Going the other direction, it's a steady five to a forward one stride. Approach on a short canter, then once you're on the fifth stride, push forward for the one stride.

Distances:
8 yards = one stride
18 bending yards = four or five strides
23 yards = five strides

Exercise 5

The adjustability exercises that you can do with this setup are good for going forward and then collecting; or collecting and then going forward. The bending lines require control and obedience from the horse, as well as patience from the rider.

Distances:
10 feet = bounce
21 yards (from oxer to oxer) = a forward four strides
22 yards = a short five strides

Jumping Exercises

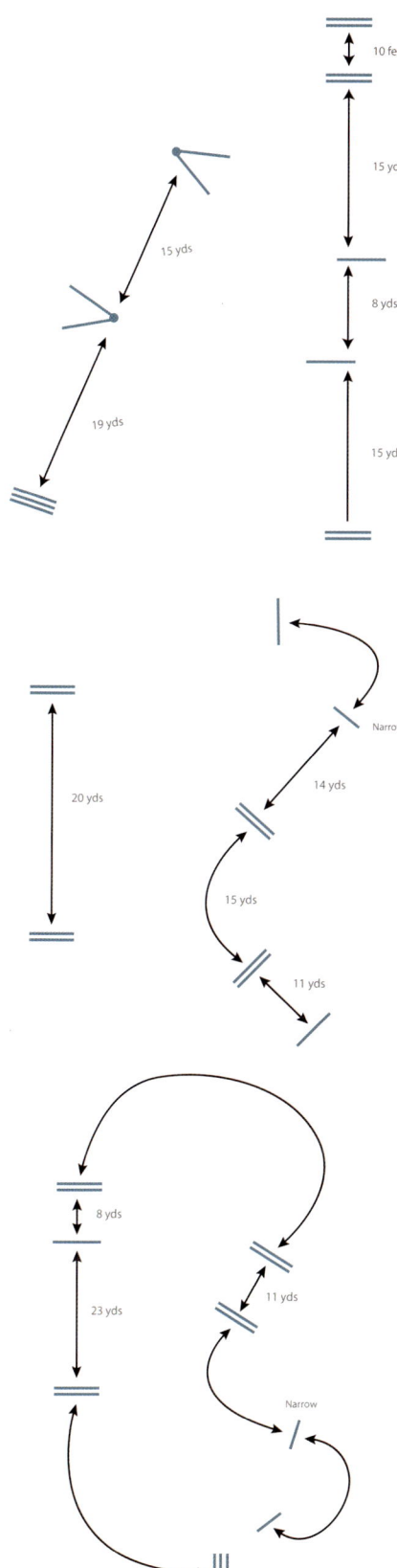

Exercise 6
This is more of an exercise to prepare for cross-country. In the line on the left, the triple bar to the corner needs a positive approach in four strides, without letting the horse get too long, then steady the horse for the three strides from corner to corner. The line on the right is 15 yards, which is a balanced three strides, to a "thread-the-needle" exercise on one stride. This laneway "through the needle" can start wider and as you progress, it can narrow to 3 or 4 feet wide.

The angled verticals require accuracy, but the horse still needs to be forward to make the striding. The oxer-to-oxer bounce requires quite a lot of power to execute, but the horse needs to be on a short collected stride. This can be ridden in either direction.

Distances:
8 yards = one stride
10 feet = bounce
15 yards = a steady three strides
19 yards = four forward strides

Exercise 7
The distance of 20 yards oxer to oxer requires a forward ride for four strides, then you come around in a controlled, shorter canter approach to the vertical on a bending line to a narrow jump, then a short three strides to an oxer. A bending 15 yards is three or four strides. With an oxer 11 yards to a vertical coming up, the best ride would be a "waiting" four strides, which helps to create the right distance for the two strides that follow.

Distances:
11 yards = two strides
15 yards = short three strides
15 yards bending = three or four strides
20 yards = forward four strides

Exercise 8
This exercise is useful if you want an extended period of jumping, the design being such that you can keep going around and around the exercise. This is sometimes helpful for horses that need more jumping to settle.

Distances:
8 yards = one stride
11 yards = two strides
23 yards = five strides

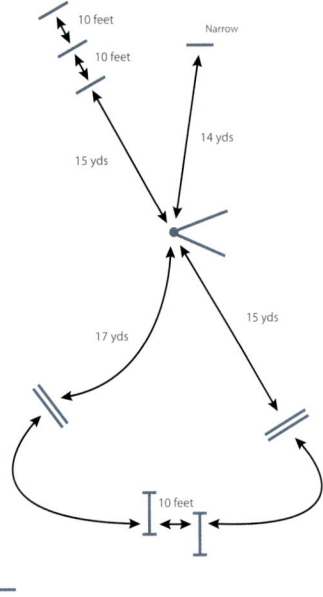

Exercise 9

If you start at the double bounces at a distance of 10 feet, they require a collected canter approach. The 15-yard distance is a nice three strides to the corner, so the horse must stay true on the line, then 15 yards or three strides again to the oxer. Head around the turn to a "thread-the-needle" bounce again, then a short distance around to the oxer. This time it's a bending 17 yards, which is a steady/"waiting" four strides, then a short three strides to a narrow fence.

Distances:
10 feet = bounce
15 yards = steady three strides
17 yards = steady/"waiting" four strides

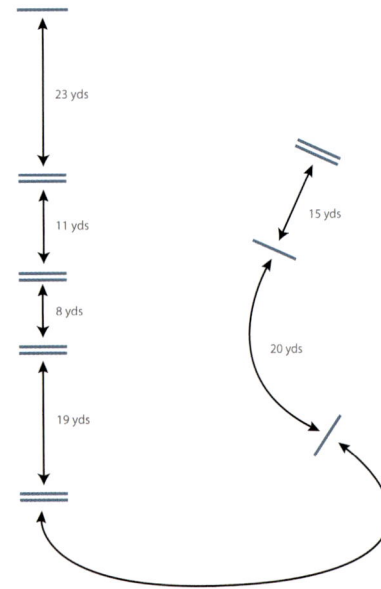

Exercise 10

This combines a bending exercise and a straight line exercise. If you start with the vertical, 23 yards is a steady five strides to two strides to one stride to a steady four strides. Follow with a big wide turn to a vertical, then 20 yards on a turn. This is better done in a "waiting" five strides because the three strides that follow are then steady. If you ride the 23-yard line in four long strides, the canter will be too forward for the short three strides.

Distances:
8 yards = one stride
11 yards = two strides
15 yards = three strides
19 yards = steady four strides
20 yards = "waiting" five strides
23 yards = steady five strides

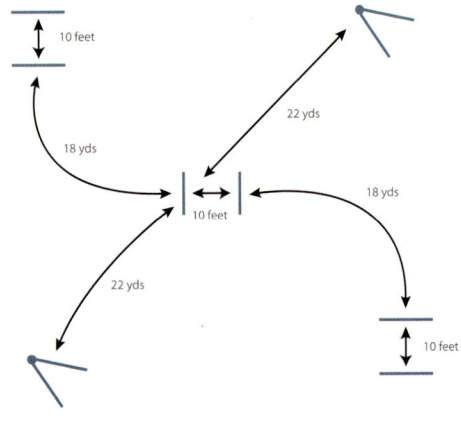

Exercise 11

The 10-foot, short bounce distance really helps the horse and rider to understand the concept of the jump "holding" the horse.
The bending 18-yard line can be ridden in an easy, forward four strides or by staying out wide for five strides.
The option of riding the apex (corner) then 22 yards to the angled first element of the bounce requires steady riding for a distance of five strides. This requires accuracy and honesty and a somewhat collected stride.

Distances:
10 feet = bounce
18 yards bending = easy four or wide five strides
22 yards = steady five strides

Appendix E

My Horse Hall of Fame

True Blue Girdwood
1983 Australian Thoroughbred (by Loosen Up out of Paramel)

This Australian Thoroughbred came with me to the United States—we literally flew over together. I've sometimes heard people say that there are certain things that happen in your life, like going to college or meeting someone, that change your life forever; for me, True Blue Girdwood is one of these cases. If I hadn't had a good horse like that when I started in this country, I'm not sure if my career would have been as successful.

He was a tough, talented Thoroughbred that still required a lot of training to get the best out of him, which helped to develop skills that I needed. He first represented Australia at The Hague in 1994 and then was on the Australian team at the Atlanta Olympics, where he was second-best horse and won team gold. Later he competed at the 1998 World Championships in Italy and had a couple of great finishes at Badminton, an incredible feat for me early in my career, and he was third at the Four-Star in Kentucky. He was an incredible cross-country horse and as fast as you could get; he always had a light mouth and could turn quickly. After the 1998 World Equestrian Games, I didn't compete him much; he did a little at the lower levels for several years before he retired at our house in Pennsylvania, where we have a small paddock, to live out his days.

Hannigan
1991–2010 Irish-bred Thoroughbred (by Western Promise out of Bleeker Lady) owned by Bruce Duchossois

Born and trained in Ireland where he was ridden by Sue Shortt, Hannigan was imported by Abigail Lufkin, and as an eight-year-old, he was very successful. He was shipped to Sydney as one of her horses in training for the Sydney Olympics. In the lead-up to the Games, he started refusing to jump and so wasn't selected for the team.

My Three- and Four-Star Horses

From 1991–2012, I have produced or ridden 30 horses at Three and Four Stars. They are:

Regal Affair	Dusky Moon	Connaught
True Blue Girdwood	I'm So Brite	Kheops du Quesnay
	Damien	
Fairdinkum	Cayman Went	TruLuck
Sky's Prospect	Hannigan	Fernhill Eagle
Show of Heart	Nova Top	William Penn
Irish Fling	Amazing Odyssey	Mighty Nice
Drizzle		Ben
House Doctor	Match Play	Atlas
Rough Cut	The Foreman	Mystery Whisper
Simply Red	Loose 'N Cool	Inmidair

Once home, Abigail decided to sell him, and Bruce Duchossois bought him for me.

Hannigan was as quiet and laid-back an animal as I've ever spent time with; most of my training was about trying to keep him in front of my leg, whether it was flatwork, galloping, or jumping. In the beginning I'd find that when I asked him to turn, since he wasn't going forward enough, he would "nap" or stop. I spent a lot of time encouraging him forward; I taught him that on a turn he had to keep going forward and take the bit through the turn. He had a huge jump, although a little bit unorthodox: He jumped with his head high in the air and wasn't super tight in front with his knees. He wasn't a fast galloper, but he was very efficient; since he wasn't strong, I didn't need a lot of preparation for each jump, so he was able to make the time at most events, including Burghley, Badminton, and Kentucky. Throughout a lot of his career he was plagued with slight soreness around his knee, which made it difficult to manage his soundness and train him for the upper levels. Because of this we retired him at a reasonably early age. In lighter work the soreness went away and Bruce did jumpers with him, my stepdaughter Lee Lee did much of her first eventing on him, including her first Prelim event, and my wife Evie fox hunted him.

Nova Top

1991 British-bred Thoroughbred (by Ra Nova out of Expo Topic) owned by Shannon Stimson

Nova Top was imported from the United Kingdom by Mimi Combs, but they didn't get along and he was stopping at the Intermediate Level. When I tried him I really liked him: He was a nimble Thoroughbred type, a bit nervous, and really jumped over himself, but was very careful. I took a chance on him and Shannon Stimson bought him for me pretty cheaply. He was a very sound horse and we worked mainly on his relaxation in the dressage. Because of his carefulness the jump really held him, and I just had to give him some confidence and ride him forward.

It clicked with him pretty quickly. I got him to the Four-Star level and he placed second at both the Blenheim CCI*** and the Rolex Kentucky CCI**** and then went on to the Athens Olympics where he finished tenth. He was a tough horse, which really showed through at the Olympics where conditions were very hot. The night before his dressage test, "Tucker" had a pretty painful gas colic; any drugs would have meant disqualification from the Olympics so my groom Sara Sadler and I, plus the two Australian vets, Denis Goulding and Graeme Potts, stayed up walking him most of the night until it passed. He recovered and put in a decent test the next day, and we were swarmed by drug testers as we left the arena! After Athens we sold him to Susanna Bordone from Italy.

House Doctor

1992 American Thorougbred (by Inca Chief out of Night House Rock) bred by Tim and Nina Gardner

Bred by Tim and Nina Gardner on their farm in Maryland and broken in by their daughter Julie, House Doctor came to me as a three-year-old. He was the most classic, beautiful Thoroughbred type: about 16.1 hands and naturally balanced and well put together. He had great natural movement and because of his conformation, dressage came naturally him. He was also a very quiet horse. He was not very brave, though—often in the early days it was a battle just to get him to start to jump, so he needed a lot of encouragement.

Because of his dressage he was successful through the levels. I took him to Blenheim in

1999 and had a pretty unlucky fall on cross-country. In 2000 he was second at the Foxhall Cup CCI*** and selected as my backup horse for Sydney, along with the Gardner's horse Show of Heart. I never really thought of him as going to the Olympics that year since he was still so green and only eight years old, but after an untimely lameness with Show of Heart, House Doctor was selected for the Australian team. I'd never been so nervous on cross-country day as at the Sydney Olympics, before negotiating the course with House Doctor, but he stepped up to the plate and helped secure a team gold medal. Two years later at the World Championships in Jerez, Spain, I had a chance to get him to be a World Champion: He was in second place going into show jumping, but was very sore after cross-country, so we didn't have a great show jumping round and ended up fifth. It was still a great effort. He had a long recovery, and then I mainly did Horse Trials with him until his retirement.

The Foreman

1996 American Thoroughbred (by Across the Field out of Four Flora) owned by Annie Jones

Bruce Fenwick, a steeplechase trainer in Maryland, brought The Foreman over for me to try and Annie Jones bought him for me. He had a great trot for a Thoroughbred, and a big, airy jump, but jumped over himself and didn't have great technique. He was also somewhat nervous as most horses off the track can be. He'd raced in Charlestown, not with a big-name trainer, and didn't win a lot of money, but he turned out to be an incredible horse for me. He was always a nervous type of horse and didn't fare well in Horse Trials since he got tense in the dressage, but in the bigger events he had an incredible record, winning or placing near the top in every Three- and Four-Star he went in. He was very quirky with roping around the dressage arena: Any time the laneway to the dressage was confined, he got nervous and took a while to get used to it. The worst was at Saumur in France where we had to go down a laneway—from that day on I'd walk him up and down there first, in-hand, to help get him used to the roping. He was always fine once he realized he wasn't going into a chute toward the racetrack!

The Foreman placed second at both Burghley and Kentucky in one year. The next year in Aiken, South Carolina, he came in from the field with a splint, which seemed pretty minor. We treated it with anti-inflammatory medication and kept him in training, which in hindsight was a pretty bad decision. A lot of the growth of the splint was not obvious from the outside, but it affected the attachment of some of his ligaments. There was always some restriction of the movement of that leg, which made him hard to manage and train for the upper levels. He did go on to win Fair Hill after the injury, but he has had lots of time in the field since.

TruLuck

1997 American Thoroughbred (by Maha Baba out of Grayfully) owned by Annie Jones and Becky Broussard

TruLuck was bought off the track by Dave Harris from Oklahoma, who sold him to a student of mine, Amy Smith from Texas. When Amy had to go to college, Annie Jones and Shannon Stimson bought TruLuck for me to ride; eventually Becky Broussard took over Shannon's share. He was an incredibly honest horse: I never had a cross-country fault with him in his whole career. He was a good mover: His conformation was a fraction downhill, but he moved very uphill and had a great gallop (although he did struggle with the flying changes). We had some great performances, including fourth at Burghley, and won individual silver and team gold at the Pan-Am Games. He had a lot of bad luck and injuries, including a broken hind coffin bone, a punctured tendon, and a crack in his shoulder, so he missed a lot of competition time. We retired him last year and now Annie Jones fox hunts him. He loves his new life.

Simply Red
1988 English-bred Thoroughbred (sire and dam unknown)

Imported from the UK by Kelli Temple and Carl Bouckaert, Simply Red was sent to me to sell because he had lost his confidence in jumping. I remember the first day I tried to jump him, he stopped at the first cross-rail. He had quite a long back, so his canter was long and hard to put together, and he was another one I took back to basics and taught not to get worried about getting close to the jumps or getting a deep distance. We did a lot of figure eights, circles, and teaching him to relax on the approach to a jump.

I took him to the Fair Hill CCI*** that year and he placed well. He went on to Kentucky the next year and to my dismay ended up a close second to Giltedge! He was always cautious and not very brave, and as it turned out he had quite bad cataracts in his eyes. The next year he landed in the middle of an apex corner with me and we decided to retire him early. He's now at Carl Bouckaert's farm in Georgia.

Connaught
1993 Irish Sport Horse (by Ballysimon out of Bromehill Rouge) owned by Bruce Duchossois

Born in Ireland and produced by Carol Gee and Paul Donovan, "Simon" was imported by Julie Richards. Once he got to the Three-Star level, she was starting a family and offered to sell him to me, so Bruce bought him. Simon always had a huge jump but was quite worried about his jumping, so he'd rush at the fences and had no idea how to get to a deep distance. I started from scratch over low jumps and tried to give him an understanding of the jump "holding" him. Our partnership still wasn't great, but I ended up taking him to Kentucky in 2004, with an eye on the Athens Olympics, and we had a pretty bad fall coming out of the sunken road. After that we did start to mesh and ended up having an incredible record at Kentucky: He never had a rail down there and was always highly placed, including winning in 2008.

Simon had tendon and wind surgeries, and it was a real struggle to get him fit enough for a Four-Star. He also didn't like to eat much, so he was always skinny, and it was hard to get him to carry enough muscle. Emma did an incredible job with him during his career, including in the heat at Hong Kong (the 2008 Olympics). As a side note, in December 2007, when he was 14 years old, we received an offer for him for $250,000; after discussing it with Bruce we decided to sell him, but he failed a vetting on his x-rays. The following year he won Kentucky and then went on to the Olympics—I've never been happier that a horse failed a vetting! He's now retired at Bruce's farm in Aiken.

Woodburn
1996–2011 New Zealand Thoroughbred (by Herewood the Wake out of Princess Heights)

Woodburn was imported by Liz Milliken and sold to Jess and Sharon Sweeley from Acorn Hill Farm. After a couple of years they decided to sell him, but he failed a vetting and they sent him to me to ride. I loved the horse from the first time I sat on him and thought he had the makings to be world class. Annie Jones and Mardy Fawcett bought into a partnership with the Sweeleys so that I was able to keep riding him.

Woodburn struggled with the cross-country at the Two-Star level and it was apparent that he got quite strong at speed, so I spent a lot of time working on getting him to stay in self-carriage when galloping. I usually treated Horse Trials as schooling opportunities and never really went fast with him; this made him more rideable, which allowed me to make the time at the major events. He eventually developed into a phenomenal cross-country horse and jumped around some of the toughest courses in the world, including a very wet Burghley and the WEG in Kentucky, and made them look easy. He was pretty highly strung and naturally nervous, which took constant management of his feeding and meant we focused on keeping him relaxed and quiet. He also had a rolled-in heel on his left front foot, which took constant attention from our farrier, especially during the summer months. Woodburn's career was cut short when he died suddenly in 2011 from a ruptured aorta while turned out in his field.

Mighty Nice

2004 Irish Sport Horse (by Ard Ohio out of Sarazen)

Foaled in 2004, I tried Mighty Nice in Ireland in December, 2010. It was late one evening and love at first sight, since he's such a stunning looking horse. He had a nice jump and great canter, but not much trot—but I was prepared to work on that. I was traveling around with Carol Gee and told her I wanted the horse and had to fly home to find someone to buy him; she actually bought him and then waited for me to find another buyer. We had him back in the United States even before she was paid back, so I'm pretty indebted to her for her kindness.

Mighty Nice had done a One-Star in France before I bought him and had pretty good basics even though he was still green. Things came easy for him and with the Olympics in mind, I decided to move him on quickly. He is a sensitive horse and wants to do things well. Most of the time in show jumping I'm trying to keep him quiet. He's fast and agile even though he's a big horse, and the dressage comes pretty naturally to him, it's just a matter of building the strength he needs. "Happy" is close to being the ideal event type, being such a big, good-looking horse with a great nature.

William Penn

2002 Irish Sport Horse (by Condios out of Cavaliers Abbey) owned by Tim and Nina Gardner

I saw him on the same trip to Ireland as Mighty Nice, in Belfast, and tried him in an indoor. He has huge movement and a huge jump, but you could tell he'd been pushed along a bit in his work and was lacking some basics. Tim and Nina Gardner offered to buy him for me to ride.

The first spring was not that pleasant for him as it took us a while to get on the same page. He would stop on me in the show jumping any time I tried to adjust his stride. After some embarrassing performances we started to work things out, and he is now turning into a reliable horse. He is very quiet and a bit along the lines of Hannigan (see p. 321): most of the time, I'm trying to keep him in front of my leg. He has a very powerful jump and it's a case of being able to have a little more say in the approach to the jump, working on getting him to come to the jump on whatever length of canter stride I need. For his size he is fast on cross-country and has great stamina.

Ben

2001 American Holsteiner (by Mr. Wizard out of Baroque) owned by Team Rebecca, LLC

A Holsteiner gelding bred in the United States, Ben was sent to Julie Richards to sell. When I was in training in Chattahoochee, Georgia, for the 2010 WEG, she asked me to sit on him for her with no idea that I'd look at him to buy later. He wasn't that impressive, so I didn't think much of it. Julie rode him the next year, and he took to eventing well: He actually had a lot of education in the dressage and show jumping but needed confidence cross-country. Julie took him to the CIC** at Red Hills, and then I approached Sarah Kelly about buying him.

Ben is a Warmblood and that comes through on cross-country—he's not a sleek cross-country machine compared to a lot of the Thoroughbreds I've ridden. Because fitness wasn't a part of his early life, a lot of my training now is to get him in shape for the Four-Star level. I've galloped him head-to-head with other horses and tried to get his heart into wanting to go fast. He's a big, robust horse with a great mind and attitude and he loves to work.

Sky's Prospect

1987 American Thoroughbred (by Tank's Prospect out of Third and Ten) owned by Tim and Nina Gardner

A spotted grey, Sky's Prospect was a steeplechase horse before the Gardners bought him, the first horse of many that I've ridden for them. He was incredibly honest on cross-country and had quite a high knee action on the flat. The main area we had to work on was his show jumping, where he was quick to go flat and low like he'd been taught for racing. He did very well, including winning the Fair Hill*** and had a top ten finish at Bramham. He also jumped around clean at Burghley, representing Australia in the Open European Championships.

Cayman Went

1994 American Thoroughbred (Easy Goer out of Secret Holdings)

A very well-bred Thoroughbred raced by Annie Jones' family, Cayman Went retired from racing early, and they ended up putting a pin in his hind ankle as a three-year-old. Annie sent him to me as a four-year-old. He took to eventing quickly. My fondest memory was at Fair Hill when he was only seven years old: My twin daughters were born late Friday night, and the next day he raced around cross-country clean. Unfortunately I had a rail down to finish second. He went on to be successful at Kentucky and Badminton but was plagued with back problems, and it became apparent that dressage was a struggle. He'd always been a brave horse but didn't want to jump off drop fences. He retired from eventing when he was only 12 and became a successful fox hunter. He was an incredible horse—he had three careers and was very good at all of them.

Mystery Whisper

2000 Australian Warmblood (by Richmeed Medallion out of Socialite) owned by Jim and Arden Wildasin

My partnership with Mystery Whisper was short but very memorable. I flew to Australia in November 2011 to look for a suitable horse(s) for Arden Wildasin. Arden and her mother, Sarah, met me in Australia. I haven't bought a lot of horses from Australia in the past, mainly because it is much easier and closer to get horses from

Europe. However, there wasn't much available in Europe at the time, and there seemed to be a good selection to look at and try in Australia.

Heath Ryan bred, broke, trained, and competed Mystery Whisper to the Four-Star level. I knew Heath from growing up in Australia and through my experiences on the Australian eventing team when he was the assistant coach for dressage. He is an incredibly accomplished rider on the flat, having represented Australia well in dressage. A couple of years back, Heath suffered a stroke, most likely caused by a blood clot caused by inactivity on a long flight back to Australia. Most riders wouldn't even consider riding in a Four-Star event after something that traumatic, and it speaks volumes about Heath's determination and heart that he was able to get to that level again.

It also made me think that Mystery Whisper could be suitable for an up-and-coming rider, who undoubtedly will make some mistakes in her riding. After two days of trying the horse out, we decided to try to purchase him.

Heath's original goal had been to get someone who was in contention for the London Olympics to buy his horse. He has Mystery Whisper's dam and also many of his brothers and sisters, whose value would increase if "Whisper" went to the Olympics.

We decided to structure a deal so that I would ride Whisper in the spring events to try to get him qualified for the US Olympic Team. If we were able to achieve this and he was selected, I would then have the opportunity to compete him in London before returning him to Arden at the conclusion of the Games.

Once he was home, it was a mad scramble to get Whisper's ownership papers in order because the FEI deadline for horse ownership is December 31 of the year before the Olympics—2011. It was still a long shot but well worthwhile for me. I had some other very talented horses but all were pretty green at the Four-Star level, especially in the dressage phase.

I set out to get to know Whisper, get him fit enough and be competitive at the world level in just a few months! Whisper was an incredible competition horse, he just loved to go to events and Heath's training on the flat was second to none. We clicked right from day one on cross-country, and he was very careful in the show jumping, but he needed a forward ride to jump big, "scopey" fences with related distances.

In the spring of 2012, Whisper and I won the CIC*** at Red Hills in Florida, The Fork in North Carolina, and the CCI*** at Jersey Fresh in New Jersey, before going on to represent the United States at the London 2012 Olympic Games.

Acknowledgments

From Phillip:

There have been so many people that have helped me throughout my riding career. My childhood riding days were spent at the Nyngan Pony Club. To all the instructors, organizers and volunteers, I thank you. Denis Piggot was my first real inspiration when he spoke to me about his experiences at the Montreal Olympics. Beth and Warrick Turner gave me my first horse job and really believed in me. Wayne Roycroft was my Australian team coach for many years. Wayne's unbelievable knowledge and dedication to his riders was unprecedented. He came to the United States before the Atlanta Olympics and spent a month coaching me, one on one, on every horse I had in the barn. I definitely would not have won any of my medals without this incredible horseman and friend. Captain Mark Phillips has been another great coach that I have been fortunate to have ridden with and been coached by. He is a great horseman and was very good and understanding as he helped me transition to the American team and system.

In the United States, I have been fortunate to ride for some of the nicest, most loyal and supportive people. Annie Jones has been my longest owner, first helping me with True Blue Girdwood. Michael Dickinson and Joan Wakefield believed in me early on and sent me a lot of racehorses to work with, which gave me a leg-up financially. Tim and Nina Gardner have supported me for as long as I can remember and made it possible for Evie and me to buy True Prospect Farm. Bruce Duchossois has been with us now for close to 15 years, and I couldn't ask for a better supporter and friend. Augie and Joyce Vettorino are great friends and supporters of the sport. The late Marilyn Riviere was a great friend to me and hosted us in Aiken for many years. The late Rebecca Broussard was another incredible person that I was fortunate to ride for. Her equestrian legacy is now being carried on by her daughter, Sarah Kelly, who I am very grateful to. I have some wonderful new owners: Tom Tierney, who is new to the sport but is very enthusiastic, and we are getting a good string of horses; George Mahoney is willing, interested and really enjoys his horses.

I will be forever grateful to Bruce Davidson, who agreed to help an unknown kid from the outback of Australia when I showed up on his doorstep. He generously connected me with Ron and Densey Juvonen who took a chance and gave me my first place to live, work and train in the US. They all remain great friends.

Kevin Keane was my first veterinarian when I moved to the United States over 20 years ago. Little did I realize then that he was one of the best vets in the country and would become one of my best friends. His help with my horses throughout the years has been invaluable. Dave Kumpf and Steve Tiechman are two genius farriers and have always done their absolute best with my horses. I have had incredible grooms over the years, Colby Saddington, Sara Sadler and Emma Ford all made the horses welfare and care their highest priority. They were also great company for me, which is important because we spent a lot of time together. My assistant trainers have also been there for me, keeping the barn and horses going while I travel: Bonnie Mosser, Heidi White, Boyd Martin, Ryan Wood and Jennie Brannigan. Lastly, my wife Evie, has stood by me through the excitement of my successes, but more importantly, is so supportive when it doesn't go right. Also, my children, Lee Lee, Mary and Olivia—without them, none of this would be worth it.

I feel extremely privileged to have been sponsored by Cosequin now for approximately 15 years. It is a great company to be associated with.

Many thanks as well to Amber Heintzberger, who, under the difficult circumstances of having a new baby and working with a very green author, did an amazing job.

Eventing is a close-knit sport and community, and I feel very lucky to be a part of it.

From Amber:

It is no small task to bring a book or a baby into the world, and the writing of this book coincided with the birth of my son William. I would like to thank Phillip for his understanding and cooperation as we conducted interviews by phone at extremely odd (usually very early) hours so that we could talk while the baby was sleeping, or while my husband or a babysitter was home to watch him. The photo shoot at True Prospect Farm with William snoozing against my chest in a baby carrier for hours was one that I will always remember.

I am extremely grateful that Martha Cook, Rebecca Didier, and Caroline Robbins at Trafalgar Square Books were also very patient and supportive as the writing took longer than originally planned and the book became longer and more and more detailed. I hope that everyone agrees it was worth the wait.

A huge thanks to my husband, Juergen Grosserhode, for helping out with the kids, William and Emily, who were not always so patient about the many hours I spent at the computer writing and editing. Thanks also to Molly Hill, Melissa Punch, Courtney Young, Elly King, Taryn Herman, and Jackie Buda for the proofreading, moral support, encouragement, and child care.

Thanks also to my parents, Leslie and Hank Heintzberger, my brother Land Heintzberger, and to my grandmother Jean Loveday, for all the years of encouragement and support, driving to events and Pony Club rallies, and putting up with my horse obsession. The many lessons learned over the years made it possible for me to write this book with Phillip.

Finally, of course, we owe the greatest depths of gratitude to the horses.

Index

Page numbers in *italics* indicate illustrations.

Adjustability, of stride, 159. *See also* Ratability
Advanced Level, xv, xvi–xvii, 69–70, 71–73, 114
Aerobic/anaerobic exercise, 68, 69, 74
Alternative therapies, 255, 262, 294–295, *296*
Anhidrosis, 269, 297–298
Anticipation, 183. *See also* Rushing
Apex fences, xii, 138–141, *139*, *141*
Apparel, for riders, 55–63
Approach, to jumps. *See* Takeoff
Apps, for smartphones, 194
Arenas
  in dressage competition, 185, 188
  training/schooling in, 73, 114, 138–139, 141
Arthritis, 31, 262, 288–291
Ascending oxers, 160–161, 206, 227, *228*
Azoturia, 269, 293, 306

Back
  of horse, 22, 91, 93, 113, 288, 291, 293–294
  of rider, 76
Balance, of rider, 112, 119
Balancing/rebalancing, of horse, 44, 161, 193–194, 212, 222–223, 224. *See also* Rebalancing
Bandages
  for legs, 48, 50, *50*, 253, *256*, *291*, 303
  for tail, *250*
Bank fences, 133, 135–138, *136*, *138*
Bascule, 26, 160, 166, 227
Bathing, 238–239, *239*, *240*, 245, 300
Beginner Novice Level, xiii, xvi, 69, 71, 114
Bell boots, 50, 281
Ben, 326
Bending, *92*, 98. *See also* Lines
Bit checks, 178, *179*
Bits, 40, 44–48, *44*, *46*, 113, 153. *See also* Contact
Blankets/blanketing, 219, 253, 255, 299, 308
Body protectors, 59–60, *59*
Boldness, of horse, 23

Boots
  for horse, 48–50, *50*, 53, 179, 253. *see also* Bandages
  for rider, 63
Boredom, 259, 268
Bounce fences, 146–147
Bowed tendons, 33, 291–292, 295, 297
Bracing. *See* Hollowing, of horse's back
Braiding, 246–250
Breaks. *See* Rest days
Breastplates, 39–40
Breathing exercises, 171
Breeches, 60
Bridles, 15, 40–44, *41–43*, 256

Canter. *See also* Leads/lead changes
  counter-canter, 107–108
  in cross-country, 126, 144–145
  evaluation of, 23–24
  in fitness training, 71–74, *72*
  pace control exercises, 114–115
  in show jumping, 154–156, *154–155*
  transitions to/from, 90–91, 104
  in warm-up, *86*, 183, 204, *204*, 226, 227
  into water, 134
Cardiovascular health
  of horse, 297
  of rider, 76
Cayman Went, 326
CCI events, xv, xvii, 71–73
CCN events, xiv
Chafing, 39, 50, 299–300
Chambon, 51
Change, vs. improvement, 22, 28
CIC events, xv, xvii, 71–73
Clipping, *242–244*, 243–245, 299, 304
Clips, on shoes, 278–279
Coats, 61
Coffin fences, 144–145
Colic, 253, 259, 263, 301, 302
Collection, 85, 99, 101, 152
Collective marks, in dressage, 188
Combination fences
  in cross-country, 142–144, 194–195
  in show jumping, 159–160, 224
Combined Tests, xvii
Compatibility, of horse and rider, 15–16, 17, 22–23, 32

Competition
  health and well-being during, 254–257, 304–308
  levels of, xiii–xv
  preparations for, 64, 79, 169, 238–239, 241, 246–257, 315
  rules, resources for, xviii. *see also* Drug rules
  scoring of, xviii, 186, 188–189, 314
  withdrawal from, xii, 19
Complementary therapies, 255, 262, 294–295, *296*
Concentrates. *See* Grain/concentrates
Concussion, legs and, 287
Confidence
  of horse, 121, 125, 164, 166
  of rider, 171
Conformation evaluation, 20–22
Connaught, 28, 44, 147, 324
Contact
  accessories and, 50–52
  in flatwork/dressage, 84–85, 91, 93, 95, 102, 104
  in galloping position, 119
  jumping and, *150*, 151, *225*, 226
  strong horses and, 113
Cool-down strategies
  for body, 297–298, 304, 306–308, *306–307*
  for legs, 74, 257, *257*, 291
Core fitness, 75–76
Corner fences. *See* Apex fences
Corners, of arena, 186, *188*
Counter-canter, 107–108
Course design, xi–xii, xvii, 198
Crookedness, in jumping, 165, 224
Cross rails, 151–152, 157
Cross-country phase
  apparel for, *56–57*, 60–63, *61*
  competition preparations, *208*, 256
  competition riding, 211, 213–219
  course design, xi–xii, 198
  fence types, 129–147, 194–196, 200
  general considerations, 4, 108, 219
  horse selection, 15–19, 29
  making time, 212–214
  schooling for, *120*, 123–129, *124*, *126*
  scoring, 314
  in short format competition, xiii
  vs. show jumping, 166
  stirrup length, 117, 119

Index

tack/equipment for, *36*, 37, 38–40, 44, 45–49, 65
training venues, 125–126
USEF rules regarding, 114
walking the course, 170, 191–201
warm-up, 203–209
Cross-training, for riders, 76–77

Days off. *See* Rest days
Death, of horses, 298
Defensive riding position, 145
Dehydration. *See* Hydration
Dental care, 268
Diagonal aids, 87, 107
Diet, of rider, 78–79
Digestive health, 253, 259, 260, 263, 301–302. *See also* Feeding/nutrition
Direction changes, 87–88, 181
Distance, time and, 196. *See also* Pace
Distances, in jumping, 156–160, *158*, 223–224, 316–320
Distractions, dealing with, 198–199, *199*
Ditch fences, 130–131, *130–131*, 144–145
Double bridles, 41, 45
Dr. Bristol bits, 45
Draw reins, 51–53
Dressage phase
apparel for, *56*–57, 60–63, *61*
competition preparations, 188, 256
general considerations, xi, 4
horse selection, 15–19, 24, 26–27
relevance to jumping, 152
riding the test, 185–189
tack/equipment for, *36*, 37–39, *38*, 41, 44–45, 48, *48*, 65
warm-up, 171, 177–185, *178*
Dressage training
basics of, 83–85, 91–93
bending aids and, 87–88
movements and exercises, 93–109
transitions, 88–91
Drifting, 26, 165, 224
Drop fences, *133*, 214, *215*
Drug rules, 285, 294–295, 299, 302
Dutton, Phillip
background, ix–x, 111
horses of, 321–327
Dutton RZ saddles, *36*

Emergency kits, 253, 301, 302–304
Endurance, xii, 74, 117. *See also* Horse fitness
Equipment/accessories
for horses, 48–53, *48–50*. *see also* Tack
for riders, 63–65
Event organizers, 11

Eventing, generally, xiii–xvii, 3–5
Experienced/educated horses
evaluation of, 27–29
in training young/green horses, 119, 121, 173
Extended trot, *99*, 101, *101*
"Eyes on the ground," *8*, *9*

Falls, xii, xvi–xvii
Farriers, 10, 272–273. *See also* Hoof care/shoeing
Fast work, 72, 73–74
Fatigue
aerobic/anaerobic exercise and, *69*
in horses, 68, 201, 217
in riders, 75, 76
Faults. *See* Penalties
Feeding/nutrition. *See also* Grain/concentrates
hay, 260–261
health issues and, 267–269, 300–302
overview, 259–260
supplements, 263
travel and, 253, 293
turnout, 264–267
water intake, 263
Feet, evaluation of, 21. *See also* Hoof care/shoeing
FEI
event formats, xv–xvi
rules of, 286, 294–295, 299, 302
Financial considerations, 6–8, 14
Finish, of jumping courses, 201, 219, 232
First aid kits, 253, 301, 302–304
First fences
in cross-country, 211, 213
in show jumping, 222, 230–231
Fitness. *See* Horse fitness; Riders, fitness of
Flashlights, 303, 304
Flatwork, 24, 26–27, 225–226. *See also* Dressage training
Flexibility, of rider, 76, *78*
Flexion, 87, *92*, 93, 94–95, 107
Flying lead changes, 108–109, 155–156, 226, 253–254
Focus
of horse, 200, 209
of rider, *231*
Footing, 73–74, 116, 117, 194, 265, 274–275
Footwear, 63, 64
Ford, Emma, 52–53, 236
Forehand, halting on, 104
Forelock, braiding of, 249–250, *249*
Forward movement, 83–84, 93, 119, 173, 185

"Forward-riding" fences, 128, 129, 195–196
Foxhunting, 112
Fractures, 295
French Link bits, 45
Front legs, jumping technique, 26, 166
Fungal infections, 241, 299, 300

Gag bits, 46–47, *46*
Gaits, evaluation of, 17–18. *See also Specific gaits*
Gallop
development of, 112
evaluation of, 17–18, 29
out of stride, 128
self-carriage in, 114–115
strong horses and, 113
Galloping fences. *See* "Forward-riding" fences
Galloping lanes, 198
Gastrointestinal health. *See* Digestive health
Girths, 38–39, *38*
Gloves, 61, 63
Goal setting, 4–5
Grain/concentrates, 259, 261–263, 267, 269, 293, 300, 301–302
Green horses. *See* Young/green horses
Grooming
for competition, 188, 246–257
daily routine, 237–238, *237–238*
Grooms, 11, 235–236, 272
Ground poles, 108, 151–152, 156, 157, 164

Hackamores, 43–44, *43*
Half-halts, 89–90, *89*
Half-pass, *99*, *100*
Halts and halting, 102–105, *103*, 185, 188, 222, 230
Hannigan, 321–322
Haunches-in, 98–99, *98*
Hay, 260–261
Head
carriage of, 50–52, 95, 225, 226
clipping of, 243, 245
Heat build-up, under tack, *36*, 37, 49. *See also* Cool-down strategies
Heels, of horse, 274, 277, 288
Helmets, 55, 58
Helpers, 11
Hickstead, 298
Hills, 74, 119
Hindquarter conformation, 22
Hives, treatment for, 238
Holding, of horse by jump, 123, 153, 162. *See also* Lines, holding of
"Holds" on cross-country course, 217–218

Hollowing, of horse's back, 47, 50, 102, 113
Hoof care/shoeing. *See also* Farriers
   after competitions, 257
   maintenance routines, 237, 238, *240*, 241, 243, 263, 280–281
   overview, 272–273
   pain management, 288
   stud use, 116, 256, 279–280, *279–280*, 281
   trimming and shoeing, 273–279
Horse fitness
   footing and, 73–74
   general considerations, 67–68, 177, 217
   muscle fitness, 74
   training plan, 68–74
Horse selection
   conformation assessment, 20–22
   general considerations, 4, 13–15, 19–20
   green prospects, 16–17
   movement evaluation, 16, 23–26, *25*
   rider compatibility, 15–16, 17, 22–23, 32
   test rides, 26–27, 29
   trail periods, 32
   upper level horses, 17–19
Horse Trials, xiii–xvi, 72
Horses
   Hall of Fame, 321–327
   as team members, 5–6
House Doctor, 322–323
Hydration
   of horses, 253, *257*, 260, 263
   of riders, 79

Ice. *See* Cool-down strategies
Improvement, vs. change, 22, 28
In-and-out fences, 146–147, 159
Injuries
   associated with eventing, 32, 39, 287–291
   prevention of. *see* Boots; Safety
   skin trauma, *299*
   to soft tissues, 18, 33, 288, 289–292, 295–297
   subclinical, 292
   treatment approaches, *269*, 290–292
"Inside leg to outside rein," 87, 107
Instructors, 8–9, 15
Intermediate Level, xiv, xvi, 69–70, 71–73, 114
International Three-Day Events. *See* CCI events

Jackets, 61
Jog presentations, 64, 254–255, 306
Joints
   health of, 73–74, 290–291
   supplements for, 262
Judges, acknowledging, *184*, 188
Jump cups, 162
Jumping
   ability, evaluation of, 23–24, *25*, 26, 27, 29
   exercises for improving, 316–320
   "holding the horse," 123, 153, 162
   out of stride, 128
   preparation for, 121
   rails down in, xviii, 166, *229*, *231*, 314
   show jumping vs. cross-country, 166

Keane, Kevin, *30*, 31–33, 283–284, *284*
Kimberwicke bits, 47

Lameness. *See also* Injuries; Pre-purchase exams
   as cause of drifting, 165
   hoof care and, 278–279
   horse selection and, 20
   longeing and, 51
   rules regarding, 255
Landing strides, 212, 213
Last fences
   in cross-country riding, 219
   in show jumping, 232, *232*
Lateral movements, 93–99
Lazy horses, 226
Leads/lead changes, 108–109, 154–156, 226, 230–231
Learning ability, of horse, 16, 102
Legging up program, 70–73
Legs, of horse. *See also* Lameness
   care of, 74, 257, *257*, 287, 289–291, *291*
   evaluation of, 21
   jumping form, 26, 166
Legs, of rider, 91, 94–96, 165
Leg-yielding, 94–96, *94*, 179
Lengthening, of stride, 101, *101*. *See also* Ratability
Leverage bits, 45
Ligaments, injuries to, 292
Lines
   exercises for, 317–320
   holding of, 126, *127*, 141, 207, 209
   walking of, *196*, 222
Liverpool fences, 162–164, *163*, 223
Logs, as jumps, 125
Long format events, xiii, xv
Long rein, riding on, *187*, 188
Longeing, 51
Lower levels, defined, *69*

Mane care/grooming, 237, 245–250, *248–249*
Martin, Boyd, ix–x, 6
Martingales, 50–51
Medications. *See* Drug rules; Veterinary care
Mental preparation
   for horses, 172–175
   for riders, 76, 169–172, 201, *205*, 224–225, 226
Metal polish, 53
Meter wheels, *197*
Mighty Nice, 325
Mistakes, recovering from, 15, 144, 188, 229
Movement
   conformation and, 20–21
   evaluation of, 16, 17–18, 23–26, *25*
   in halt, 105
   roundness and, 85
Muscles
   fitness training and, 74
   therapies for, 255
Mystery Whisper, 326–327

Narrow fences, xii, 141–142, *142–143*, 162
National Three-Day Events, xvi
Neck
   carriage of, 50–52, *95*
   conformation of, 22
Neck straps, 119, 137
Nervousness
   in horses, 211, 216–217, 225, 267
   in riders, 171, 209
Neville Bardos, x, *180*
Nosebands, 41–42, *41*, *42*
Nova Top, 322
Novice Level, xiii, xvi, 69, 71, 114

"On the aids," 105
Opening rein, 155
Option fences, 200
Orthopedic injuries, 295
OTTBs (Off the Track Thoroughbreds), 16, 33, 153, 211, 287
Outside/inside aids, 87, 107
Overbending, *92*, 95–96
Overgirths, 39
Overweight horses, 267–268
Owners, 7, 8
Oxers, 160–162, 206–207, *206*, 223, 224, 227

Pace
   maintaining, 112
   planning for, during course walk, 196–197
   practice for, 115–117, *115*

riding for time, 193, 196–199, *197*, 212, 213–214
speed development, 115
strong horses and, 113
USEF rules regarding, 114
Pads, for shoes, 274, 278
Parasite control, *42*, 268, 286–287
Patience, 102, 153
Pelham bits, 47
Penalties, xviii, 166, 314
Personality, of horse. *See* Temperament
Plank fences, 162
Planning, for success, 4–5
Polo wraps, 48, *50*
Positive attitude, 4
Preliminary Level, xiv, xvi, *69*–70, 71–73, 114
Preliminary Three-Day Events, xvi
Pre-purchase exams, 16, 17, 18, 19, *30*, 31–33
Presentation. *See* Apparel, for riders; Grooming
Probiotics, 253, 260, 263
Protein, 262
Pulling up, 217, 219
Pulse, 304, 306
Puncture injuries, *299*

Quarter marks, 250–251, *251–252*

Rails
knockdown of, xviii, 166, *229*, *231*, 314
weight of, 316
Rain rot, 300. *See also* Weather conditions
Ratability, 149–153, *151*, 164, 204–205. *See also* Distances, in jumping; Pace
Rebalancing. *See* Balancing/rebalancing, of horse
Refusals, 126, *126*, 159–160, 166, 224
Rehabilitation, 295–297
Rein styles/types, 40–41, 46–47, 51–53
Rein-back, 105–107, *106*
Related distances, xii, 157–159, *158*, 223–224
Relaxation
of horse, 211, 225
of rider, 171, 209
Repetition, learning and, 102
Resistance, 126, *126*, 186, 289
Respiratory health, 68, 72, 260, 298, 303
Responsiveness, to aids, 91, 94–96, 165
Rest days, 70, 261, 292, 293, 295–297

Retraining, 18, 188
Rhythm, 24, 88, 125–126, 152, 212, 226
Rhythm, jumping and, 151
Rider position
for bank fences, 137–138
in cross-country riding, 112, 117, *118*, 128, 129
defensive, 145
for ditches and water fences, 131–135
drifting and, 165–166
in jumping out of stride, 128–129
planning for, 195, 214–216
in show jumping, 160–164
for technical fences, 141, 142, 144–147
two-point, 74
in warm-up, 226
Riders
apparel/equipment for, 55–65
attitude of, 4, 5, 8–9, 11
fitness of, 75–79
inexperienced, planning considerations, 15–16
Riding boots, 63
Roads and tracks, xiii
Roaring, 298
Rolton, Gillian, xii
Roughage, 259, 267
Roundness, 26, 85, 91, 93, 104–105
Roycroft, Bill, xii
Rubber reins, 40–41, 52
Rubbing, from tack, 29, 50, 299–300
Runaway horses, 113
Running martingales, *42*, 50
Running out, 126. *See also* Refusals
Rushing
in cross-country, 123, 132–133
in dressage tests, 186
generally, 26
in show jumping, 153, 157, 164, 166, 226

Sacroiliac pain, 294
Saddle pads, 37–38, 53, 299
Saddles, 35–37, *36*
Safety
protective apparel, xvi–xvii, 55, 56–57, 58–60, *59*
pulling up, 217
rider fitness and, 75
rule changes for, xii
Salt, 263, 301
Salutes, 185, 188, 222, 230
Schedule planning, 14
Scoring, xviii, 186, 188–189, 314
Scratches (skin infection), 241, *299*
Seat, 117, 119. *See also* Rider position
Sedatives, 303

Self-carriage, 114–115, 153
Self-preservation, horse's sense of, 23
Shirts, 60
Shoeing. *See* Hoof care/shoeing
Short format events, xv–xvi
Shortening, of stride. *See* Collection; Ratability
Shoulder conformation, 22
Shoulder-in, 96–97, *97*
Show jumping phase
apparel for, *56–57*, 60–63, *61*
competition riding, 230–232
vs. cross-country, 166
distances in, 156–160, *158*
fence types, 160–164
general considerations, xii, 4, 18
grooming for, 256
horse selection, 16–19
rails down, xviii, 166, *229*, *231*, 314
ratability, 149–153, 232, *232*
rider position, 117, 119, 160–164
schooling for, 153–160
tack/equipment for, *36*, 37–40, 43, 45–49, *49*, 65
troubleshooting, 164–166
walking the course, 170, 221–225
warm-up, 171, 225–229
Side reins, 51
Simply Red, 324
Skin care, 238–239, 241, 243
Sky's Prospect, 326
Smartphone apps, 194
Snaffle bits/bridles, 40, *41*, 44–45, *44*, 153
Soft tissue injuries, 18, 33, 288, 289–292, 295–297
Soles, of feet, 274, 278, 281
Soundness. *See* Lameness
Speed, developing, 115. *See also* Pace
Sponsors, 6, *6*
Spooky horses, 164–165, 200, 222
Spurs, *62*, 63, 65
Square oxers, 161, 229, *229*
Squaring up, at halt, 104, 105
Stabling, 264, 298
Standing martingales, 51
Start
in cross-country, *192*, 193, 209–211, *210*
in show jumping, 222
Steeplechase, xiii
Steering, 44
Stifle soreness, 289–290
Stile fences, 162
Stirrup length, 63, 74, 117, 119
Stock ties, 61
Stopping. *See* Halts and halting; Refusals

Straightness. *See also* Lines
    in dressage, 84, 185
    in jumping, 26, 160, 165
    in rein-back, 107
Strength training, 76
Stretching
    of horse, 91, 93, 294
    of rider, 76, *78*
Stride
    adding of, 157, 223–224
    adjustability, 159. *see also* Ratability
    average length, 159
    combination fences and, 194–195
    planning for, 223–224
Strong horses, 113, 213, 214–216
Stud guards, 39
Studs, on shoes, 116, 256, 279–280, *279–280*, 281
Subclinical injuries, 292
Success, planning for, 3–5
Sunken roads, 145–146, *146*
Supplements, 31, 262, 263
Suppleness, 85
Support teams, 5–11
Suspension, of gaits, 85
Suspensory injuries, 291–292
Sweating, 269, 297–298. *See also* Cool-down strategies
Swedish oxers, 161–162

Tack. *See also* Equipment/accessories
    accessories, 50–53
    bits, 44–45, *44*
    bridles, 40–44
    care and maintenance, 52–53, 254
    overview, 35
    saddle pads, 37–38
    saddles, 35–37
"Tack walking," 296
Tail care/grooming, 238, *238*, 246, 250, *250*, 253–254
Takeoff, 125, 160, 164, 212, 213. *See also* Distances, in jumping
Teichman, Stephen, 271, *272*
Temperament
    competition effects on, 172–175, 214–217
    evaluating, 17, 18, 19, 22–23, 235
Temperature, of horse, 303, 304
Tempo, in warm-up, 86. *See also* Pace
Tendon health, 33, 49, 73–74
Terrain
    assessment of, 192, 193, 197–199
    slopes and hills, 74, 119
Tests (event type), levels of, xiii–xv
The Foreman, 26, 28, 323
Thoroughbreds, 16, 33, 153, 211, 287

Three-Day Events, xiii–xvii, 70
Three-ring bits, 47
Ties, 61
Time
    distance and, 74. *see also* Pace
    monitoring, 115, 116, 196–197, *210*, 211
Tired horses. *See* Fatigue
Top hats, 59
Trail riding, 112
Trainers, 8–9, 15
Training Level, xiv, xvi, 69, 71, 114
Training Three-Day Events, xvi
Transitions, 88–91, 181, 183
Travel preparations, 14–15, 79, 251, 253–254, 293
Travers, 98–99, *98*
Treats, 269
Triple bar fences, 161
Triple combinations, 159
Trot
    in cross-country schooling, 125, 130, 137, 141
    extension/collection of, 99, 101
    in fitness training, *70*
    improving, 97, 98
    in show jumping schooling, 154
    for spooky horses, 165
    transitions to/from, 90–91
    in warm-up, *86*, 181, *204*, 226, 227
True Blue Girdwood, 303, 321
TruLuck, 323–324
Trust, 121
Turnout, 264–267
Two-point position, 74
Tying up, 269, 293, 306

Ulcers, 267, 268, 301–302
Ultrasound, 31, 296–297, *296*
Underweight horses, 268–269
Uphill balance, 23, 85, 104
Uphill conformation, 21
USEA, xiii–xv
USEF, xiii–xvii, 114, 285

Vaccinations, 286
Ventilation, 253, 298
Vertical fences, 160, 206, 223, 224, 229
Veterinary care
    back pain, 293–294
    cardiovascular health, 297
    gastrointestinal health, 300–302
    maintenance routines, 286–287
    muscle conditions, 293
    pre-purchase exams, 16, 17, 18, 19, *30*, 31–33
    rehabilitation, 295–297

    respiratory health, 298
    skin problems, 299–300
    for unsoundnesses, 287–292
    veterinarian role, 9–10, 284–285
Veterinary inspections, 64, 254–255, 306
Visualization, 201
Vital signs, 304, 306

Walk (gait)
    in cooling down, 308
    evaluation of, 23
    in rehabilitation, 296
    transitions to/from, 90
    in warm-up, 181, 209, 211, 229
Walking, of courses, 170, 191–201, 221–225
Warmbloods, 15, 17, 153
Washing. *See* Bathing
Water obstacles, *120*, 121, 131–135, *132*, 196. *See also* Hydration
Weather conditions
    horse health and, 265, 267, 274–275, 280–281, 299
    riding considerations, 197, 255. *see also* Footing
Whips and whip use, 65, 119, 121
White markings, cleaning of, *240*, 241
William Penn, 325
Willingness, of horse, 22
Wind. *See* Respiratory health
Winging movement, of legs, 21
Wonder bits, *46*, 47
Woodburn, 113, *184*, *186*, *216*, 324–325
Wraps. *See* Bandages

X-rays, 31

Yellow warning cards, 255
Young/green horses
    competition considerations, 172–175, 196, 213
    cross-country training, 119–121, *120*, 123–129, *124*, *126*, 136
    evaluation of, 26–27, 29
    foundation building, 4, 89, 105. *see also* Dressage training
    selection considerations, 16–17
    show jumping training, 155, 162